Jazz

Michael Bean

Published by Michael Bean, 2023.

This is a work of fiction. Similarities to real people, places, or events are entirely coincidental.

JAZZ

First edition. June 7, 2023.

ISBN: 979-8223021476

Written by Michael Bean.

Dedication

To my wife, Ashley, for always encouraging and supporting me, rain or shine. I have learned to love an infinite amount because you have loved me an infinite amount.

To Levi, for reminding me that joy can be found in the smallest moments of the day.

To Noah, for designing the cover of this novel and offering all sorts of wonderful advice.

To Christian, for always reminding me that I'm going bald.

To Maddox, for constantly asking me to finish my novel so you could finally read it.

To Grayson, because Maddox made it to the dedication page and I didn't want you to feel left out.

To my brother, this novel isn't *Game of Thrones* but I think you should still read it.

To my parents, thank you for taking me to the comic book store for all those years when I was a kid.

To all of my family members, I'm grouping you all together so I don't have to list every single one of you. Thank you for loving me when I'm difficult to love.

To all my students, this is proof that if I can do it, so can you. No dream is too big.

To all my former teachers that inspired me, thank you for every bit of energy you spent trying to reach the kid that wasn't the smartest or the brightest.

To my band director, Mr. Kuni, for creating the spark that would eventually become this novel.

To Steven, for being the authority on sweet potatoes and yams.

To anyone else that feels like they also deserve a spot on my dedication page, I guess I owe you a doughnut.

Prologue

I don't remember everything Mr. Undergrove taught me.

Yeah, yeah, yeah - you know every teacher's dream is probably that every single one of their students hangs on to every idea and lesson that they are trying to bestow upon them, but let's be honest: life doesn't work that way.

Think about it: what would the world look like if every kid understood and comprehended what was presented to them in school and applied it to their life?

The federal government would probably be really efficient because members of the Senate, the House of Representatives, and the Presidential Cabinet would actually remember that those that don't remember history are bound to repeat it, and if I've learned anything about history and government, it's that the government loves to repeat history.

There'd be little signs of heart disease because after hearing about the importance of exercise and maintaining a healthy diet, people would actually apply those two practices to their lives.

I imagine there would be less smoking-related illnesses out there because c'mon, they start teaching you in kindergarten that smoking has the potential to kill you.

The economy would be thriving because everyone would take all those financial skills they sling at you in math and business classes and put them to use when it comes to spending money on things that you don't need and can't afford.

I imagine there would be better quality music for the world to listen to. Don't believe me? Turn on the radio. There's a lot of bad music out there.

Imagine a world of sports where every athlete actually listened to their coach, including the athletes whose parents are yelling at them from the sidelines to not listen to what the coach was telling them to do.

The truth is this: we don't remember everything our teachers teach us. We may remember it long enough to take a test, or maybe even long enough to take a final at the end of a semester or school year, but if it's not immediately applicable to your life, there's probably a good chance you're going to forget it.

Poof. Gone. In one ear, out the other ear, whether it's in a week, a month, or a year.

What you do always remember is how a teacher made you feel on the inside.

And that can go in a variety of directions.

My 7th grade science teacher? She yelled at me on the first day of school for writing on a paper in pen instead of pencil. The second day of school she gave me detention for writing my name on the left side of the paper instead of on the right side. On the third day of school, she told me that I was worthless because I typed my homework on the computer and printed it out instead of writing it by hand; when I tried to explain to her that my parents had just purchased a new printer and I wanted to try it out, she made me sit in the hall for the remainder of the class.

That was just in the first three days of school. I endured an entire year of that teacher.

I had science during third period in 7th grade. Every day, right at the end of second period, I'd start to get so nervous that I would feel sick and get a headache. Every day, by the time I got to fourth period and third period was behind me, my headache and nervousness would go away.

So when I think about my 7th grade experience, I can't remember anything I learned in science class, but I do remember how that teacher made me feel, which was that I was below dirt.

On the flip side of all that science anxiety was my 7th grade English teacher, Mr. Hunt. Mr. Hunt was young, energetic, waved his hands in the air a lot, and when you asked him a question, he actually appeared to be listening to you. He actually listened! How many adults out there can you name that will actually listen to a kid in middle school? Like listen to them like they're the most important person in the entire world?

Not a very long list, is it?

Sometimes Mr. Hunt would just start singing in class, almost like they do in musicals, like the moment captured him and he just had to put his hands in the air and sing out loud. He'd jump up on his desk, throw his hands up, and just wail. He didn't care if he was on key or not. Can you imagine? In front of a bunch of 7th graders too!

Mr. Hunt even dressed up as Count Chocula on Halloween that year. We had been reading about monsters and spirits and whatnot all through October; sure enough, when we walked into Mr. Hunt's class on the 31st, there he was, decked in all brown: a brown cape, brown shoes, brown pants, a brown tie, and he had even sprayed his hair brown with a temporary hair dye. He was super excited when some of us realized that he wasn't Dracula, but instead he was Count Chocula, as in the General Mills cereal. Mr. Hunt didn't break character either; he spoke with a Transylvanian accent from the start of class until the bell rang.

Mr. Hunt was the coolest teacher in all of 7th grade.

And then, he left.

We came back from Thanksgiving break to find Mr. Hunt's room completely cleaned out of all his belongings. A new teacher, Mrs. Gourd, took Mr. Hunt's place. She was bland, quiet, and boring.

Mrs. Gourd was so boring that I'm not even sure if her name was Mrs. Gourd. I think I remember that her name was Mrs. Gourd, but that could be because 'Gourd' rhymes with 'bored'.

"Where's Mr. Hunt?" we asked Mrs. Gourd.

"I'm not sure. One of the 6th grade teachers said he moved to the mountains."

The mountains? Why would he move to the mountains when he could teach us? I mean, the man dressed up as Count Chocula! How cool is that? Why would he ever want to leave us?

But do you see the difference there? My science teacher was the bane of my existence for an entire year, while Mr. Hunt brought a lot of joy to my life and the lives of a lot of students. He made me want to be at school; he made me feel like I mattered.

And Mr. Hunt was only my teacher for four months.

Mr. Hunt had been the highlight of all our lives in 7th grade. After he left, life went back to being the struggle that most 7th grade students go through when just trying to survive middle school.

But then Mr. Undergrove came into our lives in the fall of 1995. 8th grade. He was our new band teacher, and we were lucky enough to grow an entire year under his direction.

Mr. Undergrove always talked about how playing a song was a lot like telling a good story. There's the hook that pulls you in, the rising action, the climax, the falling action, and then Mr. Undergrove's favorite part: the 'point of no return', which is where the listener realizes the emotional weight of the song.

"It's a lot like watching a movie," he'd say. "You know that part of the movie where the main character or hero has that earth-shattering moment and all of time seems to slow down? I mean, every movie has that moment. Go ahead and think about it: you're watching a 90 minute movie, and right around the 75 minute mark, boom: something happens. But it's not just anything; it's gotta be something huge. Like massive. Maybe even something thrilling. Maybe a big secret is revealed. Maybe something absolutely terrifying happens that makes the hero rethink everything they've learned, and then they push on through to save the day. Maybe it's something that's extremely personal, like a moment of self-discovery."

"In *Ghostbusters*, our heroes realize they need to cross the streams of their proton packs to defeat Gozer. In *Back To The Future*, Marty realizes he has to warn Doc Brown of the Doc's eventual death. In *Superman*, the big blue Boy Scout has to fly backwards so fast that he has to reverse time in order to save Lois Lane," Mr. Undergrove would say.

"If you can build a song or a performance for the audience the same way you build a movie's story, they'll realize it at the 'point of no return'. Look at the guitar solo in Jimi Hendrix's 'Bold As Love', or George Harrison's piano solo in The Beatles' 'In My Life'. These are moments that give the song a little extra push; it's no longer a song, but instead a moment, something that you know the listener won't forget."

"That's what we're going to try to achieve here: the 'point of no return' in music. For you as musicians, and for the audience, like your parents, the staff members of this school, the students at this school that aren't involved in the band program, and the members of the community that surrounds us."

The point of no return. Yeah, right.

If anything, King's Hollow Middle School was sitting in the heart of the point of no return.

King's Hollow Middle School was the hubcap center of one of the worst neighborhoods in our small town. Built in the late 30's and into the early 40's, the school's architecture gave off a gothic vibe with its hand-cut stone statues of gargoyles and angels that decorated the rooftop. Demon heads acting as rain spouts ran parallel to the roof, their eyes bulging from their heads like someone or something was squeezing them entirely too tight. Intricate stone carvings of vines with pulsing thorns outlined the windows that stretched across every classroom. All the windows had bars covering the windows, just like a jail cell. Not only could you go to school and feel imprisoned, but King's Hollow actually had windows that made the students feel like they were in prison.

A middle school that looks like a prison? If you can't smell the irony waffling off that statement, something may be wrong with you.

A handful of small intricate holes decorated the front doors of the school as well, kind of like as if someone took a drill and just went wild with making random holes in random places. Some were small, about the size of a dime, and some were large enough to put your entire thumb in the hole.

I had never thought much about the holes at the front doors until the day Stephen, my best friend, pointed out that the holes that ornated the front of the school were bullet holes scoured into the walls from a drive-by shooting from years earlier.

Middle school. Fun times, right?

Stephen was a free spirit who came into my life in 5th grade when we were on the same elementary school soccer team together; Stephen played goalie while I played defender. At least it was like that for one game.

During the very first game of the season, an airplane heading towards our local airport flew across the sky, which caused our team to lose the game, which led to my dad punching our soccer coach, which led to Stephen and me becoming friends.

It happened in that order. No, I'm not joking.

It was the first soccer game of the season. A plane flew across the sky. Not like a jet liner or something like that, but one of those small local planes, the kind that tend to crash a lot more often than the commercial ones.

Being intrigued by the airplane, surely self-aware that by flying over a local elementary school during their Saturday morning soccer league games would be a giant distraction for all, I watched it stretch and soar across the sky like a giant eagle instead of paying attention to the soccer game that I was playing in. Stephen, playing goalie, was equally transfixed by the airplane, and also took a moment to put his focus on the sky as well. The plane seemed to be just out of our reach above the treelines that bordered our school's soccer field.

So there we were: two kids standing on a soccer field, staring up at the sky, looking at some rinky-dink local airplane flying overhead, while our parents screamed at us, our teammates screamed at us, and our coach screamed at us to pay attention as the kids on the opposite team came barreling down the field towards us. By the time we both realized what was going on, the other team had scored a goal as time on the clock expired and secured the opposition's victory.

After the game, our soccer coach gathered the entire team around him to let everyone know that he was disappointed in Stephen and me. Then he yelled at Stephen and me that he was disappointed in us. Loud. Louder than a coach should probably yell at a kid. Then the coach yelled at Stephen's mom when she yelled at the coach to back off. Then the coach yelled at my dad that he wasn't yelling after my dad yelled at the coach to stop yelling. Then the coach yelled at everyone, both kids and parents, to calm down.

Everyone got quiet and appeared to be calming down, but then the coach went back to yelling at Stephen and me about his level of disappointment. Then my dad got mad and yelled at the coach to stop yelling again, and the soccer coach yelled at him again that he wasn't yelling, so then dad took two steps forward and punched the coach right in the chest. The coach went down to the ground, and my dad, well, he just stood over him showing restraint, probably realizing he shouldn't have punched the coach like that in front of all these kids, parents, and families on a soccer field. Then the coach yelled at my dad some more that my dad was a bully.

Not long after that, the school told our coach that he couldn't coach anymore, and that my dad couldn't come to anymore soccer games. Stephen and I - we could keep playing, but our new coach, another kid's dad, moved us to midfield and told us to always keep our eyes on the ball, even if an airplane passes overhead.

On the playground the following Monday, I apologized to Stephen for my dad knocking the coach to the ground like he did when the coach was yelling at us. Surely, Stephen had to be as embarrassed as I was about the whole deal, but Stephen wasn't bothered by it.

"At least your dad was there at the game. My dad didn't even know I had a game."

"Oh."

What do you say to that? 'My dad didn't even know I had a game.' Do you follow up with 'Why didn't he know about the game?' Or 'I'm sorry' or what?

"He's got issues," Stephen added. "Like mental issues. Depression and stuff like that. He's just always mentally somewhere else. Like, not living in the moment, or whatever they say."

"Oh," again.

"But your dad seems pretty cool and all."

"Thanks."

"Hey," Stephen turned his body towards me but kept his eyes on the ground, "do you think your dad could punch our math teacher too?"

"Mr. Winslow?"

"Yeah, Winslow. He's been giving us way too much homework lately."

"In the chest, like he did the soccer coach?" I asked.

"Yeah, the chest is fine," Stephen replied, staring down at his shoes. "Or maybe in the face. Whatever."

I nodded. "No, face is cool. I'm cool with that. Let me talk to my dad and see what he can do."

"Yep," Stephen kicked a rock across the cement of the playground, "the face." He watched the rock skip and hop before settling at the edge of the grass. "Or your dad could maybe kick Mr. Winslow in the nards."

"The nards?"

"The nards," Stephen confirmed. "Just a swift kick to the nards."

"The nards. Right. I think I get you," I said, even though I didn't get him.

Stephen turned around and looked me in the eye, like really looked me in the eye, and could tell I didn't have a clue to what he was referring to.

"Ya know, like when Wolfman gets kicked in the nards in the movie *The Monster Squad*?" He leaned toward me on his legs, slanting himself on the playground surface.

I was confused. "Monster Squad?"

An aura of shock came over Stephen's face. "*The Monster Squad.* Like, the movie! You've never seen it?"

I shrugged. "Is it like *Ghostbusters*? I've seen that one a bunch of times."

Stephen put his hands up. "No, no, no. *Ghostbusters* is not *The Monster Squad. The Monster Squad* is *The Monster Squad.* How do you not know this stuff?"

"Um..." I looked around the playground, "I mean it's just a movie so..."

Stephen cut me off. "*The Monster Squad* is not just a movie! *The Monster Squad* is the greatest cinematical adventure of all time!"

"Cinematical adventure?"

"Oh jeez," Stephen rolled his eyes. "Movie. That's fancy talk for a movie. I watch a lot of them. Dad's always too busy, remember?"

"Yeah, sure, I guess. Look, I just wanted to make sure you were ok with everything that went down on Saturday on the soccer field."

"Soccer? Oh, right." Stephen scratched his head. "Forgot all about that already. Your dad is going to punch someone else, right? Isn't that how all this got started?"

"No, you asked if he could punch Mr. Winslow for you and then you said you wanted him to..."

"Kick Winslow in the nards!" Stephen screamed loudly. Some of the other kids playing nearby looked our direction. "I remember now. And you don't know what *The Monster Squad* is. And now those girls over there," Stephen pointed at a group of fellow 5th grade girls, "think we're weird."

"Look, I just wanted to make sure..."

"That I'm free on Friday night so you can come to my house to watch *The Monster Squad*? Yes, let's do that."

I stammered. "Wait.....what....huh?"

Stephen poked his finger in my chest. "You haven't seen *The Monster Squad*. I own the tape. It is now my job to expand your horizons and expose you to why the movie is so amazing, which includes an understanding of Wolfman having nards."

"Wolfman had nards?"

Stephen raised his voice. "Good gosh! Have you not been paying attention? Work with me here! Yes, Wolfman has nards! It's one of the highlights of the movie!"

"Wolfman has nards. Got it. I'll....uh....I'll..."

"Have your mom call my mom. Or I'll get my mom to call your mom. Set everything up. *The Monster Squad.* Friday night. It'll be fun."

"Look, it's not a big deal what my dad did..."

"No, I owe you. There's a reason for all this."

"What happened for a reason?" I asked.

"Call it fate. Call it luck. Call it karma. I believe everything happens for a reason." Stephen put his hands in the air and projected his voice. "I believe we were destined to be put on our soccer team together because there are greater forces at work here, and that is that of *The Monster Squad*!"

"Oh."

Again, what do you say to something like that?

"So, what's your name, kid?"

"Me? My name?"

Stephen smiled. "No, the name of the guy behind you." I started to turn my body when Stephen added, "Yes, you! What's your name? I mean, I know we're going to be hanging out on Friday night, so I should probably know your name."

"Oh, um... Mitchell. Mitchell Williams."

"Williams? Like Ash Williams, zombie slayer?" Stephen asked.

"Zombie slayer? No, I'm not..."

"*Evil Dead.* Ash Williams is the main character. C'mon, Mitchell, know your movies."

"I...I'm not up-to-date on all the movies."

Stephen put his hands on his hips. "Maybe if your parents ignored you more often, you wouldn't have that problem."

That Friday night, I went to Stephen's house as planned out by our moms. We watched *The Monster Squad* in the basement, the old tube television sitting on the floor illuminating the adventures of a group of teenagers as vampires, mummies, and various other monsters descended onto their small town. The highlight of the film: watching Wolfman get kicked in the nards, just as Stephen had promised.

"See? Wolfman has nards. Told ya."

From that day on, despite that my dad never bothered to punch anyone in front of us ever again, Stephen became my best friend. Two years later, we were on our way out of elementary school and onto King's Hollow.

Leaving elementary school had its share of thrills because we were no longer going to be 'kids', but upon arriving at King's Hollow on the first day of school, our attitudes towards the unknown dimension of middle school drastically changed. 7th grade sounded exciting, but 7th grade inside a concrete castle of gargoyles and demons in a gang-infested neighborhood was a lot less interesting than it sounded.

"You know King's Hollow has got to be crazy haunted with all those demon heads and gargoyles and crap on the building. Plus, the whole King's Hollow doomed family thing."

"What King's Hollow doomed family thing?" I asked.

Stephen cracked his knuckles. "The King family? They were one of the richest families in town way back during the Great Depression. Owned the glass factory that was out by the lake. They were always trying to give back to the community, especially during a time when people didn't have a lot. The Kings had agreed to put the money up for the new school, and construction had started and everything. When the school was on the verge of being done, a crazy ex-employee from the glass factory burned down the King's house while they slept one night. The whole family died. Crazy stuff."

My eyes grew wide; I was speechless. "That is messed up," I staggered out. "That's just, man, that's horrible." I hesitated. "What about the Hollow family? What was their deal?"

Stephen put his hands behind his head. "The Hollow family? I don't know. Beats me."

"Why'd you say 'the whole King's Hollow doomed family thing' then?"

Stephen shrugged his shoulders. "I just assumed they were messed over like the Kings were. Look at all that demon crap going on the outside of that school. And the neighborhood? It's a war zone. That's gotta explain some of it, right?"

"You said 'doomed family thing', like there was more than just what happened to the Kings."

"It made for a good story. I'm sure the Hollow family was messed up too. Had to be. It's middle school."

It turns out that nothing terrible ever happened to the Hollow family that put up the money to complete the school. The Kings had taken the entirety of the bad luck with the burned down house and all, and the Hollow family, a wealthy family of farmers, paid for the remainder of the construction of the new school. Thus, the *King's Hollow* name was born into existence.

I'm sure if the Kings or Hollow family knew that the neighborhood that would grow up around the school was going to be terrible, they'd have never built the school where they built it.

But now, here we were: in a questionable neighborhood, in a scary-looking school, with an entire legion of hormonal, moody velociraptors known as 'teenagers' roaming the halls.

That's a great recipe for disaster, right?

Looking back, maybe I shouldn't be mad at Mr. Hunt for leaving to go to the mountains. I mean, I would have if I had had the opportunity to leave King's Hollow.

But Mr. Undergrove came into our lives in 8th grade, and we had some adventures with him, all the way into high school.

AUGUST - 10TH GRADE

Maynard Ferguson plays on the stereo. It's 'Hey Jude', a song we all know, but still, it's different. It's bubbling something unseen, like the music is a slow boil that is fizzing just below the surface of our ears. Not in a painful way, but in a way that makes everything seem different. The lights above us seem duller; our seats are now slightly uncomfortable. I mean, it's still the band room, but it's no longer the band room, ya know? We're somewhere else now without having left the room.

Mr. Undergrove slightly nods his head along with the beat. Just barely. Not enough to really notice, but enough to notice that he wants to nod along in a more dramatic way without worrying what some high school kids will think of him. He's holding back. His eyes don't lie: he wants us to like this song. He wants us to really like this song. He wants us to play this song. As a band. Not as a bunch of kids playing instruments in a band. As a band. There's a difference.

It's 3rd period. Jazz band class. Northern Kent High School. 1997. 10th grade. There are only a handful of us, and, for the most part, we're all products of Mr. Undergrove's teachings from when he directed us in middle school at King's Hollow. Now, he's back in our lives, directing us again, this time in high school at Northern Kent, of all places. The band director from before Mr. Undergrove? He got canned. Well, not really. He kinda got canned, but also got promoted. Rumor was he couldn't teach a brick how to be red. We've all had one of those teachers before: a teacher that just can't teach, no matter how hard they try. The Northern Kent band director was one of those teachers, so the district shifted him to the central office where he didn't have to teach anymore and had a comfy desk to sit at, and then moved Mr. Undergrove to Northern Kent to 'fix' what was left of the band program. We're a part of what's left.

We're the kids that liked band, but didn't want to be part of the whole 'marching band' deal. We were the classy band kids. 'Classy' may be not the right word, but it sounds better than 'somewhat sophisticated'. No, that's not it either. Hey, I'll put it this way: we were in band together, but we weren't about to put ourselves out there publicly enough to be a part of the marching band getup. I mean, playing from behind the comfort of a podium on a stage is a lot less intimidating than marching in a parade, or, dare I say, the middle of a football field. Imagine your whole school sitting in the stands, all there to see a football game, and their added perk is watching you during halftime carry your instrument around at a weird angle while marching some weird half-Irish jig while playing a song from the 70s that no one really cares about? Sheesh, I wouldn't be caught dead doing that. None of us in jazz band would. Anyone could be in marching band; let the classy kids handle the jazz. Sound fair enough?

There was Kirby & Justin on percussion. My grandma always said to me that the word 'percussion' sounded silly when the word 'drums' sufficed; this isn't my grandma's story, but she's got a point. Kirby and Justin, they banged on the drums. Ian played guitar, David on the bass guitar, Kevin played the sax, while Josh, Brooks & Stephen played the trumpet. Phillip, a senior, played the trombone right alongside yours truly. Not a lot of us, but we were a class of a bunch of classy high school guys playing jazz. Classy - still not the right word.

The solo kicked in on 'Hey Jude'; our eyes grew wide as Maynard Ferguson's trumpet pitch went higher and higher. Deep down, I felt like the windows in the band room should be rattling. "What note is that?" I asked.

"Double High C," Mr. Undergrove responded, a grin smeared across his face. "Maynard Ferguson was a master of the double high C."

Brooks' eyes widened as the solo hits its climax. "Dude has some lungs," he commented.

As the song wrapped, Mr. Undergrove, still floating that silly half smile / half smirk on his face, hit the stop button on the stereo and turned his chair back towards us. He pulled out sheet music from a folder on his podium and distributed it to everyone in the band. "Holy Saint Francis," Stephen muttered, "we're doing this, huh?"

"We certainly are," Mr. Undergrove crooned back. "And all you trumpet players, we're going to get you into Ferguson's double high C territory; that's our goal. When someone hears us play 'Hey Jude', I want them to not think about Maynard Ferguson but instead the Northern Kent Jazz Band."

"Mr. Undergrove," Stephen perked up, "I hate to break it to you, but most people think of The Beatles when they hear 'Hey Jude'."

Mr. Undergrove sighed. "In the jazz world, it's a little different."

"What world are we living in?" Stephen asked. I wasn't sure if he was joking or being serious.

"Stephen, how can I even answer that question?" Mr. Undergrove responded. "Look, everyone, it's a solid, recognizable song that is moderate enough for us to master and complicated enough to really push us to make us a better band overall. On the plus side, it's one of Maynard Ferguson's signature pieces."

"You mean The Beatles," Stephen added.

"Yes, and The Beatles," Mr. Undergrove confirmed.

"Because, honestly," Stephen added, "the only person in this room that has heard of Mayonnaise Ferguson is you."

"Maynard," Mr. Undergrove corrected, "Maynard Ferguson."

"Who was not one of The Beatles," Stephen said back.

Mr. Undergrove shook his head. "No, Ferguson was not one of The Beatles."

"Oh, good. We're all on the same page," Stephen said, a grin of accomplishment on his face. "Look! We're building team dynamics here!"

"It looks that way, Stephen," Mr. Undergrove responded, raising his baton in the air, signaling for us to raise our instruments to prepare to play; Mr. Undergrove gave a few instructions, counted down from four, and soon after, the homemade jazz-infused tune of 'Hey Jude' filled the band room.

OCTOBER - 8TH GRADE

Mr. Undergrove was one of those teachers straight out of a Hallmark Production, a real stand-up kinda guy. Put us kids first, made us feel important. Not a lot of lecture, but a lot of encouragement. The kind where you look at yourself in the mirror and when you see your reflection, you want that reflection to be a better person than the dude looking back at you. We didn't buy it at the time, but man, looking back, it made sense. "Practice every day," he'd say. "Practice, practice, practice." We'd look around the room and think, 'we're practicing every day in class! What more do you want?' Mr. Undergrove could tell if you had practiced too. He'd point that out to everyone during 8th grade band class. "Do you hear that, everyone?!" he'd yell. "Do you hear that man playing his trombone? That man practiced last night! I don't even have to ask him because I can tell he practiced!" People would look back at you and then down at their own instruments, wondering what they could do to get that kind of reaction out of Mr. Undergrove the next day. That's the kind of encouragement that sticks with a person, something they remember throughout the years.

At our Christmas concert, Mr. Undergrove let us pick out what we were going to wear. He wanted it to be our decision, kind of like a democracy and not a dictatorship. Charlesey, a saxophonist, was the deciding vote: to be black & white formal, or to be formally festive and let our Christmas pride fly. Charlesey went with formally festive, so the 8th grade band broke out its red & green to the extreme for our concert. I wore my dad's Charlie Brown Christmas tie. Mr. Undergrove had on the exact same tie. "Hey! Great minds think alike!" he said. Normally, I'd be repulsed by the idea of matching with my band director, but Mr. Undergrove, well, he was alright.

We became good under Mr. Undergrove's direction. Not that we weren't good before, just not motivated. It was kind of like a movie. You know, one of those movies where all the neighborhood kids play baseball together, but they're not that good, but then this young coach comes their way and puts his faith in the kids and tells them to try hard, and so they do and they start to have faith in each other, and the next thing you know, the baseball team that wasn't that good before starts winning games, and the coach is proud of them and they're proud of themselves and the moms and dads are all proud and everyone is happy because this young coach made them believe in themselves and nothing can stop a team that believes in themselves. It was just like that, only with a band instead of a baseball team.

Mr. Undergrove could tell we had potential. He believed in us. He told us that. He told us that all the time. "I believe in you". It was kind of annoying, but, man, the guy had charisma, so when he singled you out when you were having a rough day and patted you on the back and said "I believe in you", you took those words to heart. This man believed in me. This man believed in us. He believed in us as a band. Man, he believed.

King's Hollow Middle School was going to have a homecoming football game. It was the first homecoming game King's Hollow had ever hosted. We couldn't believe it. It was like this was high school, or like something you saw on a television show. We weren't the type of school that just had a homecoming football game. Our school was a bit rough around the edges because our school sat in a neighborhood that was a bit rough around the edges. We didn't have homecoming football games, or home football games in general, because the crowd would be full of all those people that your parents warned you not to associate with: the guys that were in high school but still came to middle school games, the guys that had dropped out of high school but still hung out at middle school games, the drug dealers that had no business being at a middle school game but came anyways because that's where they could do some business, and people that didn't have a kid in middle school but came to the games because there was always guaranteed to be some kind of drama that could pull the crowd in a different direction. It was like that.

Typically, King's Hollow hosted their home football games at the high school, Northern Kent, which was situated down the road a couple of miles in a much nicer neighborhood, the kind of neighborhood that you wouldn't mind its local residents making an appearance at the football stadium. While King's Hollow had a perfectly good football stadium with nice concrete stands built directly into the hillside that surrounded the field, everyone knew and understood why the stadium was used for practices but never for actual games. You know, safety first.

Mr. Cooper, our principal, was determined that King's Hollow Middle School was going to have a homecoming game, and that game would be hosted at the school, and that, despite the odds, that it would be a success, so he went to Mr. Undergrove . "I want that band of ours to give that homecoming game some real spirit," is what I envisioned Mr. Cooper saying. Mr. Undergrove, being a first year teacher, was excited, for this was his first test as our new band director.

This is when the whole "I believe in you" business started. Our band, at this point in our young, 8th grade lives, was terrible. No. We weren't terrible. We lacked direction, focus, patience, ambition, and pretty much the rest of the formula needed to find any form of success. We weren't terrible. Our band director before Mr. Undergrove was, well, he left after one year at King's Hollow, but that's normal for middle school, right? Middle school is kind of like an emotional holding cell for teenagers. We're angry, we're emotional, we're confused, we're irrational, yet unreasonably happy all the time. We hate & love our parents. We hate & love our friends. We hate & love our teachers. We don't know what to do. So when our band teacher left after one year at King's Hollow, we didn't bat an eye. It's reality. A fresh face comes in, realizes that middle school isn't their cup of tea, and then holds the door open for the next person. Mr. Undergrove was our next person, and he had just taken on his first obstacle for us as a band: the homecoming game.

We played the 'Star-Spangled Banner'. It was our first time through. I mean, everyone and their mother knows the 'Star-Spangled Banner', but to actually read the sheet music and then actually play that music in tune with others was a bit frazzling. It kinda sounded like the 'Star Spangled Banner', but it didn't really sound like it at all. Like maybe the song had been put in a blender. Mr. Undergrove put his hands on his head. "Y'all have heard the 'Star-Spangled Banner' before, right?" He asked. There were a few muffled smirks throughout the room. We, as a collective unit, were very aware that the song had been slightly butchered in our first attempt. It was only three weeks until the homecoming game.

It wasn't just the 'Star-Spangled Banner'; it was all sorts of little numbers & songs Mr. Undergrove wanted us to learn before the big homecoming game. Every day was a mad rush to learn and master a new song, and not just master it, but maybe even try to memorize it. Mr. Undergrove paced and waved his baton and paced and waved his baton. He seemed on edge. He glared at the homecoming game flyer that was taped to his door, almost mocking him, mocking his band.

"Are you practicing?" he asked. "Like really practicing?" Mr. Undergrove was addressing Brent, our lone tuba player. "Because every week you turn in a practice note signed by your parents, but every week, you don't get any better. Something is not adding up."

Our eyes turned to Brent, pale and speechless, and then back to Mr. Undergrove, standing on his podium, a vivid look of frustration flushed across his face. "Brent, must I remind you that the homecoming game is only a week away? Must I remind you that this is our 1st official gig of the school year? Must I remind you that the entire crowd will be watching and listening to not just all of us, but you in particular? Must I remind you," Mr. Undergrove's voice got louder with each point he was making that his loud voice was mutating into a yell, "that your mother and your father will be right there, waiting with suspense to hear their son play the tuba?" Mr. Undergrove was pounding his hand on the podium. "Do I have to remind you of all this, or can you figure it out for yourself and remember to practice tonight?" Brent, sitting beside me in the back of the room in between the trombone and French horn sections, weakly nodded his head, mumbled a "yes, sir", and lifted his tuba, ready to continue to play on Mr. Undergrove 's instruction.

The buzz of homecoming was all around us. In 7th grade, there was no spirit week, no morning announcements, no hype for attendance to any school functions, no excitement amongst the football players for a single game, and no motivation by the teachers to get their students to attend a game. When Mr. Cooper had taken over as principal, all that changed, culminating in a buzz of electricity for the biggest football game that was going to take place in the history of King's Hollow Middle School. Every day, Mr. Cooper's voice boomed over the school's intercom system, a sense of excited urgency in his voice as he encouraged us to participate in every day of spirit week and to attend THE homecoming football game. THE game. THE one & only homecoming game. Featuring the King's Hollow cheerleaders AND the 8th grade band. There was weight in those words. All of us in the 8th grade band felt the weight of those words, but man, those words came down hard on Mr. Undergrove, like someone was slinging 100 lbs. of rocks on the man's shoulders.

Weekly band notes became nightly band notes. Mr. Undergrove would daily stop us one-by-one at the band room door with his hand out. "Practice notes - practice notes go right here in my hand. If you don't have it, go to my office and call your parents."

"Have you ever heard of 'performance magic'?" Mr. Undergrove asked. It was the day before the homecoming game. We weren't going to admit that we were nervous, but you could hear it in our notes that were emitting from our instruments. "It's when you mentally step up in ways that you just could not before. It's arriving. It's putting on your game face." Mr. Undergrove's eyes waved over the room at his 8th graders. "We're going to practice with vision today." He said "with vision" like this was a movie or something. "We're going to practice with vision tomorrow, and tomorrow night, we're going to play as a united band for the first time in the homecoming game. Everybody understand?" We nodded along, some of us understanding and some of us nodding because other people were nodding. "I believe in you," Mr. Undergrove said.

We met in the band room on the evening of the game to warm-up. Mr. Undergrove walked around from student to student with an electronic device in hand and asked them to play some notes on their instrument. The device in his hand made weird sounds, turned different colors, and then Mr. Undergrove would instruct the kid to twist a nozzle here or turn a switch a quarter of an inch there, and then Mr. Undergrove would get them to play another note. This time, his device turned another color and then Mr. Undergrove would move on to the next student. When he got to me on my trombone, he got me to inch out a tube on the back of my instrument until he was happy with the way my trombone sounded. "Well, for the first time, you're in tune, sir," he said with a smile that momentarily washed away the well-worn anxiety from his face before he walked on to the next kid. Tonight would either make Mr. Undergrove or break Mr. Undergrove.

AUGUST - 10TH GRADE

"You've got to go higher, push yourself."

"Mr. Undergrove, if I go any higher, I may pass out." Josh responded. "I can't hit those high notes on the trumpet."

"Then you've already given up? Just like that?" Mr. Undergrove placed his baton on his stand. "Things are a little tough and you immediately roll over & quit on all of us?" Josh, staring down at his feet in frustration, didn't respond. After a moment, Mr. Undergrove spoke up. "Ok, Stephen, can you give it a try?"

Stephen shrugged his shoulders, looked nervously over at Josh and then stuttered out, "I mean I can try, I guess, I mean, sure?"

"Do or do not. There is no try." Mr. Undergrove's face got cold and serious.

"That's a Yoda quote!" I blurted out. Mr. Undergrove shot me an eye, letting me know that now was not the time to point out that his words were *Star Wars* inspired.

"Uh, yeah, sure." Stephen nervously shrugged his shoulder. "I mean it's a note, right? It's not like I'm going to melt my brain out or anything."

"Double high C, let's go" Mr. Undergrove said.

"Double high C, great" Stephen responded. He pulled his trumpet up to his lips, took in a quick breath, a breath that seemed to sweep over all of us, closed his eyes, and played.

Notes floundered out of Stephen's trumpet. High notes, but not double high C notes. "No, like this," Mr. Undergrove said and drew up his trumpet and pierced out a screech of a note. It rattled all of us. "That's a double high C. That's what you want it to sound like."

"Oh, double high C. See, I was aiming for quadruple high C so I was kinda confused," Stephen quirked. He returned the trumpet to his lips to try again, glaring out a mangled high note devoid of life, and shrugged his shoulders. "I think I got the 'screeching canary' part down, but not quite the 'screeching canary in a blender' part that really makes double high C a double high C."

Mr. Undergrove ignored Stephen's attempt at humor. "Stephen," Mr. Undergrove said, "keep practicing. Josh, you too. I believe in you."

OCTOBER - 8TH GRADE

There was a buzz generating about the band room that morning after the homecoming game. We were all smiles, giggles, and full of pride. We knew what we had sounded like leading up to the homecoming game, and we knew what we sounded like at the homecoming game, and it was magical. The crowd had applauded our 'Star-Spangled Banner'; they had clapped along as we spouted out songs during timeouts and in between plays. During the 3rd quarter, Mr. Undergrove allowed us to go to the concession stand to take a break; while there, parent after parent complimented us. Even our 8th grade science teacher, Mr. Esposito, was complimentary of us. "You know, you guys almost sound like you know what you're doing out there when you're playing your instruments," he said sarcastically, "must be the new band teacher; he's whipped you all into an actual band in no time." Mr. Undergrove's performance magic was real, and it had been flowing through our instruments the entire game.

That next morning, we prepared for rehearsal and to bask in our musical victory; Mr. Undergrove stood silently at his podium, an emotionless face, waiting for us to have our instruments ready. When we were collectively prepared, he raised his baton, and signaled the start of our warm-up. No sign from him on our performance, no sign of any evaluation of how he thought he did, just him warming-up the band. Mr. Undergrove then passed out new sheet music. Christmas music. It was the middle of October. "We must prepare for our holiday concert," Mr. Undergrove said.

"Hey, Mr. Undergrove," someone in the percussion section said out loud, "what about last-".

Mr. Undergrove immediately cut the student off before he could finish. "WE must prepare for our holiday concert. THAT is what must happen now."

"But, I mean, last night.....that was-"

"Something that will be discussed later," Mr. Undergrove shot back, "please don't interrupt again."

The percussion section grew quiet. One thing you need to know: the percussionist section in any band is always going to be your kids that fish for attention. They're the kids that are like dogs and need to be petted between the ears every other minute. They want compliments, and they want them as much as possible. They're essential, for they keep the beat & rhythm alive. They're like the abs - you don't really need them to lie in the bed, but try to move at all and you realize how important they are. So without a percussionist section, no band is complete, and boy, do those guys know it. "Did I play my part like you wanted me to, Mr. Undergrove?" "Was my rhythm on point like it normally is, Mr. Undergrove?" "Should I play a little louder, Mr. Undergrove? I want to make sure everyone can hear the beat?" Blah blah blah.

When Mr. Undergrove shut down the kid playing the cymbals from trying to start a percussionist compliment party, we didn't mind. I mean, we know we played great at the homecoming game. Did we really need a compliment from Mr. Undergrove to justify it?

As we wrapped up practice, Mr. Undergrove spoke, continuing to keep his face free of emotion. "About last night." He paused, causing us to mentally pause with him. "Last night did not go down the way I had envisioned it." We edged up in our seats. Was this going to be a compliment, or was it going to go somewhere we weren't expecting? "Last night, I was expecting mistakes, a few flaws, some boo boos.

We're all human. You all are very human, and mistakes happen." He took a deep breath, taking all our breath with him. "I listened and looked for mistakes last night. I know mistakes happened, and odds are, you know mistakes happened, but I don't think a single person in that crowd had any clue that mistakes happened during our performances, so that's a win for us."

Our breath returned to us.

"I'll go ahead and say it: King's Hollow's football team may have lost the homecoming game, but the King's Hollow 8th grade band scored its first victory last night."

The percussionist section was the first to break into a celebratory roar. We all followed.

SEPTEMBER - 10TH GRADE

"It's a four chord progression: E, C, G, and then D. It's not hard."

Brooks sat there, dumbfounded. He shrugged his shoulders and raised his trumpet to his lips. "I don't know, man. It's just, I mean, you just want me to improvise? Just play on the fly?"

"Yes!" Mr. Undergrove said with enthusiasm. "Improvise! E, C, G, D. Play to your heart's desire while following the chord progression!"

Brooks shrugged his shoulders again, his concern dripping from his face.

"There are no rules, Brooks. You can do this. Let yourself experiment," Mr. Undergrove added.

Mr. Undergrove counted us down and we began playing again. We approached Brooks' big solo moment and braced ourselves. He slugged through it, hitting some notes correctly and some not, but he played the entire measure without stopping, without dropping his trumpet from his lips and saying "I don't know, man."

"Brooks, do you know what you just did?" Mr. Undergrove asked. "You successfully improvised a solo. You just took one step closer to being a jazz musician. Be proud of yourself."

"I don't know, man. I don't know," Brooks shook his head, while blushing, trying to hide his pride from shining through. "I don't know, man, but can we try it again?"

Mr. Undergrove nodded his head and we played through the designated solo section, allowing Brooks to take the spotlight again, this time with a little more confidence. He still missed a few notes, jumbling his way through the progression, but this time it sounded like he may have somewhat known what he was doing.

"I don't know, man, I don't know," Brooks repeated himself, a slight grin bursting from his trumpet. 'It's uncomfortable not knowing what you're gonna play. Like, the sheet music is there, but there's nothing telling you what exact note you need to play to make it sound right. It's ambiguous, and strange, and....and...and..."

"It's like asking a girl to dance with you at a party." Our heads turned back to Mr. Undergrove. "You know how to ask - 'Will you dance with me' - but it's the terror of not knowing what she's going to say. Will she accept your request and allow you to socially live for a few more minutes? Maybe. Quite possibly, if you know the girl well enough, she's not going to turn you down, but what if she's waiting for someone else to ask her? What if she knows who exactly she wants to dance with, and you may not be that person? You can get over yourself and just go over there to ask the girl, but that terror, that unexplainable doubt that sits in the back of your mind may be telling you to second-think yourself. 'You aren't good enough to dance with her' it says. 'She doesn't want to dance with you, she wants someone else: the football player, the soccer captain, the math whiz that tutors her, literally anyone else.' So now instead of listening to your original instinct of asking that one girl to dance with you, you've let all your buried doubt rise to the surface and take over. So you hesitate. And that brief moment of hesitation is when your opportunity to dance with that one girl that you've waited the entire party to dance with is now in the hands of another guy that has also been waiting, maybe with the same fears prancing through his subconscious. The only difference between you now and that guy on the dance floor is one simple fact: he chose to live his life and take a risk at asking a girl to dance while you let your inner demons get the best of you. Now you're still at that same party you've been at all night, but instead of finding joy on the dance floor with all the other people that are finding joy in dancing, you're sulking on the sidelines, wishing you hadn't hesitated, wishing you had risen to the occasion instead of fearing failure." Mr. Undergrove swept his hand back through his hair. "Playing an improvised solo is the same thing as asking a girl to dance. If you let your fear get the best of you, the audience will know it, we will all know it, and most importantly, you'll know it, because odds are, while you're thinking about your solo instead of playing your solo, the moment will pass and it'll be too late to save the day. But, if you let go of logic and fear, turn your brain off, and just pour your heart into it, man, that's what jazz is: it's letting go of your fears and just embracing that moment that's given to you. It's asking that girl, that one girl that takes your breath away, and you're asking her to dance without a single fear holding you back. That's jazz music, man, and if you can let your guard down just enough to embrace that, then magical things are going to happen."

That day, we all took turns trying to improvise a solo; some of us mildly succeeded, and some of us looked around the room with the mild shock in our eyes as we tried to figure out what playing an improvised solo was. Mr. Undergrove sat with us, directing us through our troubles, and tried to shelter the smile from his face that his eyes failed to hide.

JANUARY - 8TH GRADE

It was the first day back from Christmas break that Mr. Undergrove let us know his next plan for us: "I've entered the 8th grade band into a competition that is in May."

"Competition? Like a fight?" someone in the percussion section asked.

"No, not like a fight," Mr. Undergrove responded, then he stopped, scratched his head, and added, "well, I guess it kinda is like a fight. We're fighting to see who the best band is through healthy competition with other schools, so yes, yes it is a fight."

"We're going to fight another band?"

It's always someone in the percussion section.

Mr. Undergrove took a deep breath, closed his eyes, and shook his head. "No, we are going to play a series of songs before two different sets of judges. Those judges are going to give us a rating based on our performance on a scale of 1 to 5, with 1 being the highest, and 5 being the lowest. The judges will then take our scores from our two performances and average them together, and boom, that's our performance rating."

We all stared at Mr. Undergrove, slightly nodding our heads, a tad scared of the unknown.

"We're going to miss an entire day of school for this competition. An entire day."

The class broke into a wail of joy. We were sold.

OCTOBER - 10TH GRADE

"Great news everyone! I booked us a gig!" Mr. Undergrove rested his baton on his music stand.

"Why do you call every time we play somewhere a 'gig'?" Stephen asked. "Why not just say 'We're playing for someone', or 'we have a concert'? Gig? Who says that?"

"For your information, 'gig' is how cool musicians address the word 'concert'. Jazz musicians don't play concerts - they play gigs. Gig is just jazz talk. Like, 'yo, we're playing somewhere; come check our jive.'"

"You want us to check your jive? Is that like weird musician talk for someone's ..."

"Jesus! No!" Mr. Undergrove interrupted before Stephen could finish his sentence. "I know we are all guys here, but man, keep it PG!" Mr. Undergrove's face blushed a whole new color of red.

Stephen smirked, glancing around for approval as we all tried to hold in our laughter.

"Check out our jive. It's jazz talk. You know, like you want to sound cool, and if you want to invite someone to your gig, you've got to sound cool, right? So I always thought 'Come check out our jive' sounded really cool. Real jazzy. Maybe even classy sounding."

We were not classy.

"If I tell my mom to check out my jive, she's probably going to think I need to see a doctor about a disease on my-."

"Stephen, no one thinks 'jive' is a reference to your.....well, manhood," Mr. Undergrove said back.

"You didn't let me finish," Stephen responded. "My mom's going to think I have something weird going on down there, like warts or something. The awkward part is my uncle is a doctor and he'll be the one that she's going to want me to talk to."

"Oh, well, I guess that does make that awkward," Mr. Undergrove said. The awkwardness fell into the classroom, lingered just enough for us all to try to keep ourselves from laughing, and then floated back up into the air. "Scratch the whole 'jive' thing, I guess, since Stephen has officially made 'jive' weird."

"Hey, but in all seriousness, I think 'jive' is cool. It's a cool word, man. I'm gonna tell the girl I sit next to in Biology on Friday to check out my ji-"

"Enough!" Mr. Undergrove said, interrupting Stephen again.

"So where's our gig?" I asked. Mr. Undergrove connected his eyes with mine just long enough for me to tell he was thankful that someone was trying to change the topic.

"It's at the hospital, Mercy Medical, three Fridays from now in the evening. It's a fundraiser for the addiction rehab program."

The awkwardness fell back into the room again.

"Is that like druggies that are trying to get clean?" Brooks asked it, but we were all almost 100% positive that it was asked for dramatic effect.

"Yes, it's a program that assists people that have made questionable decisions with their life get back on their feet again," Mr. Undergrove said. "So yes, if you want me to use the words you used, yes, it's like druggies that are trying to get clean. And we are going to entertain them. The doctors, the staff, the people that are a part of the program, the patrons that are there to help raise money for the program - we will be their entertainment, and we are going to put on one heck of a show.

"Addiction rehab program? Sweet. They're gonna be digging our jive, for sure."

"Yes, Stephen, they most certainly will," Mr. Undergrove responded, "and thank you for using 'jive' correctly."

Stephen smiled, glanced over at me, and whispered, "Who says I meant it to be used correctly?"

FEBRUARY - 8TH GRADE

May 3rd. The date was written in solid blue marker on a piece of paper taped above the band door entrance. It was also above the blackboard at the front of the band room, above the door to the instrument room, and above the door to Mr. Undergrove's office. May 3rd was the date of the band competition, and it loomed over Mr. Undergrove like a shadow stalking him in the dark. We were learning six new pieces, three for each set of judges. "Are you practicing at night? I can tell when you don't practice. I can tell, especially with the flutes," Mr. Undergrove said. The entire flute section, in shock & horror of being called out publically in that manner, shot Mr. Undergrove an evil glare as a collective unit; it was the most united action that they'd accomplished in weeks. "Keep staring at me like that," Mr. Undergrove shot back in reaction, "the truth can hurt sometimes."

"Mr. Undergrove is all over his feelings nowadays." Someone brought it up at the lunch table. Someone agreed. Someone wished we weren't even entering a band competition. Someone admitted that they never practiced and forged their parents' signatures on their weekly band notes. Someone admitted that their parents just signed their weekly band notes knowing that their child never practiced. Someone wished they weren't in band at all.

I arrived at school early one day; I had bombed my math test earlier in the week and my math teacher was allowing me to make corrections as long as I came to do them before school started. Mr. Undergrove was standing outside of the band room, staring at his door, a concerned look on his face. "Would you look at that?" he asked me. On the band door, etched into the wood, was a derogatory picture of what looked like Mr. Undergrove having inappropriate relations with a tuba. I tried my best not to laugh, putting my hand over my mouth and then pretending to cough. "It's ok, you can laugh. I did." Mr. Undergrove let out a hefty chuckle, shaking his head, letting a grin break out across his face. "I mean, how does that even work? Whoever drew this has a weird sense of imagination. Good golly."

"Are you going to cover that up?" I asked.

"Nah. Whoever did it obviously wants attention. Let them have their moment of glory." I'll let Mr. Cooper know. He'll get a janitor to paint over it this afternoon."

"You're not bothered by it?" I asked. "I mean, we can cover it up with some bulletin board paper before anyone else sees it."

"The difference between an adult and a child is that an adult won't let the actions of someone trying to tear them down bother them," Mr. Undergrove said. "Someone drew that because they wanted to hurt my feelings. It's ok. It's middle school. Someone in middle school is always trying to hurt someone else's feelings. That's everywhere at every middle school in America. Remember that, ok? No matter what kind of a person you are, someone is always going to try to tear you down, especially in a middle school environment."

I nodded, not even really sure what Mr. Undergrove was trying to tell me.

"Let them have this moment. They obviously need it to feel good about themselves."

"Did you do it?" 2nd period Math class. Brent nudged me in the side. "The tuba picture on Undergrove's door. Was it you?"

“No!” I tried to whisper back. “Jeez, no! I wouldn’t do something like that!”

“I figured. Thought I’d double check.” Brent then leaned over to Caroline on the other side of us. “Did you do it?” he whispered.

“Do what?” Caroline asked without looking up from her paper.

“You know, the ‘artwork’ on the band room door?” Brent winked his left eye at her.

“No, girls don’t do that kind of crap,” Caroline said, rolling her eyes and turning her shoulder away from Brent to focus back on her work.

Brent leaned back over to me. “She’s right” he said as he put his eyes back on his assignment. “A girl probably would never draw something like that.” Brent let his statement settle into the air for a moment before he leaned back over to me. “Or that’s what they want us to believe?”

“I don’t think Caroline drew the picture,” I responded.

“Sure, sure, it may not have been Caroline, but it could have been a girl. Any girl. Any girl in the school.” Brent lifted his hands and slapped them against his head. “What if it was a united collaboration of an entire section?” His eyes widened. “I mean, there’s the flute section. Not a single guy there, and Undergrove did make them mad the other day.”

“I don’t think-“

“Mr. Brent, surely you’re done with your work by now? Surely you’re not distracted by something else in my class?” Mrs. Watson, our math teacher, asked with intensity.

"No, ma'am," Brent answered. "Trying to complete it now. I would never get distracted from my math work."

"Good, let's get to it." Mrs. Watson's eyes lowered back to her clipboard as she walked around the classroom, assisting students that may need her help.

Brent leaned back over to me. "Girls are mean. They're mean and intense. It definitely could have been a girl that drew the picture."

"Maybe. Or maybe it was a dude. We don't know."

"But, it definitely could have been a girl," Brent said back.

"Mr. Brent!" Mrs. Watson raised her voice a notch louder than before. "Please explain to me what is so interesting over there!"

"We're discussing the exact approach to how to formulate this linear equation at a precise-"

Mrs. Watson cut Brent off. "I don't want to hear another excuse! The two of you keep your mouths shut and focus on the assignment in front of you!"

We both turned our heads back to our work. After a few moments, Brent silently muttered, "That artwork? Definitely the work of a girl. Definitely."

"You don't know-"

"But I do know that a girl was capable of doing it," Brent said. "Gotta admit, the odds are it probably wasn't a guy. Unless it was you..."

"Dude, it wasn't-"

"Out! Now!" Mrs. Watson was yelling now. "Both of you! Report to Mr. Cooper's office immediately!"

Brent and I sat on the bench outside of Mr. Cooper's office. Inside we could hear him talking on the phone. I kicked my foot against Brent's foot. "All you had to do was shut up about the picture. That's all you had to do."

"Dude, I'm just saying, no one knows if it was a guy or a girl that drew that picture. It could have been a guy, but it most definitely was probably a girl."

"Oh, jeez, you're still on that theory?" I hoped Brent picked up on the annoyance in my voice.

"To assume only guys draw such derogatory pictures would be sexist, right?" Brent asked. "What better way to throw the scent off of an investigation than to draw something like that out in the public eye? It's gotta be a girl. Gotta be."

"This picture is not that big of a deal. I mean, not even Mr. Undergrove was that upset about it this morning."

"You talked to Undergrove?" Brent asked, a look of concern on his face.

"Yeah, he was super chill about it. Not even that mad. Said something about whoever did obviously needed this moment or something like that. Something about someone is always going to want to tear you down. I don't know. You should ask him about it." My words seemed to fumble out of my mouth.

"Well, it was a girl, so...." Brent's voice trailed off. The sound of the ticking from the clock on the wall above us seemed to fill the room.

"Brent, the picture on the door of the band room....it was a tuba. You're the only tuba player in the band..."

Brent's eyes widened for a brief second, half with shock, half with panic, before they narrowed back down and then focused back on his feet. "Girls draw ugly stuff sometimes too," he mumbled.

"Yeah," I nodded my head. I leaned back in my seat and stared at the doorknob to Mr. Cooper's office while Brent continued to look down at his feet. We didn't speak for several moments, letting the sound of the ticking clock fill the air once more.

"Hey Brent?"

"Yeah?"

I swallowed, and then shifted my feet. "It could have been a girl." The ticking of the clock seemed to die down. "The picture could have been drawn by a girl maybe."

"Yeah, it could have been. But it may not have." Brent's voice trailed off again.

"I know."

"Look, when we go in there..." Brent seemed to stumble on his words. "If Mr. Cooper asks why we're down here...."

"It's because we were talking too much during Math class," I said. "That's all."

Brent looked up at me, grinned slightly, looked back down at his feet, and responded, "50% chance it was a girl".

Mr. Cooper emerged from his office and motioned us to join him. A stern talking later, we were back in class under the promise to not misbehave and to try our best. "If this happens again and the two of you are sent back here at any given point in the future," Mr.

Cooper said, "you'll be spending time with me after school sweeping the halls." We assured him it would not be an issue and left it at that.

By the time band class rolled around, people giggled as they walked into the band room, the questionable picture still on display. The only people that seemed enamored by the picture was the drum section (as usual), but the stern look on Mr. Undergrove 's face that day sent the message that today may not be the day to try to make it a public discussion.

While there was talk and gossip about the artwork on Mr. Undergrove's door during lunch and into the afternoon, when the following school day rolled around, Mr. Undergrove's door was a new shade of red, and people quickly forgot that the artwork had even existed. We all moved on, and Mr. Undergrove never addressed the issue in front of his classes. In the long run, it just marked one day closer to the band competition.

NOVEMBER - 10TH GRADE

It was Friday. Three weeks had passed by in what seemed like an hour. Solo improvisation had been practiced. Notes had been conquered. Our timing was impeccable. We were ready.

It wasn't our first "gig" as a jazz band. When the school year first started, Mr. Undergrove had gotten us a performance spot at the town's annual hot sauce festival. And not long after that, we played in the school's courtyard during all three lunches, so anyone that chose to eat outside that day was exposed to some jazz during their lunch period. And right after that, we played for the local Kiwanis club at one of their monthly meetings. So we were ready for this next gig, but it was our first gig playing for former drug addicts.

"So, if these guys are former drug addicts, do we need to worry about them trying to steal our stuff?" Kevin brought up a valid point. "I mean, if my saxophone gets jacked in the line of duty, I'm not going to be able to afford to buy a new one."

"No, guys, our equipment is not going to get 'jacked' by the crowd tonight," Mr. Undergrove responded, half annoyed at Kevin's question. "Drug addicts are people, just like you and me, that have made difficult decisions with their lives and have had their share of struggles. They're trying to make themselves better though. They're grasping for a turning point, and the fundraiser tonight is about raising money for the program that gives those type of people a fighting chance. There will be some former addicts there, but there will also be a lot of local businesses, churches, service organizations, and a few corporations there as well, all with the same intention: to make sure a program like this continues to be successful."

We nodded in agreement.

"Oh," Mr. Undergrove added, "shirt and tie dress again tonight. I know you guys aren't a fan of that look, but it makes us sound better when we look professional." A few people groaned or rolled their eyes, but Mr. Undergrove continued on with our final instructions. "The fundraiser event starts at 7:00 PM, so we need to start setting up at the hospital in the gala room by 6:00 PM. That'll give us time to get all our equipment and instruments inside and arranged, and then we can warm-up and smooth out all the wrinkles before the crowd begins to roll in. I'm not sure if they're going to feed us, so plan on eating before we meet here at 6:00. We will load all of your cars with our equipment and caravan over to the hospital together."

Brooks came up with a counter-argument: "Let's meet here at 5:00, load our stuff, and then go get tacos. If you let us do that before tonight's gig, we will never fuss about dressing up in our shirts and ties ever again."

In an instant, the nervousness of playing jazz in front of a crowd of former drug addicts dissipated and excitement took over. Even Mr. Undergrove was on board with it.

"Wait," Stephen called out. "We'll call it 'Trombones, Trumpets & Tacos'! It'll be a bonding experience!"

With a united cry of joy, the evening before us just became magical.

APRIL - 8TH GRADE

I had gym class near the end of the day. 7th period. 8th period was English class with Mrs. Tolbert. Because I had one more class to sit through, I had to watch how sweaty I got during gym, because, let's be honest, no one wants to be the sweaty kid in middle school, or anywhere else for that matter, even if it is at the end of the day. The only other kid that went from gym class to English class was a 16-year-old that was still in the 8th grade named Max. He normally slept through every class, so he'd go from sleeping in the bleachers of the school's gymnasium to sleeping in a desk in Mrs. Tolbert's room. Max never did any work, so in terms of gym class, he never broke a sweat.

Our gym teacher was Coach Brier, a tall, skinny, fit but equally frail woman that looked like she had been teaching since the dawn of time. She appeared to be hard-of-hearing if someone was asking a question, but was quick to start yelling at a kid if she thought she even heard the slightest hint of profanity. She mumbled when she talked, and frequently made contradicting statements. She once told us that running was a great cardio exercise, but that it could also run us to an early grave. "How is it a great exercise if it will kill us?" we asked.

"Push-ups will kill you if you're not careful," she responded, "running is great, unless you can't run. Then it's bad."

Coach Brier didn't know any of our names, despite that she'd been our gym teacher since 7th grade. "Marshall. Marshall. Marshall?" Coach Brier was calling the role for attendance. We all looked around the gym for a person by the name of Marshall. Was this Marshall kid new? I mean, it's King's Hollow; it's a roving door of kids coming and going all the time. Kids coming that had been kicked out of other schools; kids leaving as they've been kicked out for excessive bad behavior, fighting, or drugs. Yes, we were in that type of school.

"Marshall! Answer me!" I realized Coach Brier was yelling at me. "Marshall, raise your skinny arm right now!" The rest of the class stared at me while I stared at Coach Brier, unsure of how to respond to her. "Marshall Wilton! I have called your name repeatedly! Answer me! Or so help me, Lord, I will smack you into next week!"

"Coach Brier, my name is Mitchell. Mitchell Williams."

Coach Brier squinted her eyes at me, then at her attendance notebook, then back to me, then back to her notebook. "Says here that your name is Marshall, Marshall. Care to explain that?"

"Coach Brier, my name is Mitchell. I've always been Mitchell. All last year I was Mitchell. Why would I go by Marshall now?"

Coach Brier squinted at me a little more, the wrinkles in her skin almost folding over her eyes. Her eyes then glanced back at her attendance notebook as she made a weird gruffling noise in her throat, and then Coach Brier looked at me and said, "Michael, why aren't you dressed out today?"

"Coach Brier," I answered, "I am dressed out. I wasn't wearing this when I got here. I changed in the locker room with everyone else." I then added, "And it's Mitchell. Mitchell Williams. Not Marshall. Or Michael." I flinched. Why did I correct her?

"Mitchell, go run a lap for your insubordination."

I didn't argue. I ran a lap around the gymnasium as instructed. Before the end of class, two other students ran laps for shooting the basketball from the three point line instead of the free throw line, one student ran a lap for not knowing the difference between a forward and a point guard, and Max was instructed to run a lap for sleeping on the bleachers. Instead of running his lap, Max continued to sleep.

After class, I tried to apologize to Coach Brier, but it backfired. "Michael, this is the third time this week you haven't dressed out for gym class! Now, explain yourself!"

"Coach Brier, I dress out every day," I responded. "I promise. Besides, today is only Tuesday, so there's no way I haven't dressed out three days this week."

Coach Brier raised her clipboard and whacked it against my head, just hard enough for it to sting. "Manson, you best know better talking to me like that! Now go on to your next class before I call your momma and get you expedited to the courthouse!"

I bit my tongue and went on to Mrs. Tolbert's class for two reasons: 1) it was obvious that Coach Brier had no clue who I was, or who anyone was, and 2) I didn't want to know what being "expedited to the courthouse" meant. I mean, does anyone, literally anyone, know what that means?

NOVEMBER - 10TH GRADE

5:00 PM. We all met at school dressed in our shirts and ties. Because Northern Kent only had two activity buses, and because those two activity buses were being used on this particular evening by the basketball teams, we had to load several cars with all the equipment needed for our gig, and then divide up to caravan over to Taco Bell for "Trombones, Trumpets, & Tacos." Initially, we all figured 'going for tacos' meant we would be going to the local Mexican restaurant, but that's not what Mr. Undergrove had in mind. "We're going to Taco Bell; 'real' Mexican food tears my stomach up, and I can't have that when we have a gig."

"Burritos no bueno for el stomacho," Stephen said. "Gotta hablo espanol."

"Fine, burritos make me runo to el bano."

"El crapo," Stephen responded. "It's 'el crapo.'"

Phillip took Justin and Kevin in his car. Ian took Stephen and David. Kirby rode with Josh. I opted to ride with Brooks. "Yo, Undergrove!" Brooks said as we all split up to go to our vehicles, "ride with us!" To both of our shock, Mr. Undergrove shrugged his shoulders, grabbed his trumpet case out of his car, and proceeded to join us in Brooks' SUV.

"What kind of crap are you listening to?" Mr. Undergrove asked. Brooks tapped his fingers on the wheel along to the beat of the music blasting out of the car's stereo as he drove down the road.

"That's Pearl Jam. Everyone loves Pearl Jam, man, c'mon. Pearl Jam is the bomb." Brooks smiled as he defended his musical choice to our band director, who was very much riding in the front seat of Brooks'

SUV, flipping through Brooks' CD collection, and offering criticism on each CD he recognized.

"Sucks. Sucks. Good. Blah. Blah. Excellent. Blah. Sucks. Overrated."

"Overrated?!" Brooks' voice squeaked into a high emotional pitch. "You think Sonic Youth is overrated?!" He turned down the volume on the stereo, a look of concern on his face. "Sonic Youth isn't just a band; it's like a musical movement of expression for listeners from all walks of life. They're like, ya know, progressive leaders on defining the individual. It's more than just a band making music; it's a way of thinking differently."

Mr. Undergrove looked back at me in the backseat and then back to Brooks.

"Are you in a cult?" Mr. Undergrove asked.

"What?" Brooks stammered. "Am I in a cult? Why would you ask me that?"

"Are you in a cult?" Mr. Undergrove repeated himself.

Brooks looked at me in the backseat, then to Mr. Undergrove, then back to me. "You hear this guy, man? He thinks we're in a cult, man. Asking us if we're in a cult." Brooks shook his head and then checked his blind spot as he changed lanes.

"He didn't ask me, Brooks. He asked you," I said from the back seat.

Brooks shot me a look in his rearview mirror, and then took a deep breath. "No. No, Mr. Undergrove, I'm not in a cult. I just like good, quality music, like Sonic Youth. What makes you think that I'm in a cult?"

Mr. Undergrove looked back at me. "Did you see how he hesitated when I asked him if he was in a cult?"

"Yes," I replied, trying my best to muffle my laughter.

Brooks, clearly frustrated, began to grip his steering wheel.

"Brooks, for future reference, if someone asks you if you're in a cult, and if you have to stop and think about it, then yes, you're in a cult."

My laughter was starting to get the best of me as I sputtered out a giggle or two in between gasps to hold my breath to keep me from laughing.

"Sonic Youth isn't music," Mr. Undergrove said, "it's noise with lyrics that people don't understand. Because it's different and people, especially teenagers, are so desperate to be different, they embrace it trying to be 'cool'. People will worship something, anything really, if they think it'll make them 'cool'. So you have an entire fan base of young, hormonal teenagers desperately wanting to be different embracing a band that's not that good and hard to understand, and those teenagers put that band high up on a pedestal and worship them because it makes them feel special inside because they themselves don't understand the music, but by liking the music, the general public doesn't understand the teenager, and then the teenager feels good about himself because they, like Sonic Youth, cannot be understood. It's a cycle, and it's also like a cult. Overrated if you ask me, but I'm not a teenager trying to fit in or stand out."

"Liking Sonic Youth doesn't make me a cult leader," Brooks replied.

"I didn't say you were a cult leader," Mr. Undergrove responded, "but the fact that you see yourself as a leader in a cult and not just a follower is a sign that you may be in a cult. If you can tell me three reasons why you like Sonic Youth other than the idea of liking something no one else likes makes you 'mysterious' or 'different', then ok, you can be a Sonic Youth fan that's not a part of the Sonic Youth cult."

"Well, I......I......they.....well.....ya know that.....it's just...." Brooks gripped the steering wheel even tighter as he stammered for words to use in his defense.

"Brooks, congratulations. You're in a cult." Mr. Undergrove smiled at his logical victory. I, again, laughed from the backseat as Brooks pulled into the Taco Bell parking lot.

APRIL - 8TH GRADE

Most middle schools have gym class. Some middle schools have gym teachers that don't care if you dress out or not as long as you participate. Some middle schools have gym teachers that don't care if you participate as long as you dress out. Most middle schools have gym teachers that don't care if you actually develop any skill in a sport as long as you don't give them any behavior issues.

Coach Brier broke the mold because she wanted it all.

Our grade in gym class was determined by three factors: 1) dressing out in 'gym-friendly' clothes for each class, 2) participation, and 3) actual skill in whatever sport or activity Coach Brier was trying to teach us at that moment.

I didn't mind dressing out. I participated in every class. Most of the kids participated, except for Max, who continually slept through class on the bleachers on a daily basis. But skill? That was where my struggles peaked. Dad said I was born with two left feet; Grandma said that when God was handing out muscle coordination, I was too busy getting seconds in the metabolism line. Either way you looked at it, I wasn't the best athlete. I could run, because c'mon, there's not much skill required to do that, but any sport that involved a ball was tough since I couldn't ever grasp the concept of catching, hitting, kicking, or throwing. In elementary school, I was always one of the last kids picked for any type of game. It never bothered me until middle school.

Why middle school?

Because girls. That's why.

They were everywhere: in every class, on every hall, at every game, and at almost every activity you could possibly want to do on the weekend outside of school. There was no escaping them.

And they were beautiful. So beautiful that I made it my mission to avoid them by any means possible. Talk to a girl? Girls don't talk to guys like me: guys that can't hit, kick, throw or catch a ball. Girls don't associate with guys that struggle in school, and definitely not guys that enjoyed band class. I was the type of guy that girls liked to ignore, so I tried to fly under the radar as much as possible around any girl in any of my classes. Being invisible was easy to do because it kept the spotlight on other guys. If the spotlight was on other guys, then there was no way a girl could notice if I wasn't the smartest guy in the room, or in the case of gym class, if I was 'athletically challenged'.

Coach Brier's skill tests ruined my ability to be invisible and put my lack of athletic skills front and center.

In 7th grade, during our football unit, Coach Brier took us outside to the football field where we could see three orange cones sat, each significantly apart from each other. We stood on one end of the field as Coach Brier started to give directions. "The rules are simple: you will kick the football from the line right here in the end zone. If your ball lands near the first cone, you will get a 'C'. If your ball lands near the second cone, you will get a 'B'. And if your ball lands near the last cone way down there," Coach Brier pointed all the way down the field to the other end of the field, "you will get an 'A'. Are there any questions?"

I wanted to raise my hand to ask, but thank goodness Stephen was already asking what I was thinking. "What happens if you kick the ball and it doesn't land near the first cone?"

Coach Brier placed a football tee on the ground. "You'll get three opportunities, and if you fail to reach any of the cones, then you get an 'F' for this assignment. That's fair."

Stephen responded, "So, if we can't kick a football, we're just in some serious trouble?"

"All trouble is serious, Mr. Steppin."

"Steppin?" Stephen asked. "My name is Stephen."

"That's what I said," Coach Brier confirmed.

One by one, I watched kid after kid in my gym class step up to the football tee, take a running start, and boot the football to the 'C' or 'B' cones. A few kids, mainly the kids on the school soccer team, were able to land their ball near the 'A' cone. Every girl that had gone to the tee was successful at landing their football in 'C' territory on the first try. Some girls took their second chance and pushed their grade up to a 'B'.

It was my turn. The pressure to perform was on. The more I looked at the 'C' cone, the farther away it looked. Could I kick it that far? I mean, no one had missed it yet. There was that one boy that messed up on his first kick, which was nice to see since it meant I wasn't going to be alone in my struggle, but on the boy's second attempt, his kick landed him in 'B' territory.

I stood at the football tee looking down on the ball. "Well, let's get this done, Mr. Williamson," Coach Brier said.

"It's Williams."

"No," Coach Brier said shaking her head, "the ball is brown. Are you colorblind?"

"Never mind," I mumbled under my breath since I didn't know how to even respond to her. The ball sat on the tee, ready for me to kick it. How hard could this be? Anyone could kick a football, right? I backed up a couple feet, just like everyone else had done before me. In the *Peanuts* comics, the only thing that stopped Charlie Brown from kicking the football was Lucy yanking it out from him. There was no Lucy in this scenario; just me, a tee, and a football.

"Today please." Coach Brier was growing impatient.

I pushed off with my left leg, took two big strides, and then swung with my right foot. I felt the weight of my leg hit the football, its force pushing the ball off the tee and into the air.

I looked up. A shadow moved across the blue sky, surfing on the wind, gliding with grace, almost like a bird, over the football field. It passed the 'C' cone, passed the 'B' cone, and then landed just 10 feet shy of the 'A' cone. It bounced as it hit the ground, gliding back into the air a couple of feet, and then landed again.

I stood there, in the end zone, dumbfounded. Did that just happen? I mean, this is the kind of stuff that happens in movies: the unpopular kid gets a chance to shine and no one expects him to do anything and then, boom, he scores a metaphoric homerun. I didn't need a homerun right now, because I had just kicked a football almost to the 'A' cone with ease. This is the part of the movie where the football coach, who just happens to be watching, storms the field and demands I join the football team. One week later, I kick four field goals in a game. The next week I kick seven. The last game of the season, with only seconds left on the clock, I kick the winning field goal to help the team score the championship. The crowd goes wild. My teammates carry me off the field. The cheerleaders all argue over who gets to date me. The final shot of the movie is me, standing in the middle of the field, surrounded by my teammates, championship trophy in hand, the crowd chanting my name, my parents standing on the sidelines hand in hand and bursting with pride. Credits roll. Everyone in the movie theater applauds.

Coach Brier's voice brought me back to reality.

"Well, Mr. Wilson, I've never seen that happen before."

The football sat on the field, a mere ten feet away.

No, this couldn't be right. I kicked it, didn't I? I watched the ball fly through the air. I watched it! Did I daydream all that? It happened, right?

There was some snickering coming from behind me. A few snorts. Some giggles. But then the laughter started up and just got louder and louder. I turned around; everyone in the class was laughing. Some of the girls were pointing at me and laughing. Girls were pointing at me! And laughing as they did so!

The air felt heavier. The clouds in the sky were darker. The laughter that came from my classmates resonated in the wind, carrying it for miles; kids at other schools surely could feel my embarrassment float through the town's streets.

I turned my back on the class, girls and all, still enjoying my failure. I mean, this wasn't the end of the world; in theory, I had two more kicks. Two more chances to fix this. No one had needed all three chances yet, but that was ok, because this situation could be repaired. I mean, embarrassing things happen every day. I could go get the ball, put it back on the tee, and then secure a decent grade with my next attempt. As I went to go get the ball, I noticed that the ground felt different; I could feel the dirt on the ground with my right foot: the rocky soil, the grass, and the weeds.

It turns out that me barely kicking the ball wasn't what everyone was laughing at.

I looked down; there was no shoe on my right foot.

My eyes had not played tricks on me after all. I had not imagined my glorious kick. Something had flown through the air and landed near the 'A' cone. It just wasn't the ball; it was my right shoe.

"Coach Brier, ma'am, can I ask you a question?"

"I suspect so."

"Is there any way you can count my shoe instead of the ball?"

"I can't count shoes. If I could, I'd be here until next Thursday."

"Why next Thursday?" I asked.

"I think it's obvious." Coach Brier pointed at the field like it was full of shoes littered everywhere.

"Oh. I still got two more chances, right?"

"Mr. Mark, do I look like a calculator?"

"Ok. I guess I'll go get my shoe and try again."

"You best hustle," Coach Brier said. "Today ain't got all day."

"Yes, ma'am."

The laughter continued as I walked the field to retrieve my shoe.

I gave it two more chances. While my shoe stayed on my foot, the football never got close to the 'C' cone; I was the only student to not earn a grade on the assessment. As we returned indoors to the gym, I asked Coach Brier about a chance at redemption.

"I believe the rule stated three attempts. Did you make three attempts?" she asked.

"Yes, ma'am."

"It sounds like you answered your own question."

And that's how the rest of 7th grade went: I became the 'shoe kicker' to all the kids around King's Hollow Middle School. My friends called me 'shoe kicker' when they wanted to get on my nerves. My teachers called me 'shoe kicker' when I wasn't paying attention in class. Even my parents called me 'shoe kicker' if I had not completed my house chores on time.

All because of Coach Brier's football assessment.

So when Coach Brier continuously called me by a wrong name a full year later, I was really starting to get frustrated.

"You wanna know how I deal with Coach Brier?" Max asked.

During Mrs. Tolbert's class, we were placed into partners to complete an assignment, and lucky me got placed with Max, Mr. Do Nothing. He mostly stared at his paper, then stared at me completing my paper, and then copied whatever I had wrote down, completely assuming my answers were correct. Max continuously looked around the room at some of the other groups, probably secretly wishing he had not been stuck with me, and dug his fingers into his ears, scratching them the way a dog would use his back paw to scratch their head.

"I think I know how you deal with her, Max. You sleep on the bleachers," I responded.

Max snorted loud enough to cause me to jump a little in my seat. He put his pencil down, cracked his knuckles, and then responded, "I'm awake enough to notice she don't like you too much to remember yo name. And it bothers you. So you want to know how I deal with her or you want to go back to scribbling down all this mumbo jumbo and pretendin' we don't know each other?"

I looked at Mrs. Tolbert leaning over another group's progress and then did a glance over of our progress on our work. My progress really, but Max was doing his part by copying down whatever I wrote. "Alright, how do I deal with Coach Brier?"

Max put his arms over his desk and leaned in close to me. "Coach Brier don't give no one crap that give her trouble. She thrives on worryin' the mess outta those kids that line up and just want to get their participation grade. But me? She don't want me to raise a finger cause she knows better."

I scrunched my eyebrows. "She told you to run a lap the other day for sleeping."

"And did I?" Max smiled a sly smile and cracked his knuckles again. "Coach Brier fusses at me, but it's from a distance cause she knows what I do."

"What you do?"

"Yeah, man." Max leaned back in his seat and tapped his pencil on his desk. "Two years ago. Big fight in the cafeteria. Me and some mean Oompa Loompa dude. He was beefin' about his girl that was seen talkin' to me and he came lookin' for something he didn't know that he didn't want."

"What didn't he want?" I asked, a blank stare in my eyes.

Max grew agitated. 'Me, man, c'mon. He didn't want none of me."

"Oh. Yeah. Of course."

"Oompa Loompa dude came at me, claiming I had to stay away from his girl and I best recognize. Talkin' crap. Told me he'd put a bullet in me and another one in my house for my momma. So I hit him with my chair and then broke his nose with my fist." Max clenched his hand tight, showing me his fist so I could visualize Max in action. "Three teachers came runnnin'. Pulled me off him. Dragged Oompa Loompa out of the cafeteria and me the other way. Only person that had their arms around me was Coach Brier. I won't havin' the fight end like that, with Oompa Loompa thinkin' there would be a rematch, so I threw my head back and busted Coach Brier's forehead. She let go of me and I took off runnin' out the cafeteria."

"You hit a teacher?"

Max corrected me. "Head butted a teacher. Broke the skin. Knocked her down. Now she know."

"Know what?" I asked out of curiosity.

"Know that I don't hesitate. To this day she don't beef with me. Now, I use her class to nap, and she keeps her distance."

"Did you ever get to the other guy?" I then added, "Or was the fight over?"

Max rolled his eyes. "Nah, man, Oompa Loompa had teachers protecting him, making him look like the victim. Swore he didn't start it. He knows what up though."

"So, you like never finished the fight?"

"Man, didn't you hear me?" Max asked. "He had teachers surrounding him. They took me down and got me suspended. Talkin' about how I'm a 'disturbance'. Coach Brier come up there, all bloody and junk and tells them I hit her. Got ten days at home."

"Oh." I picked up my pencil and put my eyes back down on my paper.

"That's why Coach Brier don't beef with me. She remembers."

"You head butted a teacher, and now that teacher won't 'beef with you'. What's that got to do with Coach Brier not remembering my name?"

Max smacked his lips. "Man, you don't get it, do you? You give her a reason to leave her alone. Quit being all respectful and junk. Live a little."

"Live a little. Got it."

"I've got it made. No teacher expects nothing from me," Max said.

"Except me, Max." Mrs. Tolbert had walked up behind us and had heard the tail end of our conversation. Max stiffened up as Mrs. Tolbert put her hands on Max's shoulders. "I expect the both of you to get this assignment completed before we leave here today. Especially you, Max. You've seen it several times before, so it should be easy for you."

"Yes Ma'am," we both seemed to mutter in unison.

"Good, boys, now, let's finish up." With that, Mrs. Tolbert moved on to the next group and the two of us picked up our pencils and went back to work, me completing the work and Max copying my work.

"She taught my daddy. My daddy don't like to hear bad things from her, so I best we finish." Max glared me at me a look that almost screamed, 'Don't tell anyone I'm doing my work.'

The next day, I dressed out like I normally did for gym class, but Max's words echoed in my mind. "Live a little." What did that even mean? Max told me to quit being respectful, but if I got an attitude with Coach Brier, wouldn't that just make my situation worse? I mean, right now she couldn't get my name straight for anything, but if I gave her a reason to remember my name, that would make it easier to get in trouble, right? Maybe if I showed a little attitude, maybe she would back off a little. It works for the most part for some of the girls in my class. They mostly ignored Coach Brier when she ranted and raved about following the rules to kickball, never seemed to give much effort, and would occasionally raise their voice at Coach Brier when they don't feel like participating. Coach Brier never forgot their names, and I never saw them running any laps around the gym. But it wasn't all the girls; it was just the girls that seemed to be a little rougher around the edges. It was the girls that, like Max, should have probably been in high school by now.

Coach Brier started gym class with us completing our warm-up exercise and running two laps around the gymnasium. She began the roll-call.

"Marshall? Marshall?" Coach Brier looked up from her notebook and scanned the room. "Marshall. We're not having this problem again today. Raise your hand, for Christ's sake."

I raised my hand. "Coach Brier?" I was asking for her attention. Max told me to live a little. Live a little; I can do that. "Coach Brier!" I spoke up with authority.

"What do you want, Michael?"

"Coach Bri..." I stopped myself. No need to be respectful. Just let it flow. "My name isn't Michael. And it's not Marshall, or Mark or anything else you call me. It's Mitchell. Mitchell Williams. Not Wilson. Or Williamson. Mitchell Williams."

Coach Brier put her hands on her hip. "Well, is that right?"

"Yes. I'd appreciate it if you'd respect that." My knees started to get wobbly. What was I doing?

"Well, Mr. Willis, I hear you. Now sit your tail down on those bleachers and think about the way you just spoke to me." She pointed to the bleachers where Max sat. Max's eyes connected with mine and he shook his head no. 'Sit down' my mind said, but Max's eyes were telling me to stand my ground. My eyes reconnected with Coach Brier, still holding one hand on her hip and pointing at the bleachers with the other. "Today, Marshall."

"I'll sit down when you can say my name correctly."

There was a gasp that came from some of the girls that were listening in on our exchange. Max scooted to the edge of the bleacher, leaning forward like he was part of our conversation. Two of the other boys that were standing near me inched away. Coach Brier moved both her hands back to her hips.

"Excuse me?"

"Coach Brier, I will respect your wishes and sit down once you say my name correctly." I felt myself feeling light-headed. Was I really doing this?

Coach Brier hesitated. She pulled her clipboard up to her eyes, then gave me a hard look. I didn't turn away, and I didn't dare to blink. This was our staring contest, and I wasn't about to lose it to someone that couldn't remember my name.

10 seconds. 20 seconds. 30 seconds. I wasn't going to back down. "I'm gonna say this nice and slow so you can understand what I'm saying and you won't have no questions about where I stand," Coach Brier spoke slowly and firmly. "Sit yo butt on them bleachers right

now, Mr.....” she hesitated. She didn’t know my name, so she couldn’t finish her sentence.

“Mr.....” I egged her on. “Mr. What? Mr. Marshmallow? Mason? Mr. What? First or last: it doesn’t matter.”

Coach Brier stared at me. If she had lasers in her eyes, I would have been a goner. “Mr. Williams. Sit down. And do it NOW.” She roared ‘NOW’ for emphasis.

With everyone in the gym looking at me, I sat down on the bleachers, two rows in front of Max. Coach Brier turned her back to us and returned to calling the attendance roll. “That was gutsy, man,” Max whispered, “but ya shouldn’t have sat down. Now she knows she can punk you.”

“She can punk me?”

“Yeah, man, she made a punk outta you. You sittin’ down and all. All these kids in here, man. She punked you.”

“I know y’all ain’t talkin’ while I’m giving instruction.” Coach Brier spun around. “You both made it very clear that this gym class isn’t for you, and now you both wanna talk? I don’t think so!”

“Yes ma’am,” I said. Coach Brier’s eyes shifted to Max: he did not reply, but bent down to wipe a smudge off his shoes.

Coach Brier went back to lining the other students up for an activity. Her hands were waving in the air, raising her voice at the kids near the front, fussing about dribbling the basketballs while she was talking. “She punked you again, man, talkin’ bout some ‘Yes ma’am’ junk.” Max rolled his eyes back, drew his arms into his sides, stuck his tongue out, and repeated my words ‘Yes ma’am’ in a high pitched whine. “That’s what you look like, man, standin’ up for yourself and then immediately givin' in to her in front of everybody. Punked, man." Max leaned back into the bleacher row behind him, put his foot up on the bleacher in front of him, and shook his head. After a minute, Max turned to me and said, "Man, why you still here? Get away from me. You weak."

Without a word, I moved two rows down so I was on the front row of the bleachers. I watched the rest of the students practice their lay-ups on the basketball goal for a few minutes before I glanced back at Max. His arms now sat folded across his chest, his head down, his eyeballs fluttering back and forth across his closed eyelids as he began to fall into sleep.

"Manson! What are you doing?"

I spun around. Coach Brier was a few mere inches from my face, her hands back on her hips, a confused look on her face.

"Manson, I've been calling you for an hour or so! Get off that bench and give me a lap for not paying attention!"

"Coach Brier, you told me to sit here on the bleachers."

Coach Brier squinted her eyes just a tad, made a gruffling noise, and then asked, "Mr. Manson, are those gym shoes or dress shoes?"

"Gym shoes, ma'am. They're skateboarding shoes. Vans. But they work just as well as basketball shoes or soccer shoes, or whatever sport I need them for."

"Good, then get to running. Two laps. One for not dressing out, and one for not listening to me when I called your name."

"Coach Brier, it's not that I didn't hear you, it's....." I hesitated. Coach Brier looked into my eyes with annoyance. Did I really want to go down this path again? "Two laps. I got it."

"Good. Fast laps too. None of this jogging mumbo jumbo that causes heart attacks."

As I finished my laps, Coach Brier instructed me to join one of the lines for the next basketball activity: three pointers. When it was my time to shoot, Coach Brier stopped me. "When you shoot, Mr. Willis, shoot with your legs, not your arms. And no granny shooting either." I shot the ball, ignoring my constant-changing name. I wasn't sure if Coach Brier had forgotten our verbal altercation at the beginning of class or if maybe she was showing me grace and forgiveness, but it was nice to not be sitting on the bench anymore. As I jogged to the opposite side of the court for the rebound line, my eyes rested on Max, still sitting on the bleachers. He was awake, arms still crossed across his chest, and his eyes were glaring at me, silently screaming with anger from the sidelines.

NOVEMBER - 10TH GRADE

"Kirby, I'm dead serious, the man hates Sonic Youth." Brooks was struggling to drop Mr. Undergrove's earlier suggestion that Sonic Youth was overrated.

We had pulled three tables together for the jazz band to sit together as a combined unit while we consumed our tacos and shared fellowship with each other before our big gig for the drug addiction rehab program at the hospital. Brooks, sitting across from Kirby, continued to rant about Mr. Undergrove's musical choices.

"Dude, he doesn't like Smashing Pumpkins either!"

Kirby jolted his neck in Mr. Undergrove's direction. "You don't like the Smashing Pumpkins?"

"I don't like the Smashing Pumpkins," Mr. Undergrove confirmed.

"Who doesn't like the Smashing Pumpkins?" Kirby asked. "I mean, seriously, who? They're amazing."

I made eye contact with Philip who was chuckling under his breath. "You're not into Smashing Pumpkins either, huh?" I asked.

"Nope," he shook his head, "You?"

I shook my head. "Don't tell them down there," I motioned to the end of the table. "I don't think Kirby or Brooks could handle that right now."

Brooks couldn't hear us even if we had wanted him to for he was too engrossed in Mr. Undergrove's musical tastes. "Fine, name a band, any *modern* band that you enjoy," Brooks said. "Any band. Literally any band, and we'll let you know what we think."

Mr. Undergrove took a bite of his taco. "Nirvana."

"Nirvana?" Brooks made a face like he had bit into a lemon. "Nirvana? I mean, they're not modern. Nirvana is so four years ago. Nirvana? Really?"

"Nirvana may be 'so four years ago' to you, but I think that they are modern. They had a solid five year run in the charts, and that happened in the past five years, so I'm labeling them 'modern.'" Mr. Undergrove wiped his hands off in his napkin, took a swallow of his drink, and then added, "As I recall, I saw several Nirvana CDs in your car, so maybe you like them?"

"Yeah," Brooks said as he jabbed at his burrito with a fork, "I mean Nirvana is solid. Just wouldn't consider it modern or progressive or anything like that."

"Progressive?" Now Mr. Undergrove was raising his voice into a high pitch similar to Brooks earlier when Mr. Undergrove let him know that he thought Sonic Youth was overrated. "You don't think Nirvana was progressive? That's absolutely insane!" An older couple sitting a few tables away raised their heads and looked over at us.

"I mean, they're rock and all, but I just don't know if they were game-changers or anything," Brooks said.

Mr. Undergrove's eyes grew wide and his mouth dropped. "Brooks, Nirvana changed everything!" Same high squeaky voice.

"I don't see it," Brooks replied.

"Jeez, I keep forgetting you guys are still practically kids and have no concept of history, like real-time history, except what you study in school," Mr. Undergrove said. "1990 was all pop. All New Kids On The Block. All Michael Jackson. Wilson Phillips, Michael Bolton,

Amy Grant, stuff like that. Nirvana came along and swiped all that off the table. They told the world that pop music wasn't the end-all-be-all of the industry. And they did all that with four chords. Four simple chords. F, A#, G#, C#. Just like that." Mr. Undergrove was batting out a beat on the table. "They were just three disheveled kids from Washington being loud, singing out of tune, and refusing to behave properly with what society expected out of 'popular music'. They weren't flashy, or had dance moves, but those four chords, those four simple chords at the beginning of 'Smells Like Teen Spirit' were completely different that anything the music industry had felt in years, and, God, it was just so refreshing."

Brooks wiped his mouth with his napkin. "Dude, that's stuff everyone knows. You're not telling me anything that's not public information."

"Nirvana sat on the Billboard charts because everyone in the music industry couldn't figure out how to define them," Mr. Undergrove continued. "They didn't dress a certain way to look cool. They didn't play a certain way because they were looking for notoriety. They just played, and they played music that they believed in. That's the difference between them and your bands that are trying to sell you something. There was no gimmick. Even The Beatles had a gimmick."

No one at the table spoke for a moment.

Mr. Undergrove added, "Brooks, I gave you a hard time about liking a band. I don't care if you like Sonic Youth, or Nirvana, or whatever terrible music you want to like, but if you want to like them, know why you like them. Throw away the fashion and the politics and commercialism that mucks up this world, and own the reason why you like a band." Mr. Undergrove looked around the table. "And that goes for all of us. If you like something, or you find joy in doing an activity, or playing a sport, or whatever it is, own the fact that you like it. Embrace it. If you like soccer, be proud of it and screw anyone that tells you differently. If you like skateboarding, flaunt it. If you like a band," Mr. Undergrove's eyes met Brooks', "then like that band because you like that band, not because you think it'll make you a better person." Mr. Undergrove smiled as Brooks' scowl melted away from his face.

"Look, we're a jazz band," Mr. Undergrove said. "We're already a part of something that most people don't understand. But we're here, together, right now in this moment, sitting at a Taco Bell on a Friday night because we all believe in the importance in what we're doing. This jazz band is part of who you are. This jazz band is part of who I am. Embrace that idea, because that is the difference between a musician and the people that wish they were musicians."

Mr. Undergrove took in a deep reflective breath. "Ya know, I just said something that I don't think I'd ever hear myself say. It's Friday night. It's the weekend. Look at us - a bunch of high school teenagers and a teacher on the verge of playing a Friday night gig. A paid gig at that."

"What?!" we all erupted. "We're getting paid?!"

"Well, yes and no," Mr. Undergrove responded. "The hospital is making a donation to the band program. So we're getting paid, but we're not getting individually paid. But still, we're receiving a financial transaction for our work tonight, so yeah, we're getting paid."

"It's not going towards marching band stuff, is it?" Stephen asked. "Cause I swear if those marching bands kids get our hard earned money I'm gonna'-"

Mr. Undergrove cut Stephen off. "No, no, no, the marching band isn't going to reap the benefits of your hard work. I wouldn't do that."

"So what will we use the money for?" Stephen asked.

"I've got a plan. One that I'm keeping close to my chest for the time being. Just trust me though."

We eagerly nodded and glanced around at each other, each one of us silently hoping for something amazing that the money could be used for, like new amps, or music stands, or a sweet new drum set.

"Anyways," Mr. Undergrove continued, "as I was saying, it's Friday night, it's the weekend, and here we are, on our way to a paid gig. I think it's safe to say, gentleman, that we are officially real musicians in a real jazz band."

There was a spark of excitement in all of our eyes. He was right; we could have been anywhere on that Friday night, but instead we were together at that Taco Bell preparing to play a gig. And we were to 'own it', as instructed by Mr. Undergrove. We were musicians. We were real, actual musicians.

"Wait a sec," Brooks said, "what's our name? All great bands have legendary names."

"Well," Mr. Undergrove responded, "we're technically the Northern Kent Jazz Band, so we have a name, but I guess that's up for debate. Unfortunately, at this time, we can discuss it later because we have a gig to get to and the clock is ticking."

We cleared our tables and split back up into our vehicles. The hospital was only a ten minute drive away, so there was no concern over if we needed to follow each other or not.

The time was 5:50 PM.

APRIL - 8TH GRADE

Coach Brier normally took the time between 6th & 7th period to go to her car to smoke.

Yes, Coach Brier, our gym teacher, was a smoker. Her job was to encourage a healthy lifestyle of good eating habits and daily exercise, but she also took time between each period to smoke a cigarette.

The irony was not lost on us.

Because Coach Brier was typically smoking a cigarette at her car, it wasn't unusual for me to be the first person to the gym for 7th period gym class. I had biotechnology class for 6th period in the building directly beside the gym, so within a matter of seconds, I was able to be in the gym during the allotted class transition time. There was never a class in the gym during 6th period, so I would always walk into a completely empty building, then proceed to an empty locker room, and typically be dressed in my workout clothes and back in the gym before anyone else would show up. Occasionally another guy would arrive in the locker room while I was changing, but not often. Most kids dragged their feet when walking to the gymnasium, so some days I would be by myself inside the gym for anywhere between four and seven minutes. Almost never would Coach Brier show back up in the gym until it was time for attendance to be called.

The day I got jumped, I was the first person to the gym.

At least I thought I was. The gym, as usual, appeared empty, and the locker room, as usual, was dark. I opened the locker room door, flipped on the light switch, dropped my book bag off in front of a locker and then used the restroom. I washed my hands and then headed back to my book bag; it was gone.

It was at that moment that the lights went out.

And then my lights went out.

Stephen was standing over me, slapping me on the cheek trying to wake me up. "Dude! Are you ok?" The overhead lights seemed to be a tad brighter than before. There was a loud echo to Stephen's voice, a ringing buzz sound seemed to dwarf over the commotion of the other guys in the locker room. My head throbbed.

"What on God's green earth happened to you?" I couldn't quite make out Stephen's face, but I could recognize his voice. "You look like you got hit by a truck!" I reached up to feel the area of my head where the pain seemed to be flowing from and was greeted with an overflow of warm, red, sticky blood.

"What day is it?"

"What day is it? It's Friday. Mitchell, can you even see me? One of your eyes is swollen shut!"

I reached up to my left eye to check it, but in my confusion, misjudged the distance of my fingertips to my face and poked myself right in the eyeball. Not that eye. The right eye lid, as Stephen said, was indeed swollen shut. If I pulled on the top of my eyelid, I could see out of it. "Why is it so bright in here?" I covered my good eye and stumbled backwards a step; Stephen kept me from falling over.

"Do you know what happened to you? I came in here and the lights were off and when I switched them on, you were laying over here on the floor." Stephen sat me down on a bench; another guy brought me some paper towels to place on my head. Self-awareness began to set in as I looked around the locker room. My book bag was lying face down on the floor, its zipper pulled open and empty. My notebooks that had been inside my book bag were scattered throughout the room. Two benches sat overturned on their sides. A blue football helmet with a yellow King's Hollow Cougars logo on it laid alone on the floor, blood smeared across the outside. My head throbbed at its sight. That was my blood on that football helmet, the same blood that was currently running through the paper towels I held to my head and dripping onto the floor.

"Who did this to you?"

I heard Stephen's question, but couldn't find the words to answer it as I continued to look around the room. The colors blurred a little and the floor seemed to move like small waves on an ocean's beach. The bloody football helmet seemed to levitate in the air. I looked at Stephen, then back down to the floor.

"Mitchell, yo! Who did this to you? Stay with me!" Stephen patted my shoulder. "Mitchell, I'm going to go get Coach Brier. I want you to sit still and stay here, ok?" He disappeared out of the locker room. Ignoring Stephen's request, I stood up and walked over to the sink and mirrors in the bathroom area. Two other students changing in the bathroom area took one look at me and quickly departed.

I washed my hands and then splashed water on my face. Everything seemed to burn. I looked up into the mirror and was able to see the damage: my eyelid bloated out over my eye, my nose seemed to be crooked, my head and face were gnarled and gashed, blood dripped down from several locations on top of my head. Everything seemed to be wrecked.

"Yo! You messed up, bro." Another student watched me attempt to wash the blood off my face. "You look like Mike Tyson went to town on you," he added. I nodded. "But your ear still there, so maybe not Tyson but Evander Holyfield." I tried to smile at his joke, but found smiling made my head sting even more.

Stephen stumbled back into the locker room. “I couldn’t find Coach Brier. Ran around the outside of the gym but no dice. She wasn’t at her car either. Let’s get you out of here.” Stephen tried to grab my arm to help me walk, but I pulled away from him.

“No help. I’m ok. If we walk out of this locker room arm-in-arm, I’ll look stupid. Weak.”

“I mean, you look terrible,” Stephen said. He glanced around the locker room, taking in the chaos. “Why is there blood on that helmet?” Stephen asked, but then, looking back at me, he understood. “Dear Lord,” Stephen muttered, and then said, “Let me help you. I don’t think anyone out there will...”

“Girls, Stephen. There are girls out there.”

“Alright,” Stephen put his hands in the air with a look of understanding on his face, “I respect that. But if you fall down out there, I warned you. I’ll grab your stuff for you.”

I walked out of the locker room and felt the eyes of every student in the gym fall on me. There was some gasps from some of the girls. Some whispering amongst the guys that had already seen me in the locker room and were now getting a second viewing of the damage. I sat down on the first row of the bleachers, four rows in front of Max, who was already situated in his normal gym class seat. I could feel his stare beating down on my neck as he leaned forward his elbows onto his knees. “You got messed up.”

I said nothing. I just sat there with my hands holding paper towels to my head. I didn’t want to get into it with Max, especially not today.

“You a punk, man. Now everybody knows it. You got punked real good.”

The hair on my neck stood straight up.

"Yeah, don't say nothing. Best you just sit your punk tail right there." There was a rasp to Max's voice, one I had never noticed before.

Coach Brier walked into the gym, attendance notebook in hand. Stephen, now standing beside me, was waving his hands excitedly into the air. I grabbed his arm. "I'll tell her. Let me keep a little self-pride here." Stephen nodded and put his arms down.

Coach Brier approached our class and, not noticing me, went straight into attendance. She hollered several names before landing on mine. "Mitchell Winslow. Mitchell Winslow."

I stood up. "Mitchell Williams - I'm here."

Coach Brier hesitated. She looked me up and down, marked something in her notebook, and then spoke. I thought for sure she'd ask 'What happened to you?' Or 'Are you ok? Do you need help?' Or maybe even 'We need to talk.' Instead, Coach Brier said exactly what I should have figured that she was going to say: "Mr. Winslow, you are not dressed out and you are bloody. I don't want to hear any whining when your grade is less than satisfactory at the end of the grading period." Coach Brier then made another type of mark inside her notebook and then closed it.

"Coach Brier, ma'am, I was in the locker room by myself when the lights..."

Coach Brier cut me off. "Honestly, Marshall, I don't have time for your excuses right now, but I do know that you look like you've been down the wrong side of a one-way street, so I suggest-"

"But Coach Brier," I said, interrupting her, "you see, when I was in there, the lights went.."

"Enough!" Coach Brier shot back, this time interrupting me. "I have a class to teach. We can talk later."

"But Coach Brier, when I was in the locker room, I was..."

"I said enough!" Coach Brier was raising her voice. "I don't want to hear another word about this! Now, since you are not dressed out, you clearly are not in a state that will allow you to participate, and since you want to be argumentative then I suggest that you sit down on the bleach..."

"No!" I yelled, interrupting her again. "No! I will not sit down on the bleachers! I will not drop this for another time! You're going to listen to what I need to tell you!" Coach Brier's jaw dropped open in shock, as did the jaws of everyone in the gym. I had fully hooked my audience. "I was jumped! Someone turned off the lights in the locker room, and then beat the crap out of me with a football helmet!" I let the silence of that statement linger for a second before continuing. "It happened because I was in this gym by myself! Whoever did this knew you weren't around! You weren't around! You're never around! You're such a bad teacher that I sat on those bleachers right in front of you with my face messed up and my eye knocked shut and blood dripping on the damn floor and you couldn't even tell when you called my name for attendance! Look at me! Do I look like I'm ok?"

Coach Brier stared at me speechless. The whole class stared at me speechless. Nobody knew what to say.

"I am not ok! I need you for once to be my teacher and recognize that I am not ok!"

Coach Brier took her glasses off her face and put them on top of her head. "Get out."

"Get out?"

“Get out. Get out of my gym and go to Mr. Cooper’s office. Right now.”

I thought about saying ‘Yes, ma’am’, but I did not want to give her the satisfaction of me trying to be respectful. I grabbed my book bag, stood up, and, as the whole gym watched me, walked out of the gym, my hand holding paper towels to my head as I felt the blood soak through them.

NOVEMBER - 10TH GRADE

The unloading process for a performance wasn't an exact science, but we had it down to a habit amongst the band. The drums went first, then amps for the guitars, then the music stands, then our individual instruments, and the last item was 'the ark'.

No, not like Noah's ark. It wasn't a boat.

The 'ark' was a reference to the Ark of the Covenant, where the Ten Commandments were stored after Moses brought them down from the mountain after speaking to the man upstairs. It's also the item that Indiana Jones is looking for in the movie *Raiders of the Lost Ark*, one of Mr. Undergrove's favorite movies. Our 'ark' did not contain any commandments or mystical powers; instead it was a small blue plastic crate that held all the sheet music for every band member that would be needed for a performance. The ark ensured that every band member would have their music on hand and that no one could forget or lose their music for a performance. The day of a performance, we would load the crate collectively as a band with our notebooks full of our repertoire of songs that we could play. Most of the time, we had already finalized the set list of songs that we would perform, but we would always take, as Mr. Undergrove liked to call it, our 'entire arsenal.' Mr. Undergrove's logic: "What if the gig runs longer than we expected? What if we need a few more songs to fill the time? What if the crowd asks for an encore, but we don't have all our sheet music and we cannot provide an encore? What would happen to us then? Do you want that to be our reputation: the band that wasn't prepared?"

The ark was vital to a gig.

And, on the evening of the gig at the hospital, it was nowhere to be found.

"Hey guys, where is the ark?" Mr. Undergrove's voice sounded concerned, but that of someone that can't find their keys and not the lifeblood of a jazz band's performance.

"It's in Josh's car."

"Oh, ok." Mr. Undergrove looked around. "Where's Josh?"

"Josh is....." I looked around the hospital's gala room where we had been setting up. "Josh is right......." My eyes searched the room a second time. No Josh.

"Hey, Stephen," I asked, "where's Josh?"

"I don't know. Is he even here yet? I haven't seen him or Kirby yet. Not since Taco Bell." Stephen's eyes went straight to the drum set that was sitting at the back of our designated performance area. "The drums are here, so Kirby has gotta be here somewhere."

"We put the drums in Ian's car, remember?"

"Oh, yeah. Totally remembered that." Stephen's eyes could not hide the fact that he had already forgotten that the drums got to the hospital in Ian's car. "The drums are here, though, but not put together yet, and that's normally what Kirby would be working on right now, so....."

"Kirby isn't here then. Josh's not here. This isn't good."

No one had seen Josh and Kirby since we all arrived at the hospital. We had all mentally gone straight into performance mode with unloading the cars that no one had noticed that Josh and Kirby never arrived.

Mr. Undergrove's face began to grow pale. He checked his watch. "Ok, everyone, listen up. Does anyone know if Kirby or Josh have car phones?"

Stephen replied, "Mr. Undergrove, it's 1997. No one has those things, except rich people. If they have anything, it's a pager." Stephen pointed to the pager on the hip of his belt. "Cool kids have pagers."

"Ok, fine. Does anyone know if Kirby or Josh have pagers?"

We all looked around at each other. With the exception of Stephen, none of us had pagers. "Oh, come on!" Stephen put his hands in the air. "Am I the only one here with a pager? None of y'all are ever going to get a girlfriend like this!"

"Ya know, Stephen, that's a pressing issue, I understand, but let's try to focus on the missing band members first, ok?" Stephen nodded his head and Mr. Undergrove continued. "Now, Kirby and Josh were with us at Taco Bell. Does anyone have any idea where they could have gone instead of coming to the hospital?" We all shook our heads; their disappearance was a mystery.

"Ok, here's the plan: Phillip, you and Justin get all the percussion equipment up and running. Justin, you will have to handle all the percussion parts if needed tonight. There's no time like the present to step up your drumming game."

Justin, the sole freshman of the group, nodded his head, his eyes overwhelmingly wide.

"Stephen, you and Mitchell go outside and walk the perimeter of the hospital. The parking lot goes around the entire building. You're going to look for Josh's car; do you know what it looks like?"

"Yes. Wait, no. Wait, yes. Maybe."

I stepped in to save Stephen. "I know what it looks like. We got this."

"Good. David, you and Brooks search this floor and this floor only. All entrances to the hospital are on this floor, so if Kirby and Josh are here, they entered on this floor and may be lost."

Brooks, forgetting all about his Sonic Youth frustrations earlier in the evening, piped up. "On it!"

"Good. The rest of you: finish setting up for the gig. The show must go on, with or without Josh and Kirby, and with or without the ark, which makes things somewhat difficult. I'm going to go find a phone and call Kirby and Josh's parents to see if they know anything. If anyone discovers them, or finds anything out, report back to right here, the gala room, immediately. Does everyone understand?"

We all agreed to our positions and then split up to do our individually assigned tasks.

The time was 6:20 PM.

APRIL - 8TH GRADE

Mr. Cooper leaned back in his chair. I had been through all the details of my physical altercation in the locker room, and then my verbal altercation with Coach Brier. Mr. Cooper recorded detail after detail of what occurred in the gym on a yellow legal notepad, from times of the incidents to names of students to quotes from my description of what went down between myself and Coach Brier. He tapped the notepad with his pencil, took in a deep breath, and then stood up and walked over to the fridge he kept in the corner of his office. He pulled out a blue ice pack from the freezer and brought it back over to me. "Place this on your head. It'll burn at first due to the cold, but it will make it feel better over time. Hold it to your forehead while I call your parents."

Mr. Cooper got a hold of my mom first. He went through all the main details slowly and methodically: I had been jumped by an unknown assailant in the gym, I had suffered some damage to my face and head, I should definitely get checked out by a doctor as soon as possible, and yes, yes, yes, he would do everything in his power to get to the bottom of the situation. He assured my mom that everything was going to be ok, and then looked at his watch. "Yes, I imagine it'll take him about 10 minutes to gather his belongings and report back here so you can pick him up. No worries." He hung up the phone. "Your mom is on the way, give or take a few minutes. She's going to take you to the doctor to make sure that noggin of yours is A-ok."

"Thank you, sir." I looked down at my shoes in embarrassment. Basic recap: I got jumped, I got frustrated, and then I verbally let Coach Brier have it. There was no balance there, just a bad deed done to me and then in turn I performed a bad deed by letting Coach Brier know exactly what I was thinking. No filter, no resentment, just a flow of my thoughts on Coach Brier. And now, I was here, sitting in Mr. Cooper's office.

"Do you remember a few weeks ago when you were in here and you sat in that same very chair? What class was it? Math? You and the other kid, Bishop? Bart?"

"Brent, sir. His name is Brent."

"Brent! That's right. The two of you looked at me and assured me that getting kicked out class that day was an isolated incident. You remember that?"

I kept my eyes on the floor. "Yes, sir."

Mr. Cooper sat silently at his desk for a moment. "Didn't you tell me that it was the only time you'd ever gotten kicked out of class, the only time you had ever stepped foot in a principal's office?"

"Yes, sir, I believe I have let you down. Maybe the best thing for me right now is stay away from school for a couple of days."

Mr. Cooper ignored my 'stay away from school' comment and put his hands behind his head; his eyes glanced up at the ceiling. "Well, here you are again now, this time looking like you went a few rounds with Rocky." He glanced down to create eye contact. "You have seen *Rocky*, right? The movie about the boxer? Sylvester Stallone?"

I shook my head. "No, sir, I have not."

Mr. Cooper leaned forward onto his desk and slapped it. "No way! You've never seen *Rocky*? Rocky Balboa!" He put his hands into the air, fists clenched. "Aye yo! Adrian!"

"I know what movie you're talking about, but I've never seen it. Isn't that the movie with the 'Eye of the Tiger' song?"

"Common misconception, my good man." Mr. Cooper became animated with his hands as he placed his elbows on his desk and began making movements that mimicked his words. "The song you are referring to wasn't in the first *Rocky* movie, but actually in *Rocky III*. People get that wrong about that song all the time."

"Oh. How many *Rocky* movies are there?" I asked while shrugging my shoulders.

"Five!" Mr. Cooper held up all five of his fingers on his left hand, excitement growing in his eyes. "Five *Rocky* movies. They're all good too. In *Rocky III*, Rocky fights Mr. T. You know who Mr. T is, right? You know, the guy with all the chains and the mohawk?"

"Yeah, he was a wrestler in the WWF too," I said. "I know him."

Mr. Cooper slapped the desk again. "You are absolutely correct, young man. I believe he fought alongside Hulk Hogan on a few occasions." Mr. Cooper smiled and leaned back with his hands back behind his head. "Anyways, I like the movie *Rocky* because I can relate to that character. Here's a guy that is a talented boxer, but still a potentially lost soul. He's the ultimate underdog cause he's someone the audience is rooting for even though the audience can clearly see the odds are stacked against this guy. He's someone no one believes will be successful, and then boom, he shows everyone wrong when he scores a shot at the world heavyweight champ and almost beats him." Mr. Cooper had emphasized the word 'almost', making it stretch out a little further than the rest of his words.

"So Rocky lost?" I asked. "I thought he's supposed to be the hero in the movie, like the guy that wins at the end?"

"Not everyone wins their battles, Mitchell. Rocky almost won. Almost. He gave it his all, but still fell short. But at the end of the movie, after going 15 rounds with the champ, Rocky still stood tall, so while he didn't win his match, he never gave up either. That's why I like that character. He's a fighter, but he's also a metaphor." Mr. Cooper's face went serious. "Look at you today. You're bloody, broken, a mess. But you're still here. Still on this earth. Still with the potential to stand up. Right now, you can take what happened to you and let it defeat you, or you can be just like Rocky and come back to school tomorrow, letting everyone know that you," he poked his finger at me, "are not defeated."

"That's some pretty inspirational stuff, sir."

Mr. Cooper grinned. "We will see you tomorrow then I assume?'

The pounding in my head wanted to say 'No, I'm gonna sit this one out, but "Yeah, Mr. Cooper, I'm not going to let this defeat me. I can stand tall," is what came out of my mouth.

"Good. That's what I want to hear." Mr. Cooper sighed, tapped his desk twice with his fingers, then added, "My son got jumped once. Right here, at this very same school."

I could feel my eyes widen. "Are you serious?"

"It was years ago. Before I was principal here. William, my son, was playing basketball in the gym after school with a group of guys. I don't know who they were. William never told me. We knew he knew, but, well, his pride got in the way. After a few games, things got intense. You know how it is with guys: masculinity trumps all logic. Guys just can't have fun without feeling empowered." I thought about Brent and his picture on the band room door; perfect example. "During this after school pick-up game, feelings were hurt and prides were wounded. William was a smart kid, but just never seemed to know when to keep his mouth shut. A little smack talk at the wrong time, and then next thing William knew, three of the other guys beat the tar out of him."

"Your son wouldn't tell you who beat him up?"

"Like I said, pride was on the line. We had our suspicions, and we asked, but William just told us he didn't know who the boys were. William walked home that afternoon with a black eye eerily similar to yours and a few scrapes and bruises, but he lived to fight another day. Didn't want our help. Didn't want us to report it to the school. Didn't want anyone to know." Mr. Cooper looked down at his notepad. "William wanted to pretend it didn't happen. He did that a lot - pretended things weren't happening." He picked up a picture frame off his desk and turned it around so I could see it. The boy in the picture was tall, muscular, and looked like he was in an ad that you would see in a magazine for GAP or some store like that. The boy had a smile that beamed with happiness. "William is older now. He still thinks that he can handle his issues on his own, which he's allowed to do as an adult and all, but I worry about him sometimes too, just like your parents worry about you." He turned the picture around and picked it up and held it with his two hands. "This was William's high school senior portrait. Even then he thought he could just run away from or ignore his problems. Not much has changed." Mr. Cooper placed the photo back on his desk. "I'm going to do everything I can to find out what happened to you today. I promise you that I will not let this just slide away into some dark corner and be forgotten."

"Yes, sir, I appreciate that."'

"Your mom is on the way. I see you brought your book bag with you; is there anything you need out of your locker before she gets here?"

"No, sir. But yes, sir. I mean, no, not at my locker; I have everything I need for my homework tonight, but I need to get my trombone out of the band room."

"Of course. That band sure is sounding good this year. I think getting the band to play at the homecoming game was one of the best decisions I've ever made."

"Yes, sir. Mr. Undergrove is a great teacher, sir."

"That he is. He's passionate. Finding good teachers is always a plus, but finding passionate teachers is like winning the lottery." Mr. Cooper handed me a note to go to the band room to grab my instrument. I thanked him, grabbed my book bag and headed for the door.

"Mitchell?"

"Yes, sir?"

"I have to ask one more time, just to clarify: are you sure you can't think of a single person that may have had it out for you? A student giving you issues around school? A bully? Someone that doesn't like you for not letting them copy your homework?"

I hesitated. My mind went through all my classes, all my friends at school, even all the kids in 6th or 7th grade; I came back to one single image: Max, sitting on the bleachers, staring at me with rage in his eyes after Coach Brier allowed me to return to gym class. His words rang in my ear in his raspy voice - "She punked you."

"Mitchell?"

"No one that comes to mind, sir."

"Alright." Mr. Cooper leaned back into his chair. "Go grab your instrument and come straight back to the office. Your mom should be here in just a few minutes."

NOVEMBER - 10TH GRADE

"Not his car. Not his car. Not his car." Stephen and I walked from parking lot to parking lot, checking every single row of cars looking for Josh's small, blue, two-door Honda Civic. The car was rusty and old; its dashboard shook whenever the car went past 40 miles per hour; one time, the car ran out of gas a half mile away from a gas station, causing Josh to have to push it the rest of the way. "Dude, let's be honest: Kirby and Josh are stranded on the side of the road," Stephen said. "No gas, or the car broke down or something. Some trucker has picked them up, but the trucker is really an alien or something out of *Men in Black* and is keeping them as pets."

"That's morbid," I replied. "We got to keep looking and hoping they are here somewhere." I checked my watch. "6:30. We have to pick it up."

There we were: two high school kids in collared shirts and ties running the rows of a hospital parking lot on a Friday evening searching for Josh's car. We had circled back towards the entrance that we started from. Our shirts were untucked, our foreheads slightly sweaty; we gasped for breath from the running.

"Mother trucker!" Stephen yelled. "Those idiots better get here soon. Freakin' ark! Of all the cars!" He put his hands on his head and paced in circles. "Do you think they stiffed us? Like went to do something else? Who does that? And with the ark too!"

"I don't know. A part of me is mad at them because they have the ark, and a part of me is wondering if something is wrong," I said. "Was there something huge going down tonight that they didn't want to miss?"

Stephen rolled his eyes. “Man, if there was something huge going down tonight, I’m pretty sure I would have known about it. I mean, c’mon, I’ve got a pager for a reason.”

I put my hands on my hips. “Does that pager really get you girls’ numbers like you claim it does?”

“Mitchell, man, I’m telling you - girls? They love a man with a pager. Trust me. They think it makes a guy dangerous or something. Works like a charm.”

“Don’t drug dealers all have pagers?”

“That’s what my mom asked.”

“What did you tell her?”

“That I’m not a drug dealer.”

“But don’t all drug dealers have pagers?”

“You sound like my mom.”

“Does your mom know where Josh and Kirby are at this moment? Cause if so, sounding like your mom may be a good thing.”

Stephen, despite his frustration, tried his best not to grin.

When we got back to the gala room, all of our instruments and equipment were up and ready for the fundraiser. Mr. Undergrove was pacing the floor, his face paler than before. Brooks and David were back from combing the main floor of the hospital; they had no luck locating Kirby and Josh. “Please tell me some good news.” Mr. Undergrove’s eyes were wider than I had ever seen them before. “And why are the two of you so sweaty?”

"We didn't see Josh's car," Stephen replied, "but the good news is we got lots of exercise running the parking lot, so ya know, our abs are happy."

"Oh," Mr. Undergrove replied, "I'm not sure what to say to that."

"Any word on parents?" I asked.

"Kirby's parents did not answer the phone, so I left a message. Josh's dad is out looking for them now." Mr. Undergrove checked his watch again. "6:50. We need to warm-up. All we can do from where we are right now is pray that Josh and Kirby are safe, and hope to goodness we can wing this thing." Mr. Undergrove pointed to the main entrance across the gala room. "Those doors open in ten minutes. It's time for us to quickly put together a plan of action."

"Mr. Undergrove," Stephen spoke up, "don't forget that we still don't have sheet music."

"Can your pager produce us some sheet music in the next ten minutes?" Undergrove asked.

"No. I don't think it does that."

"I guess we will have to rely on jazz to get us through the evening. Jazz may even help us look more attractive to the women," Mr. Undergrove said.

"Hey!" Stephen said. "Are you making fun of me? Mr. Undergrove is making fun of me!"

As a collective unit, we picked up our instruments and warmed up by playing several scales.

The time was 6:55 PM. The gala would begin in less than five minutes.

APRIL - 8TH GRADE

I entered the band room. Mr. Undergrove was in the middle of teaching one of his sixth grade classes - his least favorite. "You should just see them," he had told us. "It's not that they can't play, it's that they choose NOT to play. They don't even try to sound good. Plus, it's the end of the school day - 7th period - mentally, they're already gone."

When I walked into the room, it was quite obvious that they were mentally elsewhere. Mr. Undergrove was attempting to teach them how to play 'Soul Man', the 1967 hit that is the universal go-to song for any band in their earliest playing stages. I didn't hear the upbeat, jazzy, catchy 'Soul Man' that Mr. Undergrove hoped for; the version I heard sounded like a television losing its cable reception during a hurricane. The trombone section was playing too fast, the entire clarinet section was off by one beat, the drums could not establish a regular rhythmic beat, and the tuba section would play too fast for a bar before playing too slow for a bar. The whole class was a mess.

Mr. Undergrove saw me first. He had just cut the band off to give them some direction when his eyes caught me exiting the instrument room with my trombone in hand. "Great Caesar's ghost! What happened to you?! You look like death!"

The whole classroom swung their heads around to get a look at me, followed by several 'ew's, several 'oh man's, and a few of the Lord's names all taken in vain.

"I was....I was..." I didn't want to say 'jumped' in front of a class full of 6th graders; I had my dignity to worry about, so I improvised. "I was in a fight. If you think I look bad, man, you should see the other guy. Can't even recognize him."

"Are you serious?" Mr. Undergrove's face was full of both concern and anger.

"Serious? Of course. Awesome fight. I won. Definitely."

"Are you being suspended?"

"Suspended? Why would I be?" I asked, and then added, "Oh, because of the fighting! Oh, no, I didn't get suspended because the other guy started it, see? I just finished it." Then, for self-reassurance, I added, "yeah, I finished it."

"So what are you doing here then?" Mr. Undergrove asked.

"I'm.....uh.....I'm leaving early. Ya know, to make sure my brain wasn't knocked loose or anything like that. The other guy is too," I said, hesitated for a moment, and then added, "because he is way more messed up than me. That's just how it is."

The look in Mr. Undergrove's eyes told me he wasn't buying my story, but didn't press the situation. "Ok, well, let me know how it turns out. And don't forget to practice tonight. That is if you can see your sheet music out of your eye."

Not a single eye in the room blinked as I nodded and left the band room.

The next day at school, people still weren't blinking as they stared at me. My face was a mixture of black, blue, and slightly green bruising, and my head bore eight stitches between two separate cuts. The doctor that put the stitches in told me to try to comb my hair away from the cuts to help them heal faster, but the moment my mom dropped me off at school, I ran my fingers through my hair to try my best to cover them up.

The thing that grabbed most attention from the people in the hallways was my black eye, which seemed to engulf the majority of the left part of my face. There was nothing I could do to my hair to cover that up, because it stretched from the arch of my eye lid down over my cheekbone. It wasn't that I had a black eye; it was that my black eye was so big that it was impossible to ignore.

It seemed like every kid in every single class stared at my face, including the teachers. There were whispers, but nobody even bothered to ask me about it, except Mr. Undergrove. When I walked into the band room, he took one glance at me, asked me how much it hurt, and then slightly grinned. "If that monstrosity is still on your face when we go to the band competition, maybe it will create some sympathy with the judges."

NOVEMBER - 10TH GRADE

A quick poll revealed that some of us had our music memorized completely, some of us had our music memorized somewhat, and some of us didn't have our music memorized at all.

"Ya know, I never thought the idea of the ark would ever backfire on me like this. It's not like we completely forgot it. We packed it; we just placed it in the wrong car." Mr. Undergrove ran his fingers through his hair, almost like he was trying to comb the stress out. "I guess this is what I get for calling the ark our 'fool-proof' plan for facing the possibility of someone forgetting their music."

The doors to the gala were beginning to open. A wave of men in suits and women in fancy dresses began to trickle in. The gala room was decorated with elegant table coverings, candles, flowers, and dim lighting. On the far east side of the room sat a table filled with luxurious vacation packages, a laptop computer, several bottles of top-notch wine, and other various gifts that would be the focus of a silent auction. The south wall of the gala room was the location of what appeared to be a never-ending buffet, filled with a swirling concoction of wonderful smells of various meats and steaks, shrimp, an assortment of cheeses, and too many desserts that the eye or stomach could handle. The northern wall of the gala room was home to the bar area, which Mr. Undergrove had reminded us numerous times was off limits to us. The band, the entertainment for the evening, was set up in the western corner of the room. Tables littered the room for guests, each covered in a soft white cloth that featured candles and flower pedals.

"Well, here goes nothing. Instruments up. 'Let It Be' from the top with the best of our ability." Mr. Undergrove raised his baton and began to count down from four.

Stephen put his trumpet down from his lips and interrupted Mr. Undergrove's count at 'one'. "Mr. Undergrove, what do we get if one of us is able to find Josh or Kirby?"

"Huh? What? What do you mean?"

Stephen smirked. "Look behind you."

Frantically weaving through the crowd of fancy suits and dresses were Josh and Kirby, a panicked look on their faces; Josh was tightening the tie around his neck while holding his trumpet already by his side, already out of its case. Kirby followed right behind, both arms wrapped around the blue ark, hugging it like it was a kid's first gift that they're allowed to open up on Christmas Eve.

You ever held a heavy object, like a 50 pound sandbag, for an extended period of time? Whether you have it slung over your back, or cradled in your arms, you're tired when you finally get the chance to set it down; you can feel the weight in your arms, your back, and your legs still lingering even though you're no longer holding that weight. Like carrying that one bag of sand for that long of time feels like it was much, much more than just a bag of sand. That's the way we all felt when Kirby and Josh came running through those gala doors, especially Mr. Undergrove , who looked like he was so happy he was going to faint.

A chorus of cheers erupted from all of us. Before Mr. Undergrove could ask, Josh was stating: "Long story short, we got lost. Went the wrong way on the interstate, but we're here."

"Wrong way down the interstate? Why were you on the interstate? The hospital was only a couple minutes away from Taco Bell! You should have followed..." Mr. Undergrove stopped himself mid-sentence. "Ya know what? Not important. You're here. You're safe. That's what matters. Quickly, everyone grab their music from the ark. Chop chop!"

One of the doctors at the fundraiser allowed Josh to use his cell phone to call his parents to let them know of his location, while the ark was opened by Kirby, who then proceeded to call the roll of band members as he distributed the folders of sheet music, our line-up of songs for the evening already selected and organized so we could immediately jump into playing once everyone had their music. Mr. Undergrove stood by, watching us finalize our set up, hands in his pockets, relief on his face. "Thank goodness we didn't have real Mexican food tonight," he told us. "Between that and the stress of Kirby and Josh going missing, I would not have survived the night."

"Mr. Undergrove," Stephen piped up, "did you just tell a poop joke? I mean, c'mon, that's definitely a poop joke."

Mr. Undergrove laughed, like a barrier of weight that once rested on his shoulders no longer restrained him. "Stephen, I believe I did." He picked up his baton, "Instruments up everyone. 'Let It Be' from the top with both our sheet music and the best of our ability." Mr. Undergrove raised his baton and we raised our instruments. Mr. Undergrove's arms lingered in the air for a moment as his baton hesitated. "Remember, tonight is not about us as individuals, tonight is about us as a band helping make a positive impact on others." He smiled; we all smiled. We were moments away from disaster, but now on the verge of resurgence. "Remember: I believe in you. In all of you." His baton went into motion. "And from four, three, two and one."

Jazz music filled the air.

MAY - 8TH GRADE

May 1st arrived. Mr. Undergrove had grown a beard.

Is 'beard' the right word?

Mr. Undergrove had an excessive amount of hair located in the areas of his face where most men have beards.

It was terrible. Long in some areas, short in others. Parts of the beard were black like the hair on his head, while the rest of the beard featured an array of orange, brown, white, and gray. It was like the beard didn't know what color it wanted to be, so it was exploring its options.

"Mr. Undergrove?" It was Kimberly, a clarinet player, her hand raised in the air. She was a natural leader, the top clarinet player, and someone that all the guys at King's Hollow seemed to have a crush on. She was a volleyball and softball player. Fearless. Smart. Witty. Her seat in the band formation was at the front of the classroom by Mr. Undergrove.

"Yes, Kimberly, how may I help you?"

"What are you going to do about your beard?"

"What am I going to do about my beard?" Mr. Undergrove repeated Kimberly's question with a sense of cluelessness.

"Yes, your beard. What are you going to do about it?" She asked with assertion.

"What would you like me to do about it?" Mr. Undergrove's eyes narrowed, starting to catch on with what Kimberly was hinting at.

His eyes met hers and narrowed down, almost like they were projecting the question 'How dare you?'

"Well, we're playing in a band competition in two days. Don't you think..." her voice trailed off, but she maintained eye contact, well aware that Mr. Undergrove was catching on to what she was implying.

"Don't I think what, Miss Kimberly?" Mr. Undergrove responded with intensity.

"Don't you think that you should shave?"

There was a slight gasp that blanketed the room. No one spoke as we watched the confrontation between Kimberly and Mr. Undergrove play out like a wild west duel. Here was a kid, a 14 year old kid, openly questioning an adult in a way that a mother would address her child. While we could all visibly see that maybe Mr. Undergrove needed to shave, none of us had the boldness that Kimberly currently possessed.

"Why do you care what my beard looks like?"

"I think you need to show your beard some love, that's all. If you want a beard, keep your beard, but the least you could do is...." Kimberly hesitated.

"The least I could do is WHAT, Miss Kimberly?" Mr. Undergrove was raising his voice; his ears were turning red.

"Make it even. That's all. Make it look like you own the beard, and not the other way around. Isn't that what you always tell us to do? Own the music, and not let the music own you? The audience can tell if you own the music? I'm pretty sure your words apply to this situation."

The gasp that had blanketed the room moments before now weaved and wrapped itself around every single person inside the band room. No one spoke, partly out of shock of the events taking place in front of us, partly in suspense of what would happen next.

"You think....you want me to.....my....." Mr. Undergrove stammered as he was at a loss of words. He stared at Kimberly, confused.

"Don't know what to say to that, do you?" Kimberly said with a grin. It was a million dollar grin. The kind of grin that could stop a clock.

Mr. Undergrove blushed, shook his head in defeat, and acknowledged Kimberly's victory. "Yes, Miss Kimberly, I guess it would be appropriate to 'own my words'. Maybe I should trim my beard up before the competition." He continued his stare down with Kimberly, slightly grinning.

Kimberly's assertion melted from her face and turned into a smile, a sparkle of victory dazzling in her eyes.

Mr. Undergrove arrived at school the next day beardless.

NOVEMBER - 10TH GRADE

"So here's what happened," Josh took a drink from his water bottle while Kirby enthusiastically told their story. "We left Taco Bell, and Josh, well, Josh thought we could just jump onto the interstate heading south because he thought we were heading to the hospital in Cornell County, one county over.

"It's true," Josh commented. "That's the hospital I was born at, so in my mind, that's where we were going."

Kirby shrugged his shoulders. "And I didn't know any better to tell him any different. I guess that's my bad for not paying attention to Undergrove when he talks."

"And you get straight A's on all your grades, right?" I asked.

"Straight A's across the board," Kirby confirmed, making a wave motion with his hand like he was running it across the surface of the table.

It was our 'intermission' of the gala; we had played a solid 50 minute set, and Mr. Undergrove had given us a 15 minute break to refresh ourselves with bottles of water that the hospital had provided for us. A large crowd had filled the room; doctors, nurses, business owners, lawyers, all dressed in their finest, socializing and fraternizing with each other. People roved from the bar to the buffet to the tables to the silent auction to the bar to the buffet to the tables and then back to the silent auction.

"Even I knew what hospital we were going to," Stephen said.

Kirby ignored Stephen's comment. "Anyways, we get onto the interstate, and then we get to talking, like deep, deep conversation stuff. Like mind-altering stuff."

"What kind of stuff?" I asked.

"Dude, deep thoughts, man!" Kirby pushed his hair back. "We were having one of those conversations where we were both equally engrossed in what we were talking about that we didn't even realize time had passed."

Josh chimed in: "Kirby was telling me all about the ghost in the movie *Three Men and a Baby*."

"There's a ghost in *Three Men and a Baby*?" It was almost a universal reaction from all of us.

"There's a ghost in *Three Men and a Baby*," Kirby confirmed. "Saw it with my very own two eyes.

"There's no ghost in *Three Men and a Baby*," Stephen stated. "That's just an urban myth babysitters make up to get kids to have nightmares."

"Dude, I saw it. It's there." Kirby pounded his finger with authority on the table. "It's a ghost. He's there in a scene one second, and the next, poof, he's gone. The actors in the scene don't even notice. Ghost kid. I'm telling you."

"If there was a ghost in the movie, the director and the film editors would not have used that take. They would have noticed it in the freakin' editing process."

"Stephen, man, I'm telling you. It's there. I've watched that movie a hundred times," Kirby shot back.

"I've seen the ghost," Brooks said. "I know what you're talking about, Kirby. Watched that junk not but a year back. It's there."

"See?" Kirby triumphantly bragged, "I'm not the only one who knows about the ghost. It's there. Go to Blockbuster; rent it. I'll accept your apology when you get done watching it."

"Whatever, man." Stephen rolled his eyes.

"It's the scene where Ted Danzig and his mom are talking. She comes to his apartment, and when he opens the door, you can see the kid in the left hand corner of the screen standing behind the curtain. He's there one moment, and then gone the next."

"Danson," Stephen said.

"Huh?"

"It's Ted Danson, not Danzig. Danzig is a rock band. Ted Danson is the actor."

"That's what I said." Kirby seemed agitated at Stephen's correction.

"No," Stephen stretched the 'o' sound for emphasis, "you said Danzig."

"Danzig, Danson, why does it matter?"

"It matters if you like the show *Cheers*."

"Anyways," Kirby shifted his body back to the rest of the band, "the ghost boy is in that scene. Check it out."

"Hey Kirby," Stephen asked, "if you guys thought you were going to the Cornell County hospital, why didn't you turn around and come back when you realized we weren't there?"

"We tried," Kirby said. "We got to the Cornell County hospital, waited for everyone to arrive, and when no one else did, we drove around the hospital several times looking for everyone else. We realized our mistake when I sent Josh inside to the information desk at the front door. When the lady there didn't know anything, we put two and two together and realized we were at the wrong location. That's when we tried to head back." Kirby hesitated. "I assumed Josh knew the way."

Josh chimed back in, "I got us back on the interstate, but not the direction we needed to go. We went south instead of north."

"Both of you guys get straight A's, right?" I asked again.

Josh looked at me. "Yes, but why do you keep asking that?"

"No reason," I muttered.

"We were in Creedmoor when we discovered the error of Josh's driving," Kirby continued. "We got off the interstate, turned around, and headed back. We thought about stopping at a payphone to call someone, but we didn't know who to call."

"We also didn't have any money for a payphone," Josh added. "I didn't have any quarters in my car. My dad always told me to keep some spare money in my glove box for emergencies; I guess I should listen to him more."

"I still don't get how you didn't know that we were playing at Mercy Medical. Mr. Undergrove went over that detail again and again in class," I said.

Kirby shrugged his shoulders nonchalantly. "We never thought about it. I assumed Josh knew; he assumed I knew. When we left

Taco Bell, Josh got on the interstate and I figured he knew what he was doing."

"Plus, the ghost in *Three Men and a Baby* story," Josh added.

"Plus, the ghost in *Three Men and a Baby* story," Kirby confirmed and repeated.

Stephen stood up from the table. "In the future, remember that we're all a part of this band. All of us. You two could have royally messed up the entire evening tonight because neither one of you bothered to pay attention to where we were playing."

As Stephen walked away, Kirby commented, "I know we had a close call tonight, but why is Stephen so mad? We didn't miss the gig, did we? I mean, technically, we saved the day. Josh and I are heroes. 'What once was lost now was found.' If anything, he should be thanking us. Everyone should be thanking us. Y'all didn't have the ark; this gig wouldn't have happened without our divine intervention."

With those comments, I also excused myself from the table.

MAY - 8TH GRADE

May 2nd. One day until the band competition.

Mr. Undergrove slammed his baton on the music stand, knocking out the beat for the percussion section.

"Dah dum dah dum dah dum dah dum. You know, it's that nice, steady beat that we've been working on since August. That one." The drummers, all in unison, blankly stared back at Mr. Undergrove, unsure how to respond. "Yes, sir, Mr. Undergrove, sir. Yes, we understand what you're telling us, sir. Yes, we can do exactly what you're asking us to do. Thank you for correcting us, sir," Mr. Undergrove said to the drummers sarcastically, hoping to get a response; the percussion section did not respond to Mr. Undergrove's sarcasm, but continued with their blank stares. "Do any of you understand me? Give me some type of response, please. A blink, a nod, anything."

"Yes, sir," one of them mumbled, followed by a coercion of other "Yes, sir" responses.

"Well, I guess that's settled. Here we go, everyone from the top." Mr. Undergrove raised his baton and signaled for us all to start. Six measures in, Mr. Undergrove cut us off again, this time focusing on three flute players that missed their cue. Five minutes later, the trombone section was off beat, and three minutes after, Brent, our tuba player, was playing the wrong song. Before the end of the class, two saxophone players changed the reeds on their instruments, our two French horn players realized that they were playing each other's instruments, and a trombone player had broken off his water key. With every minor mistake, with every minor bump, with every minor obstacle, Mr. Undergrove's ear got redder and redder. By the end of class, we had not played any of our six songs that we had been preparing for the competition all the way through without some type of significant mistake. If Mr. Undergrove had been a stick of dynamite, he was on the verge of exploding.

Mr. Undergrove put his hands over his face, took three long, deep breaths, and then addressed us. “I strongly encourage each and every single one of you to take your instrument home and do several things: 1) I want all of you, from the saxophones to the trombones to the clarinets to the trumpets, to practice tonight. Real practicing. Real effort. Practice with sincerity. Practice with vindication.”

Corey, a fellow trombone player, leaned over to me. “What’s ‘vindication’ mean?”

“It means to do something in order to prove a point.” I replied.

“Gotcha.” Corey responded. “I’m gonna save that word for later.”

“You don’t recognize that word?” I asked, but before Corey could respond, Mr. Undergrove had continued.

“2) I want all of you to get a decent night’s sleep. Please go to bed. Please do not stay up all night playing NBA Jam or whatever game suits your style.”

A percussionist raised his hand. “What about Mortal-“

“NOW is not the time for that,” Mr. Undergrove said, cutting the percussionist off, “now is not the time for jokes, or to make fun of yourself. Now is the time for us to shine, and judging by how we all played today, we need to be worrying about waxing up and utilizing our skills that we already possess, and not making jokes about video games.”

You ever hear that phrase about being so quiet that you could hear a pin drop? It applied to this situation.

"3) When waking up in the morning, I want everyone to take a shower; please remember to use soap on your body." He had to say that because, well, it was middle school; there's always that signature stinky kid in middle school that doesn't understand the importance of soap and shampoo. "Afterwards, you will put on fresh clothes, your performance clothes at that." Performance clothes, according to Mr. Undergrove, meant a black or white dress for the girls and black pants with a white shirt and some type of tie for the guys.

"4) You will eat breakfast. This is not a suggestion. This is an order. You must eat breakfast."

A flute player, Kristy, raised her hand. "What if we don't eat breakfast?" A good number of girls throughout the room, raised their heads and nodded along with the question, almost as if Kristy was speaking on their behalf.

Mr. Undergrove, keeping his cool because the question was not asked to throw him off course, responded, "If I have no gas in my car, could I drive to Raleigh, which is about an hour away?"

Kristy, eyes wide at being asked such a strange question, looked around the room, waiting to see if anyone was going to respond before she realized that the question was directed to her. "No, no you can't do that."

"And your body works exactly the same way. You cannot operate at your full potential without fuel. Tomorrow morning, put fuel in your body in preparation for the competition. Again, this is not a request, it is an order. For you. For every girl in this room. If you're worried about bikini season," Mr. Undergrove added, "then I assure you, one morning of eating breakfast will not ruin anything for you."

Kristy nervously nodded at Mr. Undergrove's answer before making eye contact with several other girls in the room that all had the same nervous looks in their eyes.

"You ain't got to worry about me, Mr. Undergrove," Miranda, a fellow flute player, responded. "Lord, I pity the person that gets in between me and my chicken biscuit."

Mr. Undergrove, whose ears were fading back to their normal color, laughed. Miranda laughed and the rest of us slowly trinkled in with our own laughter. The tension that had taken the room released its grasp just enough to allow Mr. Undergrove to say one last thing.

"Remember, as I've been telling you all year long, I believe in you. I believe in every single band student in this room right now, I believe in this band, and I believe in everything this band program does to make people's lives better. Don't ever forget that."

That afternoon, Mrs. Tolbert, our English teacher, asked everyone to pull out their homework from their notebooks so she could do a spot check on who had completed the assignment and whose mothers that she needed to call. Corey pulled out his homework, a triumphant smile on his face. "Ah, Mr. Corey," Mrs. Tolbert said out loud, "I see you actually completed your homework for once. I'm sure your mother will be so excited to go a day without hearing from me."

"Mrs. Tolbert, not only did I complete my homework, but I did it with vindication," Corey stated.

"Mr. Corey, look at you trying to use a vocabulary word from three weeks ago. I'm oh so proud."

Corey eyed me from a row over from him, and then looked back at Mrs. Tolbert. "Of course I would never forget a word like 'vindication'. In fact, tomorrow, Mrs. Tolbert, our band will perform with vindication in our band competition."

Mrs. Tolbert, sensing what was going on, responded, "Don't push it, Mr. Corey. No one likes a suck-up."

We giggled. Minutes later, the final bell rang, releasing us from school for the day.

NOVEMBER - 10TH GRADE

The hospital's gala room was filled with all sorts of people in their fancy dresses and suits; I felt just as fancy just by standing in the room with them. The bar was overflowing with patrons drinking the night away. "Alcohol sells," Mr. Undergrove had said earlier in the evening, "but only for adults, not for you guys."

"This is a fundraiser for the addiction rehab program and they're serving alcohol?" Stephen asked.

Mr. Undergrove rolled his eyes. "Ironic? Yes. Disturbing? Yes. Typical adult behavior? Dead on the spot. My wrestling coach used to yell at us to lose weight and he was obese."

Stephen laughed and looked over at me. 'Kinda like Coach whatshername at King's Hollow. She'd tell us that smoking will kill us and then smoke like a train outside of the gym by her car.

"Coach Brier," I said.

"Coach Brier," Stephen snorted. "How could I forget?"

The buffet was restocked every couple of minutes with fresh meat, chicken, cheeses, and desserts. I watched plateful after plateful walk by me, and then felt my stomach rumble; the tacos at Taco Bell were great, but man, I'd love to be able to get a swipe at the buffet.

"The music has been fantastic, Mitchell." I felt a hand grip my shoulder. I turned around to the sight of a familiar face: Mr. Cooper. The last time I had seen Mr. Cooper was two years earlier on the final day of 8th grade at King's Hollow.

"That band of yours is really killin' it. That's great music that you're playing. I'm glad you stuck with band. I've seen too many kids with musical talent get to high school and immediately ditch their instruments for 'cooler' things." He pointed over to the rest of the band. "That group over there is a good group of people. If you guys trust each other, you all can be unstoppable."

I nodded. Mr. Cooper's words echoed Mr. Undergrove's comments from earlier in the evening. "What brings you to the gala tonight?" I asked.

Mr. Cooper shifted his feet a little, looked down at the drink that was in his hand. He hesitated for a moment, keeping his eyes on his drink before lifting them to meet mine. "Do you remember that afternoon a few years back, the day you sat in my office and we talked? I believe it was the day you..."

"Got jumped?" I cut him off. "Yeah, I remember. That was when you told me about *Rocky*."

Mr. Cooper nodded. "Good memory. I'm impressed."

"My memory is pretty useless when I'm in school. Never works when I'm taking a test."

Mr. Cooper smiled. "That I can relate to." He laughed nervously. "That day we talked - I told you about my son, William. Do you remember?"

"Yes, sir, I remember."

"William was strong-willed, passionate." He paused for a moment. "He was also incredibly stubborn. I'll admit, as his parent, he probably got his stubbornness from me." He paused again; I could tell by his eyes that he was searching for the right words to use. "William had some personal demons that he struggled to deal with. The kind of demons that can take over your life if you let them.

William never wanted to ask for help, but I could tell he was drowning." Mr. Cooper looked around the room. "I'm here tonight to help support this program. William went through it," he paused again, "several times."

"Oh," I didn't know what to say.

"This program gave William time that he wasn't going to have if he had continued to live his life the way he was living it." The room seemed to go quiet; while the crowd still stood around us, my mind had silenced them as I focused on the gravity of Mr. Cooper's words. "This program gave him a chance at redemption, and it gave me my son back. I had time with him that I didn't think I'd ever have."

"That's great," I smiled at the hopefulness of Mr. Cooper's message. I looked around the room. "Is William with you here tonight?"

Mr. Cooper took a deep breath. That's when I realized I knew the answer to the question without him ever answering it.

"It's kind of like I told you with *Rocky*; sometimes the hero of the story doesn't always win."

"Oh, gosh," I replied. "I'm so sorry."

Mr. Cooper nodded. "I appreciate that, I really do." He hesitated again, and then added, "Sometimes our demons are just too much for us to handle alone. When William was here, in this program, he became alive again. I saw hope, and he saw it too. It was when he thought he was strong enough to leave the program, when he thought he could do it all on his own, by himself, no family, no therapy, not relying on someone to talk to, that's when he struggled. The first time, he came right back here, and it saved him. He knew it too. He knew he wasn't ready. But when he chose to leave the program a second time, he thought he was strong enough, but the burden of trying to live life without any friends or family to lean on along the way, well, that burden is more than some can bear." Mr. Cooper looked back down at his drink in hand and then back to me. "That's why I'm here tonight - to make sure the addiction rehab program has all the tools it needs to help anyone that chooses to get help. To make sure another family has more time with their loved ones that may be dealing with the same demons William once faced." He swallowed. "It's my way of honoring William. To make sure his battle was not in vain."

Mr. Undergrove was waving for us all to reassemble at the band area for our second set. I turned back to Mr. Cooper. "I'm sorry for your loss."

"Did you ever get a chance to check out *Rocky*?" Mr. Cooper asked.

He remembered.

"No, sir," I answered, "I never did. I know you said you loved that movie, but I just haven't gotten around to viewing it."

"That's too bad. It's one for the ages, that's for sure. I have a whole laundry list of movies that I want to see. I mark them off one by one every time I go to Blockbuster Video."

"I understand, sir," I said, "I'll keep that in mind for the future."

"Good. You do that. The band sounds great. Keep with it, will you? Music is an outlet. Use that outlet as long as you can."

"Yes, sir. I will. It was good to see you," I said.

"It was good to see you too, Mitchell. And don't forget: see *Rocky*. Make it a priority!" He pumped his fist in the air and raised his voice. "Yo! Adrian!"

I laughed. People around him turned and stared. It obviously didn't bother him. I shook Mr. Cooper's hand and returned to the rest of the band.

"Hey, was that Mr. Cooper?" Stephen asked.

"Yeah," I picked up my trombone, "it was Mr. Cooper. He's pretty cool."

"Was he quoting *Rocky* over there? It sounded like he was quoting *Rocky*."

"Yeah," I laughed as I sat down. "He was definitely quoting *Rocky*."

"Sweet. That's a good movie." Stephen fiddled with his mouthpiece on his trumpet. "Sucks that Rocky loses in the end. Never saw that coming."

"Yeah," I repeated, looking down at my feet, "sometimes you don't see it coming." Mr. Cooper's words from earlier then echoed through me. "Sometimes, the hero of the story doesn't always win."

A moment passed, me adjusting the music on my stand and Stephen adjusting his mouthpiece. "Hey, man," Stephen said, "that's some deep stuff. 'Sometimes the hero of the story doesn't always win'. I like that. Gonna save that one for a rainy day, or when I finally confess my love to a girl and she laughs. Whatever happens first."

With the entire band back together, we quickly finalized our second set play list; Mr. Undergrove raised his baton, counted us down, and once more, jazz music filled the gala.

MAY - 8TH GRADE

I sat in Mrs. Watson's math tutoring session until 4:00. All the band kids did. Mrs. Watson had planned on giving us a test on May 3rd, and when she realized all the band students would miss her test, she pitched a fit, right there in class. "None of you will be going to any type of band competition unless you take my test first!" She was pointing her finger in the air, voice raised in anger, almost like a bad guy in a movie swearing revenge on the hero as the bad guy's plan goes down in flames.

"Does she have the power to do that?" I asked Brent at lunch.

"I don't know." Brent leaned back in his seat and scratched his head. "Maybe? No, there's no way she could enforce that. Unless she can. Then we're all in a sticky situation. Maybe not, but probably so."

"I'll handle it," Kimberly said. "We've worked too hard for too long for grumpy Mrs. Watson to keep us from going to this band competition."

And Kimberly did just that. She talked to Mr. Undergrove, who in turn talked to Mrs. Watson, who in turn talked to Mr. Cooper, who in turn talked to Mr. Undergrove, who in turn talked to Mrs. Watson, who in turn told us that in order for us to be excused from her class on the day of the band competition we would have to take her math test one day earlier, but it had to be after school. No ifs. No ands. No buts. We all thanked Mr. Undergrove for talking some sense into Mrs. Watson, but as we sat after school to complete the test as the rest of the school's population went home, we were all rethinking how lucky we were to be in this situation.

By 3:50, all of us were done with the math test, but Mrs. Watson being Mrs. Watson refused to release us early. "I told all of you 4:00, and I'm going to keep you until 4:00." Yeah, she was one of those teachers.

Brent nudged my arm. "Don't forget to take your instrument home."

"I know," I responded. "I take my trombone home every night.

"Oh." Brent said, folding his arms in front of his chest. "Well, don't forget to practice. Like really practice."

"Dude, I know. I heard Mr. Undergrove today. I'm gonna practice. You make sure you practice."

"Oh, I'm going to practice. You don't need to worry about that." Brent turned to Caroline to the left of him. "Hey, make sure you take your flute home. And practice too."

"Brent, I know. I've been practicing." Caroline held up her flute case that was sitting beside her book bag.

Not satisfied with her answer, Brent responded, "Practice a little more than what you normally do. Flutes sounded rough today in class. You all have come so far this year. We don't need anyone to relapse."

Caroline's eyes widened and then narrowed with anger. "Maybe you need to practice too, jerk." Caroline turned her body away from Brent.

Brent leaned back towards me. "Women. They can't take a compliment even if they wanted to."

"I'm not sure that you were complimenting her," I responded. "You were kinda mean."

"Yeah, I guess. But maybe not." Brent turned around and waved his hand to get another student's attention at the back of the classroom. "Hey, you need to make sure you take your flute home. Seriously!"

At 4:00, the door to Mrs. Watson's room flung open and an entire herd of 8th graders stampeded out, similar to a pack of wild animals.

Some of us headed to the band room to gather our instruments before heading out to our rides. Inside the band room was Brent and Kevin, and Kevin was getting an earful.

"All I'm saying is this: make sure your mouth piece is ready to go with a fresh reed before the competition tomorrow. We can't afford for your instrument drama before we play. It won't look good for us, and I promise it will be even worse for you." Brent had puffed his chest out and was trying his best to stand as tall as possible so he could attempt to stare Kevin down.

"Instrument drama? My reed broke today - it could happen to anyone!" Kevin responded loudly.

"Yes, I know that, but didn't your reed just happen to break right before the Christmas concert? And didn't it also just happen to break when Mr. Undergrove called you out that one day for not paying attention?"

"What are you implying?" Kevin's eyes now darkened as he became very aware of the physicality of Brent's questioning. Kevin now straightened his back, making him an inch taller than Brent, and glared down. "Why are you giving me the runaround? Last time I checked, you, our lone tuba player, was playing the wrong song today during class, something you have a history of doing when you're trying to get on everyone's nerves!"

Brent didn't back away from Kevin. "We all have our moments," Brent said, sniffing his nose. "I won't be having any moments tomorrow. And you better not either. Think about it when you practice tonight." Brent turned around as he reached the band room door. "And you will practice tonight." With that, Brent was gone.

"What the he-" Kevin stopped himself when he saw Mr. Undergrove walk out of his office and into the main part of the band room. "Heck. I saw saying heck. No way would I ever say anything different."

"Sure you were, Mr. Kevin, sure you were," Mr. Undergrove responded without looking up from his podium.

"What the heck is Brent's problem?" Kevin had turned back to face me. "I mean, I didn't do anything to him!"

"I don't think it's you, Kevin," I responded, "he has ripped into a few people today about practicing."

"He needs to practice just as bad as anyone needs to!" Kevin's voice was agitated and squeaky. "He was on a completely different song than the rest of us today. I mean, what the-" Kevin stopped himself. "Heck. What the heck crawled up his butt?"

"Maybe Mr. Brent is feeling a bit of performance anxiety." Mr. Undergrove spoke from his podium, his eyes fixed on papers in his hand. He did not look up, but continued to talk. "Maybe Mr. Brent is recognizing the importance of leadership. Maybe Mr. Brent is finally starting to be aware that he could have done better in class today, and now he's trying to compensate for it by encouraging others to do the right thing."

"It's just that today in class, Brent-"

Mr. Undergrove cut Kevin off. "Today in class, Brent was acting like he normally does. Now he's putting pressure on others. Maybe this is Mr. Brent's reaction to guilt. Maybe Mr. Brent realized the errors of his ways and now he wants to redeem himself, but just doesn't understand how to talk to others. There are certainly worse things out there." Mr. Undergrove put down his papers on the podium. "Does all this make sense? Brent's actions are in line with someone that may be searching so desperately for redemption in the eyes of his peers. You, Kevin, are obviously someone Brent feels he must correct. You pointed out the one thing he didn't want you to remember and he reacted with a threat and now you are frustrated." Mr. Undergrove stood up from his podium and walked to his office. "Surely, between the two of you, you will figure out Brent."

Kevin looked puzzled. "So, basically, what you're telling us is that Brent is scared."

Mr. Undergrove turned around as he reached the door to his office. "Scared. Anxious. Determined. Confused. He's everything right now. Just try to be supportive. He needs that right now. We all do." Mr. Undergrove entered his office and sat down at his desk, eyes still fixed on his papers.

"Supportive," Kevin said under his breath. "Hmph."

The phone rang 7:00 PM that night. It was Kevin.

"Dude, you practiced yet?"

"We just finished dinner," I answered. "That's next on my list."

"Alright, just checking."

"Didn't you get mad earlier today when Brent told you the same thing?"

I could hear Kevin smiling through the phone. "Yes, yes I did. And Mr. Undergrove told us to be supportive, so I'm doing what I can to help Brent's mission by calling as many people as possible to remind them to practice."

"Does Brent know?"

"Brent will get a call from me before the end of the night, as will as many people as I can find in the phonebook. You're my 11th phone call."

"You want help? I can take a section or something," I offered.

"Take the trombone section. I'll contact the rest. Can you handle that?" I mean, counting you, that's seven more people. You're the first one I called, so that will help me having to call seven less people."

"I can do that."

"If there's someone you can't get a hold of, call me. I'm pretty handy with the phone book."

"How can you be handy with a phone book?" I asked.

Kevin hesitated. "That's a good question. I'm not sure. I just said it, ya know? Seemed like a good thing to say."

"Well, you're weird."

"Dude, you're weird," Kevin responded.

"Dude, you don't know how to keep a reed on your saxophone," I said. There was a silence on the phone; I could hear Kevin breathing, so I knew he was still there. "Hello?"

"I'm here. I just don't have a comeback."

"Oh. Ok, I've got trombones," I confirmed. "Plus I gotta practice."

"Hey, Mitchell?"

"Yeah?"

"My reed won't break tomorrow. Don't worry."

"I won't. Go, call people. Practice."

The line went dead. I grabbed the phone book from my mom's office cabinet. "Pretty handy with a phone book," I chuckled to myself as I picked up the phone to one-by-one call the rest of the trombone section.

NOVEMBER - 10TH GRADE

We had been asked to play three sets of music at the Mercy Medical's addiction rehab gala fundraiser. Halfway through our third and final set, a bald man with glasses approached Mr. Undergrove while we were in between songs, whispered something in his ear, made a few arm gestures pointing in our direction, smiled, patted Mr. Undergrove on the back, shook his hand, and then walked away, motioning a thumbs up to another person at one of the tables. As we ended our third set, Mr. Undergrove checked his watch, leaned in closer to us, and asked us a question. "Does anyone have any pressing plans that they need to get to?" We looked around at each other confused. "What I need to know is this: does anyone need to leave? I know it's Friday night and all, and I know your social lives are beckoning you, but the man over there," Mr. Undergrove pointed at the bald man with the glasses, "is one of the doctors in charge of the fundraiser, and he wants us to play one more set. Said we were awesome, and he's willing to make it worth our time. So, what I need to know is this: do you guys have time for another round?"

"When you say 'make it worth our time', what do you mean?" Stephen asked.

"He's going to make a larger donation to our jazz band than before. Almost double."

Brooks spoke up for all of us. "So do you want to create our next set's playlist now, or after a quick five minute break?

Mr. Undergrove's theory about keeping our music notebooks well stocked with a 'full arsenal' of all the songs we could play came in handy that evening. We had covered a lot of our more difficult pieces, like Louis Armstrong's '12th Street Rag' and T.S. Monk's

'Round Midnight', some of our favorites, like Frank Sinatra's 'Fly Me to the Moon' and John Lennon's 'Imagine', and songs we weren't crazy about, like David Sanborn's 'Hideaway'.

"Here's the almighty question: do we play songs that aren't exactly 'crowd favorites' that we can play well, or do we play songs that are significantly easier that this crowd may dig?" Mr. Undergrove asked.

Stephen reacted first. "Mr. Undergrove, sir, are you asking us if you want us to put the crowd to sleep, or to rock their socks off?"

Mr. Undergrove smiled. "It's a fancy fundraiser, which is why we've been leaning on some of our more sophisticated pieces, but to answer your question, yes, do you guys want to rock their socks off?"

We all nodded with excitement and smiled. Stephen, being Stephen, took it one step further.

"Hell yes!"

He immediately realized what he had said in the company of our teacher, froze in fear for a moment, looked down at the floor, then muttered, "Sorry, Mr. Undergrove." He then added, "Please don't tell my mom."

"Stephen, your excitement is wonderful. Your language sometimes is questionable, but your heart is in the right spot. I think we can all agree on that. So let's take that energy and blow the roof off this place."

We opened our fourth set that evening with Sam The Sham & The Pharaohs' 'Woolly Bully', jumped straight into The Marvelettes' 'Please Mr. Postman', and then followed it with renditions of The Troggs' 'Wild Thing', Frank Sinatra's 'I've Got You Under My Skin', and Sam & Dave's 'Hold on, I'm Coming'. We had gone from jazz band mode to rock mode in a matter of minutes.

Our final set came to an end for two reasons: 1) the doctor that asked us to play an extra set requested that it last about 30 minutes, and 2) we had run out of songs to play. Literally every jazz song we had learned, practiced, and mastered over the past two years had been utilized. We were spent, done. We had never stretched ourselves in terms of a performance like that before. Four sets.

"That was such an endurance test," Brooks said as we packed up. "Not even a lot of professional musicians can hammer out four sets in a performance. Imagine trying to watch Sonic Youth play four sets in one evening. That would be madness. Sonic Youth could do it though. I bet they could."

"The Beatles." Mr. Undergrove said. We all looked his direction. "The Beatles could have played four sets, each set completely unique and diverse, and we would never hear the same song twice."

"The Beatles? Huh." Brooks shook his head. "They're just a pop group from the 60's. I don't know about all that. They're definitely not as diverse as Sonic Youth."

"Oh, for the love of everything!" Mr. Undergrove said, his eyes wide with shock. "You're kidding me right? You've got to be kidding me? You're seriously still riding this Sonic Youth train as far it goes, aren't you? It's completely ok to like a band AND recognize the greatness of other bands. You're not betraying your favorite band by also liking another band, or acknowledging what they brought to the table BEFORE your favorite band even existed."

"I'm just saying," Brooks said as he placed his trumpet in its case, "The Beatles may have been diverse, but they're probably not as diverse as Sonic Youth."

"Have you ever even listened to any of The Beatles' albums?"

"Well, not exactly, but I know what they're capable of as a band. But Sonic Youth, they've released roughly 11 albums in about 15 years, so I just don't see how a band with that magnitude of music composure can-"

Mr. Undergrove cut him off. "13."

Brooks looked at him confused. "13 what?"

"13 albums. 13 albums in eight years. That's what The Beatles did. They put out 13 albums in eight years. Plus toured. Plus made five movies." Mr. Undergrove leaned in close to Brooks. "I'm not saying Sonic Youth isn't diverse, or that they don't have a large variety of songs in their arsenal, or that they couldn't put on an entertaining show, but I think in this situation, The Beatles win."

"Well, 13 albums doesn't mean they were great or anything."

Mr. Undergrove took a deep breath. "No one in all of music history has had the massive success in such a short period of time. No one has made and recorded that many albums, made that many movies, or had as many hits as they did in the span of time that they did it in. No one. No. One." He then added, "Not Nirvana, or Madonna, or Hootie & The Blowfish, or Sonic Youth, or 2Pac, or New Kids On The Block, or anyone."

Our eyes jumped from Mr. Undergrove to Brooks, awaiting a response or an acceptance of defeat. Brooks stood there, soaking in the suspense.

"I don't think it's fair to put The Beatles over Sonic Youth, because let's be honest, none of us know what kind of massive success Sonic Youth could experience in the coming years. I mean, they could completely erase all of The Beatles' accomplishments from history and..."

Mr. Undergrove threw his hands in the air. "How can someone that claims to love music know so little about music? You've never listened to The Beatles and you're willing to put Sonic Youth over them just because they're not Sonic Youth! I can't argue with you anymore!" With that, he grabbed two stands, and walked them outside to the vehicles we were reloading.

I looked over at Brooks. "Have your parents ever told you that you're impossible?"

"No. Why?"

"Just wondering. I'll make you a copy of *Meet The Beatles* - that's a fun album."

"Why do I need to meet them?" Brooks asked confused.

"No, you're not meeting them. It's just the name of the album: *Meet The Beatles*. It was their first big hit album in America."

"That's a dumb name for an album," Brooks said.

"It was like their introduction to American audiences. That's where they got the name from. Like a meet and greet type situation."

"Dumb," Brooks said, and then added, "Sonic Youth has better album titles."

"Name one." Brooks was starting to get on my nerves too with his love for Sonic Youth.

"*Washing Machine*."

"*Washing Machine*?" I asked.

"*Washing Machine,*" Brooks confirmed.

"Like the thing you put dirty laundry in for it to be washed?"

"Yep. *Washing Machine.*"

"Oh goodness," I said, and then following Mr. Undergrove 's pattern, I grabbed my instrument and a music stand to take out to pack in one of the cars.

The hospital's gala room was cleared of all our band equipment. Several doctors stopped by and thanked us for the performance. Mr. Undergrove kept giving us the credit for being an awesome group when really he should have taken the credit; we were nothing without his leadership.

"You ever think about which people in the crowd tonight were people supporting the addiction rehab program and which people were actually a part of the program at some point of another?" Stephen asked as he undid the buttons at the top of his shirt. "I kept looking out at the crowd thinking, 'Were you a user? Were you a user? What about you? Were you a user?' I mean, Mr. Cooper was here. Was he a user at one point, or was he just here for the heck of it? Makes me wonder, ya know?" He paused. "Like how much do you really know about people? Everyone has demons in their closet, just some let them out and some don't."

I thought about Mr. Cooper standing in the crowd tonight, watching us, mingling amongst the guests. I thought about his son, and the melancholy that rested on the surface of Mr. Cooper's words.

Dear God. The man had to bury his son. His own son.

I turned back to Stephen. "I think there's more to almost everyone than what we probably see on the surface."

He nodded. “Kinda of like Transformers. You know, ‘more than meets the eye’, that kinda business.”

“Yeah,” I agreed, “just like Transformers.”

“Gentlemen,” Mr. Undergrove called us around him, “it’s time. Let’s get all our material back to school and then the weekend is officially ours. Josh & Kirby: please follow the rest of the cars back to school. Please do not go the wrong way down the interstate,” he paused, and then emphasized, “again.”

“Who saved the concert, though?” Kirby smirked. “Who showed up at just the right time with the ark and completely saved the day? Huh? Someone? Anyone? Oh, that’s right,” Kirby turned to Josh, “it was us. Me and you. Heroes, correct?”

“Heroes. Maybe we need to redefine that word,” Stephen said as he jabbed me in the side with his elbow and laughed. “Heroes, my...” he stopped himself when he realized Mr. Undergrove was glaring at him.

“Thank you for not using the language that I believe you intended to use,” Mr. Undergrove said. He eyed Kirby and Josh, and then returned his gaze to Stephen. “I’m with you; they could use some humility. While they did ‘save the day’, they were also the cause of the panic.”

“Josh and Kirby almost ruined the evening,” Stephen said back.

“And then they swooped in and changed the narrative,” Mr. Undergrove responded. “The world is full of people like that: people that create problems just so they can fix those problems and feel good about themselves.” Mr. Undergrove patted Stephen on the back. “Let them have their moment. We all learned the importance of the safety of the ark to avoid situations like this in the future. Tomorrow, none of this will matter except in our own history books." With that, we packed up our instruments and loaded our cars.

MAY - 8TH GRADE

It was the morning of the competition. May 3rd. Waking up and seeing the date on the calendar in my bedroom made me feel like I was about to ride a rollercoaster in the front seat. The band room was a flurry with 8th grade band students buzzing about. Instruments were being loaded onto the activity bus; folders were being checked and double checked to make sure every band student had all their music for both sets of judges before being loaded into the ark; Mr. Undergrove was walking around with an attendance roll, checking kids' names off as he saw them enter the band room. He had six extra ties dropped around his neck; if a boy showed up either not wearing a tie, or had on a tie that looked like it was on its final days, Mr. Undergrove would remove a tie from around his neck, already pre-tied for easy application, and swap it out. "Today is not a day for looking like you're trying to get by; today is a day to look like you're aiming for excellence," Mr. Undergrove said.

It was earlier than usual - 7:30. School wouldn't start for another 30 minutes, but here we were, 40 8th grade band students running around with the excitement of the first day of school. Mr. Cooper was standing out by the buses, watching us load all our instruments. He had rolled a large red cooler out of the school and sat it beside the back door of the bus, and then instructed two of the drummers to load it to take with us. "Compliments of me for your competition today. I want you all to do your absolute best, so for the ride there, that cooler is loaded with enough bottles of water, oranges, and bananas for every student to enjoy." Mr. Undergrove shook his hand, thanked him, and then instructed everyone to use the restroom before we departed.

"What if we don't need to use the restroom?" Brent asked.

"Use it anyways," Mr. Undergrove shot back. "Try, because the moment we hit the road, we're not stopping." Mr. Undergrove's eyes floated over the entire band. "For anyone. For any reason. Go. Use it now."

Mr. Undergrove counted heads as we loaded the bus. 40 8th graders collectively sat at the edge of their seat, eager for departure. "Does everyone have their instrument?" Mr. Undergrove asked.

"YES, MR. UNDERGROVE!" We yelled in unison.

"Is the ark loaded? "

"YES, MR. UNDERGROVE!"

"Did everyone use the restroom?"

"YES, MR. UNDERGROVE!"

"Does everyone have their money for lunch?"

"YES, MR. UNDERGROVE!"

"Are we ready to rock this competition?"

"YES, MR. UNDERGROVE!"

"Do all of you want to give me $20 each?"

"YES, MR. UND.....wait...." was heard throughout the bus.

Mr. Undergrove smiled, tapped the shoulder of our bus driver and sat down. With that, the bus rolled ahead out of the parking area in front of the entrance by the band room. Mr. Cooper stood outside by the curb and waved. We were officially on the road for our hour-long journey to the band competition.

As we left King's Hollow, CD players accompanied by travel CD holders came out of book bags and soon headsets covered the ears of most of the bus riders. A few of the flute players broke out a game of UNO, and a handful of kids with Nintendo Gameboy systems soon became the envy of the entire bus.

Our road trip took us to a high school in Snowfield, a snoozy, exorbitant community enriched with doctor offices, golf courses, fancy coffee shops, law offices, and tennis courts. Coming from King's Hollow Middle School, we would certainly be the fish-out-of-water in the Snowfield environment.

We passed a sign that read 'Welcome to Snowfield!' with an exclamation mark; underneath it read 'America's favorite town'. Headsets and CD cases retreated back into our book bags as the bus pulled up to an enormous building covered in glass and metal. A Snowfield High auditorium sign welcomed us into the correct parking lot, where we saw bus after bus from all sorts of different schools. Band kids, hundreds of them, swarmed the parking lot and on towards the auditorium doors. As our bus found its parking spot, Mr. Undergrove reminded everyone to stay seated while he checked us in, and then slipped off the bus and into the crowd.

We all, collectively, people watched out the bus windows, with the guys particularly noticing the amount of girls that flowed out of the buses from other schools.

"I don't think I've seen so many cute band nerds in my entire life."

It was Stephen.

"I mean, look at all of them! One cute girl after another. Out there is my future girlfriend."

"Definitely," I agreed. "Are we going to actually try to talk to any of these girls from different schools?'

"Oh, I'm getting someone's number before I leave here. It's happening."

"Gotcha," I agreed. "Hey, can we do that thing where you try to talk to a girl and I just awkwardly stand near you and don't say a word? I'm good at that."

Stephen nodded. "I'd expect nothing less," and then added, "but I'm going to need you to definitely stick close to me today. You still got one heck of a black eye from the spanking you received in the locker room, and if I know anything about girls, they love a good sympathy story." Stephen put his hands in the air like he was broadcasting a headline on a newspaper. "Teenage stud survives locker room beat down to score bodacious girls at band competition. It's got a great ring to it."

It was true; my face still bore 'battle scars' from my incident in the locker room earlier that week. But Stephen was right: the girls apparently enjoyed a guy that appeared as 'damaged'. I had had more conversations with more girls in two days than my entire time in middle school. In class, in the hall, before school, after school; after the first day, all the whispering awkwardness amongst my classes seemed to fade and everyone wanted to hear a first-hand account from the guy that survived what was now being labeled as 'the worst beat down in the history of King's Hollow'. Overnight, I went from a 'nobody' to a superhero. Everyone at King's Hollow knew my name.

Despite my new popularity, no one is ever thrilled about looking in the mirror and seeing a bruised face. While the swelling on my cuts and bruises has almost completely gone away, my left eye was as shiny as any black eye ever seen, if not shinier; my mom told me that I looked like a dog out of the movie *101 Dalmatians*. On the positive side of my massive black eye, my stitches in my head could be covered up by my hair, which the doctor told me not to do, but I did it anyways. You almost couldn't see my stitches if you weren't looking for them. Almost.

"I'm not sure about the 'teenage stud' part," I said.

Stephen put his arm around my neck. "Mitchell, man, any guy that can take the beating that you took and get back up again automatically qualifies for the 'teenage stud' category. I'm telling you, girls love that kind of stuff. If anything, today I'm going to be your wingman today while the girls give you their number." Stephen's eyes returned to the window. "They're not going to see 'Mitchell Williams - awkward 8th grade band nerd'; they're going to see 'Mitchell Williams - mysterious tough guy from King's Hollow'.

"You all are disgusting." Kimberly crossed her arms and shot us evil looks. "You act like there's not a bunch of girls on this bus right now with you. You're too busy gawking out the window at girls you'll probably never see again."

Stephen turned. "But the girls out there don't know how many times we've been rejected by the girls in here. The girls out there? They know nothing about us. They don't know I'm failing math class. They don't know that Mitchell sucks at basketball. We could be anything we want to be to them." He leaned closer to Kimberly. "I could be Prince Charming for all they know. That's the magic of meeting someone new: they're a mystery. I could be someone's new mystery man." Stephen turned his eyes back to the windows. "And one of those beauties could be my mystery woman."

"What if your mystery woman is a psycho and plans on locking you in her basement?" Kimberly then looked at me. "And you, Mr. Stud muffin, what if she has a best friend that is a vampire and you're on the dinner menu?"

Stephen and I looked at each other. "So, in this weird scenario you've established, while Stephen gets locked up in a basement, I actually have a girlfriend?" I asked. "Vampire or not, that's a win for me!"

Without taking his eyes off the window, Stephen responded, "Vampire girlfriend? It'd never happen. Mitchell is formerly trained in the ways of *The Monster Squad* and would effectively handle any demonic creature or blood sucker with efficiency and then come rescue me from the psycho girl's basement." He turned his head towards Kimberly. "Try again."

Kimberly rolled her eyes. "Guys are so stupid."

I turned around and sat down. "You're right. We are being jerks. I'll talk to you."

"Thank you. See, Stephen, some guys can be gentlemen."

Stephen was still looking out the window. "Not my cup of tea. Not when there's a whole auditorium filled with hot girls. Looks like at least half of them are high school age too."

"High school girls?" I asked.

"High school girls," Stephen confirmed. "High schools probably looking for a mysterious stud muffin to woo them and make them forget about their everyday life for awhile."

I turned back to Kimberly, who noticed the visibly distraught look on my face. "Oh gosh, go look."

I shook my head, took a deep breath, and then said "A gentleman doesn't need to look."

Kimberly smiled. "That's right. Thank you for being polite."

"Sure," I nodded, "a gentleman."

Kimberly stared at my black eye taking up the majority of the left side of my face. When she realized she was staring, she immediately shifted her eyes down at the floor of the bus.

"Did it hurt?" she asked, "When you were being jumped? I mean obviously it hurt, but like did you realize what was happening when it..." Kimberly paused for a second. "Never mind, that was an incredibly stupid question. Of course it hurt. I shouldn't have..."

I cut her off. "It's ok. My face is just a little more decorated than others."

We awkwardly sat across the bus aisle from each other, neither one of us speaking. I finally broke the silence.

"So, will you go out with me?"

"Huh? What?" Kimberly's face distorted with disgust. "Uh...um. No?" She let the 'o' in 'no' carry out a tad.

"Are you asking me or telling me?" I asked.

"What do you mean? Asking or telling?"

"Well, I said 'Will you go out with me?' and then you said 'uh...um. No?' Like you weren't sure and you were asking. So are you telling me no, or asking me no?"

"Um...well..." Kimberly clearly was confused of what I was asking her. "No. Just no."

"Just no? Like there could be other options?"

"No, Mitchell."

"I figured." I sat up in my seat and turned back to the window with Stephen.

"Hey, I thought you were a gentleman?" Kimberly asked.

"I was, but you won't go out with me since the charm of my black eye isn't working on you, so I'm going to be like Stephen and explore my options."

Stephen fist-pumped me. "That's what I'm talking about! The women in this bus don't appreciate the gems that are sitting in front of them. But you know who will appreciate us?" He pointed out the window at the crowds of band students outside of the auditorium. "They will. One of those beautiful women out there."

Kimberly crossed her arms back, and scowled in her seat. "Boys" she muttered under her breath.

"Men," Stephen corrected her. "We're becoming men."

"Boys." Kimberly said again, thing time intended to mock Stephen.

"As a man, and a gentleman, I will not lower myself to your standard of arguing with you." Stephen smiled. "But I will gladly recognize that you are a beautiful woman."

Kimberly rolled her eyes, got up, and changed her seat.

Mr. Undergrove returned to the bus and we all returned to our seats. A nervous sweat gleamed on Mr. Undergrove's forehead as he addressed us.

"Here's the deal. There are 12 other schools here with us at the moment. They'll be rotating those groups to filter us out of here in a timely manner before the next wave of bands come in. So, when we get off this bus, just bring your instrument with you. No book bags. No gaming systems. No CD players. Just your instrument in its case. We will walk over to the auditorium's doors and they will tell us where to sit inside."

"They're two areas where we will be performing," Mr. Undergrove continued. "The first will be inside the auditorium, where all the other groups that are here will watch, which means we must be quiet and we must be respectful during the performances." Mr. Undergrove's eyes then drifted to the drum section. "Can you all handle that?"

There was a few groans and grunts, but we managed to squeeze out a collective "Yes, Mr. Undergrove" with not quite the enthusiasm that we had when we left King's Hollow earlier this morning.

One by one, we exited the bus, instrument case in hand.

DECEMBER - 10TH GRADE

It was a week away from Christmas; the buzz of holiday cheer could be felt everywhere you turned around, almost like a static floating in the air. In between classes, Frank Sinatra's *A Jolly Christmas* album played on the school's intercom. Some of the teachers had decorated their doorways with wrapping paper and wreaths. Mr. Undergrove , wanting to contribute to the holiday hoopla, had purchased a 4 foot white plastic Christmas tree for the band room; it had lights on it that twinkled in rhythmic waves and all the band classes took a few minutes one day to create paper ornaments for the tree. When the tree lights were turned on and the band room lights were turned off, it gave off a red glow that looked like something out of the *Charlie Brown Christmas* special. At the end of every class, we'd kill the classroom lights for a few moments just so we could bask in its groovy aura.

Then, one of the assistant principals told Mr. Undergrove that the Christmas lights were a fire hazard and had to be removed. The next day, as a prank, one of the annoying 9th graders in marching band thought it would be funny to steal the ornaments off the tree. He hid all the ornaments in a plastic grocery store bag, then, forgetting that he was pulling a prank, left the bag in the cafeteria, where one of the janitors found it, and thinking it was just a bag of wrinkled up paper, threw it away. So in a matter of two days, we went from having an amazingly awesome Christmas tree in the band room to just a white plastic tree lacking all sense of identity. It was all very aggravating.

"Emergency meeting! Emergency meeting!" Mr. Undergrove called out as he fluttered out of his office at the beginning of class. "Everyone grab a seat! We have to talk about a last minute arrangement!" He carried a post-it note with him with information scribbled on it.

"Big question: what is everyone doing on Friday night?"

We looked around the room at each other. I spoke up. "This Friday, as in the last day of school before Christmas break?"

"Friday, as in my birthday?" Stephen added.

"Friday, as in the last day of school before Christmas break. And Stephen's birthday apparently. The Downtown Development Commission has asked that we play at the Christmas Tree lighting ceremony in front of the library. The ceremony is at 8:00 pm that Friday night, but they want us to play for the 30 minutes leading up to the ceremony and then another 20 minutes after the ceremony is over. 'To establish and maintain a Christmas mood' is what the guy said on the phone. Anyways, I told him that I had to talk to all of you before I gave him an answer, being that it's such a short notice and school is technically out as of that afternoon."

"It's my birthday, Mr. Undergrove," Stephen said, "I don't know..."

"Ok, Stephen's out because of his birthday," Mr. Undergrove said. "We can swing missing maybe two people, possibly three before we become a mess. Anyone else not able to be there?"

"You didn't let me finish," Stephen said. "What I was trying to say was that Friday is my birthday, and I don't know what my parents will say when I tell them that the party they're throwing me will have to be pushed back a couple of hours."

"Oh," Mr. Undergrove said, a wave of shock on his face. "Well, that's not what I expected you to say. Maybe I should be a little better listener."

"Never judge a book by its trumpet," Stephen replied.

Mr. Undergrove's brow wrinkled. "That......how can.....what?"

Stephen winked. "Write that down, big guy. It's great advice."

"I'm not sure what that means, but sure, why not? Moving on: anyone else have a conflict?"

We all shook our heads. We all had planned to be at Stephen's house Friday night for his birthday, but it looked like now we had his blessing to be late.

The next day, Stephen announced to the band that we were all to report to his house after our gig on Friday night. "I told mom that we had to push it back to at least 9:00 PM before the party could start, so bring both a dose of birthday and Christmas cheer." He then added, "And girls. Bring some cute girls with you. Maybe we'll pick some up at the Christmas Tree lighting. Ya never know."

"This is all so stereotypical commercial conforming holiday brainwashing," Brooks said. "This tree lighting ceremony happens every year, and every year we're forced to believe that we have to attend this annual town tradition that reeks of forced family values, obligatory consumerism, and government control."

"How is a Christmas tree lighting ceremony 'government control'?" I asked.

"Because the town's government puts it on every year, duh," Brooks responded sarcastically.

"That's not....that's..." I took a deep breath; there was no point in arguing. "Sure, whatever."

We had a string of holiday jazz covers in our arsenal of songs that we could perform at the ceremony, but with the Christmas tree lighting only 72 hours away, Mr. Undergrove went into full stress mode to make sure we were ready for the gig. What we thought would be a relaxing couple of days before Christmas break turned into a grueling marathon of practicing during the entire class period without a single second to lose, holding two emergency practice sessions after school, and then putting in practice time at home.

"Ever notice how we're completely selling out the identity of the jazz band just to satisfy the burden of some overhaul of a temporary seasonal fad?"

It was lunch on Friday. Brooks sat at the table, fiddling with his plastic spoon as he pushed his soup around inside the foam cup. Soup day at Northern Kent's cafeteria always fell on a Friday, and always seemed to be a bit magical, for soup day was a collaborative effort of the rest of the week's uneaten vegetable sides and meats. Cooked all morning long in a tomato broth, the soup consisted of: corn, green beans, carrots, peas, potatoes, broccoli, hamburger meat, rib meat, chicken, and pepperoni.

It was the best soup anyone had ever concocted.

Every once and awhile, you may find a spare piece of pineapple floating in your cup; this was a rare and celebrated occurrence that was welcomed like a winning lottery ticket.

"Our identity?" I took a bite of my soup.

Brooks elaborated. "Yes, the identity of the band. I mean, we're just some corporate sell-outs now. Playing the hospital gala. Now this seasonal exaggeration of a commercial holiday. It's just so mind-numbing."

I leaned over my bowl of soup. "I think you may be thinking a little too hard about all this. We're just a bunch of teenagers that play jazz music and jazzy covers of songs from the 50s and 60s. We don't have an identity." I took a bite of soup. "The gala gig brought some money into our account. Mr. Undergrove said this Christmas tree lighting may get us a small donation since the professional band that was originally hired for the ceremony backed out."

"Exactly. We're just chasing dollar signs," Brooks said.

"What else are we supposed to do?" I asked. "We're teenagers. Personally, I'm pumped for tonight. My parents would never take me to the downtown Christmas tree lighting ceremony when I was younger."

Brooks rolled his eyes. "Well, you're going to find out real quick that it's just some overhyped live-action commercial for the town."

I thought for a moment, and then responded, "You know you're going to be a part of that overhyped live commercial, right? Like, an integral part of it. You better get used to that idea before this evening."

Brooks rolled his eyes again and then took a bite of his soup. "Yeah," he nodded, "looks like it. I just hope they don't turn on the fake snow machine this year. It's so lame."

I almost choked on my soup. "Fake snow machine?! That's awesome!"

Brooks broke off a piece of his bread, dipped it in his cup of soup, and then ate it. "Mitchell, man, I wish I could be like you and be so easily amused."

"Thanks, I guess?" I wasn't sure if that comment was a compliment or an insult.

"So, did you invite any girls to Stephen's party tonight?" Brooks asked the question without looking up from his food.

"Stephen is the guy who is really good at doing that kind of stuff. He's been mentioning it to every person he's passed in the hall for the past three days. I assume he's got it covered. I'm just more of a wingman type of guy."

Brooks giggled. "You remember that time in 8th grade when we went to that band competition and Stephen's one goal was to try to find a girlfriend?"

I nodded. "I'm pretty sure I couldn't forget that day even if I wanted to."

Brooks nodded. "Oh, yeah, I forgot; you probably don't want to remember that day." After a moment, Brooks added, "But nonetheless, you gotta channel some of that energy before tonight. You can't buy that type of swagger just anywhere."

I sighed, shook my head, and took my last bite of soup. "That black eye was lightning in a bottle, in both good and bad ways."

School released that afternoon to a flurry of excited teenagers emptying their lockers, Christmas music blaring over the school's intercom, laughter, cheers, teachers waving, and then there was us in the jazz band, packing up everything needed for the gig that night from the band room. Speakers, drums, instruments, and stands were all packed carefully into our available vehicles amongst the members that could drive; Mr. Undergrove insisted that the ark be placed in his car. "It's not that I don't trust any of you," Mr. Undergrove said.

"It's just that you don't trust any of us," I replied.

"It's just that, after the hospital gig, I don't trust any of you," Mr. Undergrove said with a smile. "On that note, we've been so busy getting ready for this gig tonight that we failed to talk about something important: are we doing 'Trombones, Trumpets, & Tacos' tonight?"

Stephen spoke up for all of us. "It's my birthday, and I say 'Yes', and if you don't like it, well, you can..."

Mr. Undergrove cut him off. "Keep it PG."

"...go somewhere else. Anyone that doesn't like tacos, they can go somewhere else. Mr. Undergrove, you have got to let me finish my sentences. Have some faith in me."

"History has taught me otherwise, but I do apologize for always cutting you off when I think something vulgar is on the verge of coming out of your mouth."

"You're not sorry," Stephen smirked.

"You're right," Mr. Undergrove laughed. "I'm not."

MAY - 8TH GRADE

As we entered Snowfield's auditorium lobby, Stephen grabbed my arm. "Dude, stick close to me and follow my lead."

I nodded, and then fell back with him to the back of the line of the band as we shuffled from the lobby area cramped with other bands waiting to be seated into the massive auditorium. Our entire band, as a collective unit, stopped in our tracks and gazed at the elaborate room. Kevin, standing in front of Stephen and me, turned around and said 'This isn't an auditorium; this is a freaking concert hall." Elaborate cushion seating, hand-painted nature murals lining the walls, aisle lighting, surround-sound speakers, an elaborate stage; you name it, that auditorium had it.

I turned towards Stephen. "I know leaving King's Hollow to come to Snowfield meant that we'd be going to Snowfield, but I never thought about what Snowfield might look like. This is something else."

"We're not in Kansas anymore, Toto," Stephen then added, "Let's go find us a 'Dorothy'.

'Dorothy?" I asked.

"*The Wizard of Oz*. Stay with me."

As the band filed in to their seats one-by-one, Stephen's eyes moved rapidly throughout the room, almost like he was scanning every minor detail of the auditorium and the all the groups that occupied it. He tapped my arm and motioned me to follow, leaving our band mates behind. We went back five extra aisles away from our band, and then zigzagged across two more aisles to the other side of the auditorium, sitting down in two empty seats in the middle of an entirely different band from an entirely different school.

"Stephen, what are we doing?"

"Play it cool, man, and just follow my lead," Stephen repeated.

Stephen took a deep breath, straightened his arms out and then relaxed them, and then leaned back in his seat to face a group of four girls sitting directly behind us. "Well, hello there." Three simple words, but somehow they were different, like all traces of puberty had been removed from Stephen's voice and been replaced with a boom of a transcendent baritone. He sat taller in his seat, his shoulders back with subconscious confidence. A sly grin speckled his face. Stephen had transformed himself from an awkward, strange 14-year-old boy into a swaggering, smooth-toned young man.

The four girls noticed. They responded with smiles and excitedly nervous grins as they were introduced to this calm, cool, and collected version of Stephen.

Watching Stephen shift personalities was like watching the wolf man transform in *The Monster Squad*. Only less murder.

Stephen shot me a look out of the corner of his eye, visually sparking a reminder in my head of his advice: 'follow my lead'.

I sat up in my seat, rotated my shoulders back just as Stephen had, then turned around, resting my arm on the back of my seat so I could face the girls.

"Oh my gosh! What happened to your eye?" The blond girl asked. Before I could respond, Stephen had already begun to take control of the narrative.

"Oh, man, let me tell you all about what happened to my boy Mitchell here. Just a few days ago, Mitchell got jumped by three guys in the gym locker room. He walked in on them making some kind of drug deal and they tried to keep him quiet by ganging up on him." He leaned in closer to all four girls. "They underestimated who they were dealing with. He fought all three of them off single-handedly." The jaws on all four girls dropped as they looked closer at my face, noticing every scratch, cut, bruise and gash.

They looked at me like no one had ever looked at me before. I felt a weird flutter in my stomach.

"You fought off three drug dealers?" one of the brunette girls asked.

Before I could answer, Stephen had grabbed the reins of the narrative again. "Three guys. All gang members. I crap you not!" Stephen had turned his entire body around in his chair. "And get this: one of those dudes was trying to beat him with a football helmet. Don't believe me? Look at his stitches." He elbowed me in the side. "Show these young ladies your stitches."

I leaned my head forward and moved my hair so my stitches were visible. Two of the brunette girls covered their mouths with their hands out of shock; the third brunette girl squinted her eyes out of disgust and turned away. The blond girl put one hand on the side of her face, and then, with her other hand, put her hand on my shoulder. "Oh my gosh, you poor thing." I looked up and her face was level with mine.

Stephen continued. "Anyways, I was there when the tide turned. Mitchell was getting his tail handed to him, and then wham! An adrenaline rush hit him and Mitchell jumped up off the floor and opened a can of whoop-ass on all three of those dudes. Beat their tails until they ran. Some serious Macho Man Randy Savage stuff went down. It was so epic! Legit true story. None of those guys have been to school since it happened. Almost like ol' Mitchell here scared them off." Stephen patted me on the back for extra measure.

The blond girl's hand stayed on my shoulder during Stephen's somewhat-true, somewhat not true story; she then became aware that her hand had been resting on me for an awkward amount of time and pulled it back to her side. She smiled.

"So you beat up three drug dealers from your school AFTER they jumped you?" One of the brunette girls asked, her eyes wide.

"I....uh...well, yes," I said. I then, following Stephen's advice to follow his lead, added, "I couldn't let them get away and possibly jump some other innocent kid in the future. Someone had to stop them."

All four girls immediately and simultaneously made an "awwww" sound, like all four girls were connected in some unseen emotional manner. Their eyes and their smiles both grew wide.

"I'm Lauren," the blond girl said. "And this is Katherine, Julie and Chassidy." The three brunettes all smiled and waved. "We're from Trenton. Where are you guys from?"

"King's Hollow," Stephen answered. "The roughest and toughest school in the south. You name it, we got it: gangs, fights, drugs, the works."

"Oh, I'm not sure where that is," the brunette named Julie said. "Is it close to Trenton?"

"It sounds terrible," Chassidy said.

"It's about an hour up I-85," Stephen said, ignoring Chassidy's comment. "But Trenton, that's a swanky school, right? I mean it's gotta be swanky because the four of you are beautiful." He then added, "My name is Stephen by the way; you've already met my associate, Mitchell."

I cringed at Stephen's line, as did Chassidy, but Katherine and Julie giggled. Lauren was still looking at my face, right at eye level, and smiling.

"Does your eye hurt? I mean, that's a big black eye," Lauren asked.

"It hurt when it happened, but not so bad now. It's alright, though, you know? If this is the worst thing that ever happens to me and if it means some little scrawny kid out there won't ever have to worry about being jumped again, then it was worth it."

Lauren's smile grew even brighter. She put her hand on the side of my face, near my black eye. "You're like a superhero."

"So what instruments do the four of you play?" Stephen asked. "I know we're at a band competition and all, and the last thing anyone wants to talk about is instruments, but we're here, right? Might as well talk about it. Might as well make it official that we're all band geeks here."

The girls all giggled in agreement. All four of them were flute players, the official instrument of girls everywhere.

Think about it: how many guys do you know that play the flute?

Yep, I couldn't think of anyone either.

Stephen told the girls he played the trumpet. "And what about you?" Chassidy asked.

"I....um....trombone?" I stumbled out with nervousness. I sat back up in my seat, and with confidence, said, "Trombone. I play the trombone."

"Trombones are the best,' Chassidy said as she leaned forward and tapped my hand. "My ex-boyfriend plays the trombone, and I swear it's like the easiest instrument to pick up. If I could go back and pick a different instrument, it'd be the trombone."

'Oh, ok." What do you say to someone you just met that already has brought up their ex-boyfriend? Do girls think guys enjoy hearing about ex-boyfriends? Spoiler alert: we don't.

A short man with a balding head and extremely tiny glasses stood at the end of the row of the girls and motioned for the entire row to stand. "That's us," one of the girls said. They grabbed their instruments; Lauren hesitated to stand up.

"It was great meeting you," Lauren said.

"Uh.....I.....yeah." I couldn't talk, like an invisible force grabbed my tongue. "Great meeting you."

"I hope that black eye of yours brings your band some good luck. Maybe we will see you two after we get through our first set."

My ears started to grow warm, and my tongue felt stuck in my throat. "We will definitely find the four of you in a little while," Stephen said, sensing my nervousness resurfacing.

Lauren smiled, squeezed my hand, and then the four girls left with the rest of the Trenton band.

Once they were out of hearing distance, Stephen elbowed me right in the ribs. "Well call me a carpenter and paint me red, but I think they liked us!"

"You think?"

"Dude, did you not see them go gah-gah over your black eye?"

"Um....yeah, I guess." I could feel my face burning red hot and the flutter in my stomach was beginning to churn. Was I getting sick?

With the seats behind us empty, Stephen leaned forward to talk to two girls that were sitting directly in front of us. The room seemed to be moving like waves in the ocean, and I could feel my sweat seeping out my pores, like a dam about to burst. What was happening to me? "I'll be back," I told Stephen. Stephen shot me a look, probably confused as to why his wingman was abandoning him, but when he looked at me, he probably realized I wasn't feeling my best.

As I stumbled up the aisle of the auditorium; Mr. Undergrove emerged from the shadows of the darkened aisle and stopped me. "Where have you been?"

I pointed to Stephen a few aisles back, and muttered, "Girls. Talking to girls."

Mr. Undergrove's eyes focused on Stephen, still in deep conversation with the two girls in front of him. He returned his eyes to me, "Are you ok?" he asked.

"I need to use the restroom," I said.

"There's one in the lobby. Do you need someone to go with you?"

I shook my head. "I got this. I just need a moment."

I could feel my heartbeat in my head. The room continued to sway and swing as I found my way to the lobby's restroom, and then to a stall, and then, much to my disdain, I got sick.

What do I mean by saying '*I got sick*'? Well, that's easy: puke. And do you know what the worst part about getting sick is? The half second right before it happens. Tell me I'm wrong.

Instantly, I could feel the air around my head cool down, and my heartbeat slowed to just a whimpered thud that climbed back into my chest.

I washed my face off, dried it with some paper towels, then washed it again, holding my face under the sink faucet, letting the cold water refresh and restore me. I looked up at myself in the mirror; my black eye stared back.

When I returned to the auditorium, Stephen had relocated back to a seat with the rest of our band. "You ok?" he asked.

"Yeah, just some stomach issues. I'm good now." I sat down beside him and saw that Stephen had also moved my trombone case when he moved seats. "What happened with those two girls you were talking to?"

"Ah, 1) they were kinda stuck-up. Bridgetown Middle girls. That's the school that we always play in soccer that acts like a bunch of snobs. Apparently the snobbery isn't just limited to soccer. And 2) they were in 6th grade. I don't have time for sixth graders."

"Right."

"And 3) Undergrove busted me. Came over there and cramped my style in front of those girls. Right in front of them. I mean, c'mon, Undergrove! Respect the game, man!"

"What'd he say to you?" I asked, hoping to hear that Undergrove didn't let Stephen know I was the one that had alerted Mr. Undergrove to our different seats.

"Just that I needed to return to our band's location. He played it cool, but at the same time, didn't play it cool, ya know?"

"Yeah," I said as I nodded my head, even though I really didn't know.

The Trenton band was taking the stage; front and center was the flute section, which included our four new female friends. Stephen leaned in close to me. "We're on the move again, c'mon." We got up from our seats, but instead of trying to sneak away as we did before, I followed Stephen as he went straight to Mr. Undergrove. "Mr. Undergrove, is it cool if we go sit on the first row right in front of the stage? I'd think it'd be pretty neat to be that close to make note of all the little things other bands are doing. In fact, if you look up front, there's enough empty seats up there if everyone wants to go."

Smooth, Stephen. Very smooth.

Mr. Undergrove thought about it for a second and told us that we could go, but we had to report back in 10 minutes. "Ten minutes," Mr. Undergrove said, "and not a second more. They're going to be calling us soon to get ready to take the stage."

We slid into our seats, exactly where we could see all four girls on the stage. A grin broke out across Chassidy's face when she saw us. She then nodded to the other three girls toward our location in the front row. When Lauren made eye contact with me, she winked, and I immediately felt a strong wave of heat flush over my face. That churning in my stomach slowly crept back up, but not nearly as strong this time.

When one of the judges announced the band's name, Stephen and I froze in our seats.

"Our next band, contestant number 114, Trenton High School."

"Did he just say high school?" I asked. "Like 'high school' as in Trenton High School?"

"Trenton High School. Holy proton packs. Trenton High School," Stephen said under his breath.

"When they said Trenton, I thought 'Oh, Trenton, that's nice, wherever that must be,' and I figured they were a middle school like us, but they're not. Those girls are high school girls, man. High school girls!" I was freaking out; this was out of our league.

Stephen cracked his knuckles and then leaned back in his seat, deep in thought. "High school girls," he said. "You know, when I saw that high school girls were here, I didn't imagine we'd actually meet high school girls that would be into us. It was kinda like a pipe dream. Some of that 'aim for the moon—even if you fail, you'll land amongst the stars' type deal." He sat up straight in his seat. "But, and there's always a but, I told them we were from King's Hollow, and they didn't bat an eye. They must not know that King's Hollow is a middle school."

"Or," I said, trying to be optimistic, "they know King's Hollow is a middle school, but being the lovely, caring girls that they obviously are, they don't care that we're in middle school."

Stephen rolled his eyes. 'C'mon, dude, don't kid yourself. If you were a high school girl, would you waste your time on a middle school guy?"

"Good point."

"And also," Stephen added, "we don't know that these girls are loving and caring. Every girl appears delightful at first, and then, when you let your guard down, they rip your heart out and eat it for breakfast."

"Kinda like the vampire girls in *The Monster Squad*?"

"Exactly like the vampire girls in *The Monster Squad*."

Trenton High School's band began to play. We watched from the front row as the four girls we had met moments before performed. "They're good," I said to Stephen.

As they wrapped up their first song, Stephen and I stood up and clapped. Most of the other bands had been clapping for bands that were performing, but no one in the auditorium clapped with as much vigor and enthusiasm as Stephen and I. The four girls, our entire world at that moment, giggled and blushed. Chassidy waved at me. I waved back, and then as I looked at Lauren, she winked at me again. Because I didn't know exactly how to wink, I also waved back to her. I then felt that weird flutter in my stomach return, and the room began to get swirly.

"Hey Stephen," I said, not taking my eyes off of Lauren, "is it normal that every time we see these girls, I feel like I'm going to throw up?

"Isn't it a great feeling?"

I took a deep breath, and the flutter swirled around my insides, sparking my entire body from my legs all the way into my chest.

"It's the best feeling in the world," I confirmed.

DECEMBER - 10TH GRADE

We stood in line at Taco Bell, all of us, when I realized that, with Christmas only a few days away, Taco Bell was not playing Christmas music in their restaurant.

"What is this that they're playing?" I asked Mr. Undergrove with disgust in my voice. "It's not Christmas music, I know that."

"Pink Floyd," Mr. Undergrove confirmed, "'Comfortably Numb.' Great song, but, you're right, not appropriate for the season. They could use some holiday merriment in their music selection, that's for sure. I'm sure Brooks will have something to say about this." We all looked at Brooks, whose confused look was shining through.

"Don't look at me. I think Pink Floyd is overrated."

"What if I told you that Pink Floyd is weird, trippy, misunderstood, and has a devoted cult following, just like Sonic Youth? Would you like them then?" Mr. Undergrove said, making a good point.

Brooks changed his expression. "Maybe I need to listen to more of their stuff. I've only heard one of their songs."

"But based off that one song, you classified them as 'overrated'?" Mr. Undergrove asked.

"The song I heard was overrated, so yeah, that makes the band overrated."

"I'd love for you to one day write down your rules for rating music," Mr. Undergrove said. "That'd be an interesting read."

We all sat down, tables pushed together for companionship, a bunch of high school kids dressed up in dress shirts and Christmas ties on a Friday night, eating a not-so-classy meal before an outdoor Christmas concert in the downtown area. The music overhead shifted from Pink Floyd to MC Hammer's 'Can't Touch This', and Stephen rapped along, reciting every lyric with punctuality and precision. Even Brooks laughed at the silliness of the moment. It was one of those moments that felt like you'd want to remember it forever.

"So, Mr. Undergrove," Kevin spoke up, "you told us before the hospital gala gig that we'd be getting paid and that you had a plan, but we've haven't heard anything about that plan yet. Care to spill the beans? You can consider it your Christmas gift to us."

Mr. Undergrove took a sip of his drink, cleared his throat, and looked around the table. "Am I correct that all of you are signed up to take jazz band during third period next semester?"

We all nodded our heads. Originally I was scheduled to take some computer class second semester, but I got it switched so I could have jazz band year-round.

"Good," Mr. Undergrove continued, "I know a few more students will be joining us when second semester starts, which is great because every musician brings something different to the band. But, yes, I told you before the hospital gala that we were financially compensated for our performance, and I purposefully waited to tell all of you what our jazz band program was going to do with that money because I wanted all my ducks to be in a row before I let the cat out of the bag about where we were going to go with it."

We all perked up. "We're going somewhere?" I asked.

"Well," Mr. Undergrove, "we have the potential to go somewhere. It's going to require us to do more fundraising, but it's completely manageable. The school is offering to pay for some, and by some they mean a very small amount, so we're responsible for the rest. I have a few relatively simple ideas for us to pursue that could be easy money-makers."

"Are we going to a jazz band competition?" Stephen asked.

Mr. Undergrove grinned. "Yep, we're going to a jazz band competition. First week in April."

"Will we miss school for it?" Josh asked.

"Yep. You'll miss school." Mr. Undergrove continued to grin, almost like there was something more that he wasn't telling us.

"I'm good with a competition, especially if we're missing school," Stephen said. He then tapped my arm and added, "Last time we went to a competition, you had your black eye chick magnet. We're going to have to try that method again. You can punch me; I'll punch you."

Everyone went back to their food, but Mr. Undergrove just sat there with the same mischievous grin shining on his face. "Doesn't anyone even want to know where this jazz competition is?" Mr. Undergrove asked; all our eyes returned to him.

"Is it in Snowfield? That's where that one was that you took us to in middle school."

Mr. Undergrove shook his head. "No, Kevin, but good guess. Think bigger."

Josh spoke up. "Durham? That's a big city that's nearby."

"Nope," Mr. Undergrove said. "Think bigger."

We all searched our heads. Stephen suggested Tiffin, but Mr. Undergrove immediately shot that down as well. Where could he be taking us?

"I'll give you a hint: Frank Sinatra sang a song about this place."

As we racked our brains, Kevin's eyes grew wide, and he immediately yelled out: "Kokomo! You're taking us to Kokomo! We're going to a band competition in Kokomo!" He jumped out of his seat in excitement and started dancing, but his celebration was cut short by Mr. Undergrove.

"We're not going to Kokomo, Kevin."

"But you said Frank Sinatra sings about this place. Didn't he sing 'Kokomo'?"

Mr. Undergrove put his hands on his face and shook his head. "Kevin, that's the Beach Boys."

Kevin stood there in silence before awkwardly returning to his seat. "Well, I was way off."

"Frank Sinatra, guys. Frank Sinatra. It was his most famous song." He then added, "And no, it's not Kokomo."

I made eye contact with Stephen, and just like that, the same thought jumped into our minds at the same time. His face lit up with excitement. "No way...." stumbled out of my mouth.

"Undergrove! Are you taking us to New York City?" Stephen asked, trying to somewhat contain his excitement in the event that he, like Kevin, was way off on his guess.

Mr. Undergrove continued to grin. "Like I said earlier, we're going to need to do some pretty big fundraising, but yes, if all goes according to plan, we'll all miss four days of school in April for the National Miles Davis Youth Jazz Competition in New York City."

An eruption of joy broke out from all of us.

MAY - 8TH GRADE

The entire King's Hollow band stood in a long line stretching down the large hall that ran parallel to Snowfield's auditorium. We were assembling our instruments, checking our music folders, and watching Mr. Undergrove flutter around as he used his electric tuner to check as many instruments as possible, all while trying to stay silent while Trenton finished up on stage.

"You nervous?" Kevin asked.

I shook my head. "Nah, we got this. We've put in the work. Now, we're going to put on the performance."

"I thought you'd say something like that." Kevin reached his arm out and we bumped fists.

"How many people did you get ahold of last night on the telephone?"

Kevin smiled. "All but five. Three of those were answering machines, one never picked up the phone, and one dad hung up on me."

"Hung up on you? Why would a dad hang up on you?"

"I guess he thought I was trying to woo his daughter. What he didn't realize is that I just wanted her to woo her instrument."

"Gentlemen," Mr. Undergrove said, "let's take a look at what you all have going on here." Mr. Undergrove had me blow out a C, and then he had me adjust one of the tuning slides at the end of my trombone. While he was helping Kevin tune his instrument, the Trenton High School band was leaving the stage, walking right by us in the hall. Student after student walked past me as I nervously fiddled with my instrument. Then, a wave of girls came out of the stage door. I tried to look for any of the flute players Stephen and I had met earlier, but there seemed to be a hundred girls walking by in black dress pants and white shirts. It seemed impossible. Then, I felt a punch on my arm. Not a hard punch, but a playful punch, just enough to get my attention.

"Hey!" Chassidy said. "Did you like our performance?"

I kept my eyes on the mass of students floating by. "You guys rocked. I mean girls. You girls rocked," I corrected myself as I made eye contact with her. "The whole band rocked, but the flutes especially rocked." She smiled and then squeezed my arm.

"Hey, this is my friend, Kevin," I said, motioning for Kevin to step forward. "Kevin, this is Chassidy. She's from Trenton."

Chassidy waved, Kevin waved back, and then Chassidy turned back to me. "Good luck out there. The first time you walk out on a stage that big it's a little nerve-racking, but you get over it quick. The smaller theater that you play in for the next round isn't near as intimidating."

"There's another theater here?" I asked, trying to hide the shock in my voice; this school had not one but two theaters!

"Duh. Have you never been here before?" Chassidy asked. "They have this auditorium for concerts and assemblies, and then a smaller theater for their drama program. Does King's Hollow not have that kind of stuff?"

"Um....not exactly."

"You must not know anything about King's Hollow," Kevin added.

Katherine, Julie, and Lauren joined us; Lauren stood beside me and, like Chassidy just moments ago, bumped my side with her elbow, a grin on her face. "What'd you think? Did we do good?" Lauren asked.

"I told Chassidy that you all rocked. You should be proud."

Lauren grinned. "I'm sure you guys will be great. I mean, you've got the good luck of your black eye."

"Did he tell you how he got his black eye?" Kevin blurted out, inserting himself into the conversation. "You should have seen how gruesome it was the day it happened! Mitchell walked into the locker room and—"

"They know how I got it, Kevin, but thank you," I said, cutting him off.

"And I think it's cute," Lauren piped in, playfully elbowing me in the side again.

I could feel my face flush with heat, and my stomach did a somersault.

"Ahh, look, he's blushing!" Kevin declared. "I've never seen you blush like that before! Your face is bright red!"

'Dang it, Kevin, shut up', I thought, but the words were stuck in my throat.

"Your friend is right; you're blushing," Chassidy added. "And Lauren is right too. It is kinda cute. I like that in a guy."

I blushed even more. My face was so hot that even my black eye felt like it had steam coming off of it. Was the room getting smaller? Why was it so sweaty in here? Was the floor moving? Why couldn't I breathe? How long had it been since I had said something?

"Where's Stephen?" Katherine asked.

"He's around here somewhere," Kevin said, "but allow me to introduce myself..." Kevin started talking to the girls, and he just kept on talking and talking and talking, all while I stood there, trying to focus on getting the ground to stop moving and my face to stop burning and my heart to stop thumping so darn loudly in my head. And also to not concentrate on the fact that Lauren had her hand rested in the corner notch of my inner elbow, right where the forearm and bicep meet. She stood closer to me, almost leaning on me, but not quite leaning on me, ya know?

"Gentlemen, I believe you all have a few songs that you need to get ready to perform." Mr. Undergrove's voice brought me back to reality and shook me a little, too, as he approached our small gathering in the hall. "I know these young ladies may have your attention, but I know they have places to be, and so do you. You can be social later."

The girls took their cue and began to move toward the door that led back to the auditorium. Lauren squeezed my hand as she left, leaned close to me, and whispered "good luck" into my ear.

Kevin shook his head, a grin spread across his face. "Dude, how do you know those girls?"

"Stephen and I met them in the auditorium. They're nice."

"Yeah," he smirked. "They're real nice. How'd you get two of them to dig you that quickly?"

"Two of them?"

"Yeah, man, you blind or something? Two of those girls got the hots for you. It's written all over their faces. You didn't notice?"

"I....uh....huh?" I was tongue-tied. Two girls?

"Man, I don't think you look like you're doing alright. You look like death warmed over."

The room still seemed to be moving, like waves on the ocean, more so now than ever. "Two girls?" I asked again.

Kevin started to laugh. "You look like crap, but you're hung up on the 'two girls' part. Figures." He walked over to me, put his hand on my shoulder, a grin stretched across his face. "You better shake whatever bug that has you feeling flushed because the blondie and one of the brunettes have it for you, and they got it bad, Mr. Black-eyed beauty." He patted me on the shoulder and then returned to making sure his saxophone was ready. "And before you say it," Kevin added, "yes, my reed is straight and ready to go. Don't worry. They'll be no mistakes on my end today.

I could hear my heartbeat thumping in my head again. Two girls? Images of Lauren flashed through my head: Lauren touching my shoulder, Lauren winking at me on stage, Lauren jabbing me with her elbow, Lauren squeezing my hand. Ok, yeah, Lauren may like me. I liked Lauren. That was clear, although incredibly awkward to admit; it's hard to admit that you 'like' someone, like a layer of vulnerability is being stripped away from you. But two girls?

Then it hit me.

Chassidy.

When she told me that her ex-boyfriend played the trombone, she was telling me that she was single. She waved at me while she was onstage. While I was looking for Lauren in the crowd of Trenton students, Chassidy found me first. She told me that my blushing was something she liked in a guy.

Kevin saw it. Why didn't I notice it?

Two girls. An hour ago, when we arrived at this band competition, I had four things going for me: a trombone, a good friend in Stephen, a sense of adventure, and a sympathetic black eye. Now, I had two girls, two high school girls, vying for my attention.

I placed my trombone back by its case, asked Kevin to keep an eye on it, and then found the bathroom off the back of the auditorium hall, where I got sick.

Again.

DECEMBER - 10TH GRADE

Mr. Undergrove telling us that we were going to go to New York City for a jazz band competition is the greatest thing that could have happened for our town's Christmas tree lighting ceremony. It was cold out, the wind was blowing, the crowd was wrapped up in heavy coats and blankets, but the Northern Kent High School jazz band seemed to be on fire that night. We were energized with thoughts of the Big Apple, and we all wanted to prove to Mr. Undergrove, to ourselves, and to the crowd that was at the lighting ceremony that we deserved that trip to New York. So, when Mr. Undergrove opened his trunk to get the ark and also revealed he had gone to the dollar store to buy all of us Santa hats to wear during the performance, none of us, not even Brooks, objected to it.

"This is so festive, I might burst with holiday happiness," Stephen remarked. "So far this birthday, I've gotten Taco Bell, no school for two weeks, news that we're going to New York, and now a Santa hat." He then yelled out, "Happy birthday to me, and happy birthday to baby Jesus!"

"Stephen, keep it down, man. Not everyone celebrates Christmas," Kevin said. "There could be Jewish people here too, ya know?"

"It's a Christmas tree lighting ceremony, Kevin," Stephen responded. "I'm pretty sure it'll be ok. Jewish people celebrate Christmas too. Maybe not baby Jesus, but Christmas and Santa Claus, and all the ho-ho-ho stuff."

We were stationed in front of the library, right in the heart of our downtown area. A semicircle drive that pulled right up to the front door of the library was the backdrop of the ceremony, with a giant decorated but unlit white spruce tree standing in the grass area inside the semicircle. There were lights strung throughout the streetlights, the windows of the library, the trees in front of the library, and obviously the Christmas tree itself, all unlit, all seeming to vibrate with excitement as they, like us, were eager for the Christmas season to metaphorically descend upon us.

Under Mr. Undergrove's direction, we started playing at 7:30 p.m. Because the ceremony would not officially begin for another thirty minutes, the crowd was sparse, mostly city officials that were part of the ceremony's planning process. We were still amped on the news of New York City, so when Mr. Undergrove selected for us to begin with a rendition of "Frosty the Snowman," Kirby, feeling the same level of excitement that was pulsing through all of our veins, sped up the tempo of the established beat on the drums, forcing the rest of the band to speed up with him, resulting in a slightly more rock-and-rollish rendition. Despite Mr. Undergrove's evil eye that he gave to Kirby the entire song, Kirby never slowed down the tempo, a smile shining as bright as a Christmas star across his face; he knew Mr. Undergrove was upset with him, but he didn't care.

When the song ended, Mr. Undergrove, half mad, half as excited as the rest of us, stared at Kirby, trying to contain a smile with a disappointed frown. "Kirby, while I appreciate your desire to improvise with the tempo, at a gig in front of an audience is not the time to try it out. That's why we have practice; that's the time to try out new ideas, not when you're in front of a crowd and the rest of the band is at your mercy."

Kirby spun one of his drumsticks around his pointer finger, trying to contain his grin. "Sorry everyone," he said. "Guess I got caught up in the moment. It must be the Christmas spirit."

Mr. Undergrove let his guard down and broke out into a full-blown smile. "It did sound cool. I liked the energy. 'Frosty' has never been spunkier."

8:00 PM came. We wrapped up our first set with a Brenda Lee inspired version of 'Jingle Bell Rock'. The crowd had swelled to close to 300 people, all braving the cold and the wind for the annual tradition of lighting the Christmas tree. Several people spoke, including the mayor, who thanked us in front of the crowd, which got us a roar of applause. "Gotta admit, that feels good," Kevin said.

When it was time to turn on the lights to the tree, there was a big countdown from 30; the crowd counted along, each number louder than the one before. When the numbers got down to single digits, the crowd was practically screaming. Kirby's drums seemed to rattle with excitement as we inched closer and closer to the end of the countdown.

At 'one', time seemed to stop for just a second; the crowd stopped, the wind stopped, the cold stopped, everything halted. There was this peaceful silence that floated in the air. It tingled between the people, it swirled around the giant tree, it seemed to wrapped itself around every single one of us in the band, and then it lingered for much, much more than a second.

The lights came on, making the giant tree burst with hues of red, green, purple, orange, yellow, and blue. The trees that lined the library, the windows around the library, and all the street lamp poles all seemed to come alive with a multicolor spectacular. A giant six foot plastic Santa on the library's roof, once shrouded in the darkness of the night, now glowed with pride as it overlooked the area where the town's Christmas tree sat. Frank Sinatra's 'Have Yourself a Merry Little Christmas' blared over the speakers while people gawked at the beauty of the tree.

Then, it happened, just as Brooks had predicted: fake snow. Just like the plastic Santa on the roof of the library, two machines, hidden by the dark of the night, roared to life from behind the Christmas tree and began to burst out tiny soap bubbles that drifted down onto the crowd, giving the appearance of snow; the crowd 'oohhh'ed and 'aaaahhhhh'ed.

A local church choir sang a few songs. The mayor thanked everyone for coming, and then invited the crowd to stick around to enjoy hot chocolate and cookies sponsored by one of the local churches. Mr. Undergrove gave the signal, nodded his head, raised his baton, and our second set boomed into the night air, starting with a snazzed and jazzed up version of 'We Three Kings'.

We played our second set for the allotted 20 minutes; when we finished, the crowd was still alive enjoying the lights, cookies, hot chocolate and music, so we played another 15 minutes of songs.

"Going above and beyond is always a good thing," Mr. Undergrove said, "but going above and beyond when you have an audience is always a smart thing."

"I can't believe it snowed." I said to Brooks as we were in the process of cleaning up our equipment. "I mean, I knew you said it was going to possibly snow, but wow, it snowed."

"Fake snowed," Brooks said. "It fake snowed."

"Hey, fake snow is snow. Any type of snow is good with me."

Brooks grinned, and nodded his head. "Sure. I'm with you on that."

Maybe it was the hot chocolate, maybe it was the giant tree and all the lights, maybe it was the festive music, or maybe it was that we were out of school for two weeks, but Brooks, often expressing his polarizing opinions, didn't argue, criticize, or complain. He actually got along with everyone that night.

It was a Christmas miracle.

MAY - 8TH GRADE

We took to the stage. Being a trombone player, I sat near the back of the band, which meant I couldn't exactly see into the seating area of Snowfield's auditorium, and I had no clue if Lauren or Chassidy were watching. Out of sight, out of mind; I could focus on playing and not on the fact that two incredibly beautiful and completely out of my league high school girls were supposedly into me.

We had two rounds of judges that we had to survive. This was just the first round, for later, as pointed out to me by Chassidy and Mr. Undergrove; the second round would take place in a smaller theater.

What kind of school has not one, but two theaters? What is this? *Lifestyles of the Rich & Famous*?

I sat up in my seat so I could at least try to peer out into the auditorium, but the stage lights made it impossible to see anything but the darkness of the auditorium. The stomach pain was gone, my face felt cool, and the ground was no longer moving. All I needed to do was to play my trombone with heart and clarity. That was my one job.

Mr. Undergrove walked out on the stage, bowed to the judges in the front row, stepped up to the podium, and raised his arms, signifying for us to raise our instruments. With his hands up, he closed his eyes, took a deep breath, and when he opened his eyes, Mr. Undergrove said what he'd been telling us all school year: "I believe in you, in all of you."

Every kid tried their best not to smile behind their instrument. Here we were, at a band competition, something that if Mr. Undergrove had told us we were going to do on the first day of school, we would have laughed at him.

Our first number: 'Air for Band', a number I wasn't crazy about, but Mr. Undergrove insisted that we played it well. We had technically learned it back in November for our Christmas concert, and we had been concentrating a lot of effort into perfecting it for the competition. "Trust me," Mr. Undergrove had said a lot, "the judges will appreciate it."

As we finished 'Air for Band', Stephen turned in his seat in the second row and gave me a thumbs up motion. He then pointed to the audience and gave me another thumbs up. I could only assume one thing: he could see into the crowd, and that certain people from Trenton were watching us.

Our next two numbers were 'Kentucky 1800' and 'Yorkshire Ballad', both collectively not our favorites, but both were songs that Mr. Undergrove labeled as 'judge-friendly', whatever that means. "Adults have a weird sense of music, trust me," Mr. Undergrove had told us weeks earlier. "But judges, especially band competition judges, have a very odd taste in music. Sometimes when you go to these competitions you have to play songs that aren't that fun to play, but make the judges happy."

"Why do we need to worry about the judges so much?" Brent blurted out loud.

"Great question, Brent. Glad you asked. Also, thank you for not raising your hand," Mr. Undergrove said sarcastically. "But to answer you, I need to ask you a question: when you play UNO, do you play to win, or do you just participate for farts and giggles?"

"Farts and giggles?" Brent had a confused look on his face. "What's 'farts and giggles'?"

Mr. Undergrove rolled his eyes. "Ok, never mind that part. Do you play UNO to win or lose?"

"To win," Brent said back. "Who plays UNO to lose?"

"No one, that's who. And that's why we're going to the band competition with these music selections: to be successful. I don't want to take an entire day to go over there and get our butts whooped."

"UNO. Gotcha." Brent said.

And so we followed Mr. Undergrove 's lead by playing our first set comprised of three songs that no one in the band was nuts about playing. But we could play them well, so that's all that mattered.

As we exited the stage back into the large hall, Stephen grabbed my shoulder. "The girls watched us. All four of them."

"That's great, man." I said as I felt that twitch in my stomach return.

"And we also might have just a slight problem." Stephen held up his pointer finger and thumb and pinched them slightly close together while leaving space between. "There's a slight chance that when we got done with our three songs that when the judges thanked us over the microphone that they may have mentioned that we were King's Hollow Middle School." Stephen shook his head. "They gave it away. They gave away our dirty little secret."

"I'm not sure if it's a dirty little secret," I finally responded, "we just hadn't mentioned to the girls yet that we're in middle school."

"Dirty little secret," Stephen repeated.

We left the back hall area and returned to the auditorium. The number of bands there seemed to have swelled, and almost every seat appeared occupied with a kid with a band instrument, all sitting in respect and silence as they waited for their chance to perform.

"Let's talk damage control," Stephen said as we sat in the back row of our assigned section, perfectly situated at the end of the row in the event that we had the chance to relocate when Mr. Undergrove wasn't looking. "The girls were on the front row for our performance, but now they're not. They could possibly now know that we're just middle schoolers. What kind of spin can we put on this?"

"Spin?" I asked. "Are you a politician or something? We can't spin this."

We didn't have the chance to discuss it any further, because it was at the moment that the empty seats behind us became occupied with four familiar female faces.

"Well look who it is!" Stephen said, a calm and confident smile spread across his face. The goofiness and awkwardness of Stephen had melted away once more, revealing a smoother, edgier Stephen. It was all very Dr. Jekyll and Mr. Hyde.

"You guys did fantastic," Chassidy said, squeezing my shoulder as the girls sat down. Lauren was sitting directly behind me, with Chassidy beside her. Katherine and Julie both sat behind Stephen.

"It's not a question of if we were fantastic or not," Stephen said as he turned his body and propped his elbow up on the back of his seat, "but the level of fantastic that we achieved."

"Is that so?" Chassidy asked, seemingly smitten with Stephen's remark. "We were pretty impressed with how your band sounded, coming from King's Hollow and all, the 'roughest and toughest school in the south'. Isn't that how you described it?"

Stephen nodded with impressed approval. "I'm a very quotable person. It's a trademark of importance."

"You're very full of yourself," Chassidy said with a smile on her face.

"Yes, as a matter of fact, I am full of myself," Stephen replied. "I try to keep myself full of myself at all times. My own bones. My own intestines. My very own blood, type B for those of you out there wondering." Stephen then leaned over the seat a little closer to the girls. "I don't want to brag or anything, but I have my very own stomach too. Newest model on the market. Digests food at the drop of a dime." Stephen then snapped his fingers. "Don't get me started on my bowels."

The girls just stared at Stephen in strange silence, not sure what to make of his comment.

'There it is', I thought to myself, 'the awkward Stephen that I know.' Mr. Hyde was beginning to lose its power over Dr. Jekyll's body.

"Oh, well, that's good, I guess," Chassidy finally replied. "Too bad you don't have an irresistible black eye like this cutie over here." Chassidy then rubbed her hand over top of my head and through my hair, gently scratching the back of my head with her nails.

Lauren's eyes grew wide. She looked at Chassidy, and then she looked at me. A small sign of uncomfortableness rushed across her face and then relaxed away as quickly as it came.

Lauren was realizing what Kevin pointed out to me earlier: two girls, both friends, were vying for the same guy.

I gotta admit: it was nice to see someone freaking out about this situation besides me.

"So, how do you think you all scored on your first performance?" Stephen asked.

“Oh, we crushed it. Superior all the way. We always get superior ratings. Every year.” Chassidy said. “Honestly, the judges probably knew we were going to get a superior rating the moment they saw the name ‘Trenton’. We have that kind of reputation.”

“Oh really?” Stephen asked.

“Really,” Chassidy replied, almost with a ‘matter-of-fact’ bluntness.

“Well, if you don’t mind me saying,” Stephen said with a sly smile on his face, “it looks like you’re the one who's full of yourself now.” Stephen then winked at Chassidy. Chassidy, slightly annoyed at Stephen’s comment, didn’t reciprocate his smile or wink; instead she turned her head away from Stephen and then rolled her eyes. Only Lauren and I saw the gesture.

“What about you guys?” Lauren asked. “What do you think you guys scored up there?”

I looked at Stephen and Stephen looked at me and neither one of us knew what to say. “I mean, I know we did well,” I said, “so I’m gonna say ‘gold’? Is that a rating? Gold, silver, bronze?”

All four of the girls burst out laughing. Lauren put her hand on my shoulder and her head on my arm as she laughed.

“What’s so funny?” I asked.

“You’re too much,” Chassidy replied. “Gold? Really? That’s not how it works.”

“How does it work?”

“Do you guys really not know?” Chassidy said.

"Does it look like we know?" Stephen said bluntly. "We've never been to a band competition before."

Chassidy shot Stephen a harsh look, like any warm feelings she may have had for him were quickly fading.

'For him', I thought selfishly to myself, 'hopefully not for me.'

Jeez, did I just think that? Did I really just throw my best friend under the bus internally for a girl? Isn't there a saying out there about 'all is fair in love and war'?

"There's five scores you could possibly get," Lauren said. "Superior, excellent, good, fair, and poor. Obviously superior is the way to go. I'm sure you guys were up there."

"Our luck will be a 'fair' rating," Stephen said. "Mr. Undergrove will explode."

"We did better than 'fair', I'm sure of it," I said. "Although Mr. Undergrove exploding does sound funny."

"Like Wolfman, when he's shoved out that window with dynamite in his pants."

"Yes!" I blurted out a tad too loudly. Several students around us put their pointer fingers up over their mouths, signifying they wanted us to lower our voices.

"What are you guys talking about?" Lauren asked; all four girls had the same confused look on their faces.

"It's from a movie, *The Monster Squad*," I said. "You ever seen it?"

"*The Monster Squad*?" Lauren shook her head; the other girls looked equally confused.

"Monster Squad?" Chassidy asked. "Like a team of Monsters playing basketball or something?"

"No, no, no," Stephen shook his head. "It's about a group of kids, or teenagers really, or young men, if you will, that head off an invasion of monsters that descend upon Baton Rouge, Louisiana. All the classic monsters are there too, like a mummy, Dracula, the creature from the black lagoon, or if you want to call him Gill-Man, then that's fine too."

"Ugh," Chassidy cut Stephen off. "Sounds stupid."

"You got to be kidding me," Stephen shot back. "*The Monster Squad* may be the greatest cinematical adventure of all time!"

Chassidy's face scrunched up. "Cinematical? What?"

I leaned forward towards her. "Movies. He's talking about movies."

"So why didn't he just say 'movie' instead of, well, whatever he said."

"Because *The Monster Squad* is more than just some movie! It's art! It's adventure! It's horror! It's action! It's everything you'd ever want in a movie!" Stephen was peaked at his excitement. This was the guy I knew shining through, not some ladies' man character. But at the same time, he was obviously annoying our company. The girls were tolerating Stephen less and less every minute that went by that he spent talking about the cinematic merits of *The Monster Squad*. Even Lauren, whose hand was still resting on my shoulder from earlier, had a look in her eye that said 'save us, please'.

I reached over and patted Stephen on the shoulder. "Stephen, obviously these girls are unaware of the magic of *The Monster Squad*, which is totally their loss, but since we can't do anything about that at the moment, why don't we enjoy the time we have together talking about something else?"

"It IS their loss, isn't it?" Stephen nodded. "Good point."

Lauren squeezed my shoulder and mouthed the words 'thank you' to me.

It was at that moment that the realization of Lauren maybe liking me spread to Chassidy, who eyed Lauren's hand resting on my shoulder and began to make the connection that Lauren and I had made earlier. Her eyes grew wide momentarily, and then narrowed, almost like a villain plotting out an evil disposition that would derail all of humanity.

"So, Mitchell, did Lauren tell you that her ex-boyfriend is here today?" Chassidy asked. "He's in band with us. Plays the tuba. Big guy. Plays football, wrestles, and plays baseball." A grin curled across her face. "But I'm sure she's told you that already."

A look of shock sat perched on Lauren's face, like someone she didn't expect to betray her had just stabbed her in the side. "No," she finally said. "I don't see why he needs to know that."

Chassidy leaned back in her seat and looked at me, a sly smile creeping across her face. "I mean, you probably need to know. I told you my ex-boyfriend played the trombone, but he's not here today. He quit band after first semester ended. But Lauren's ex-boyfriend? They just broke up, and he's here. So I think the least we should do," Chassidy shot Lauren a look out of the side of her eyes, "is warn you. He tends to be, what's the word, Lauren?" Chassidy looked at Lauren like she already knew the answer to her own question. "Temperamental. That's it. He tends to be temperamental."

"Which is why we broke up," Lauren added, a look on her face that seemed to be struggling as to why Chassidy was bringing any of this up in front of two guys that they just met.

Chassidy looked at her nails. "I just thought they should have the head's up, you know, just in case." She then smiled at Lauren and me. Lauren had moved her hand back into her lap, and inside, I felt a rage of awkwardness drape over me.

"Let me tell you ladies this," Stephen said, slapping me on the shoulder, "if anyone is going to mess with us, we can handle ourselves. This guy right here can't be beat, and me, I'm the ultimate tag team partner. If we were wrestlers, we'd be the WWF tag team champions." Stephen had drifted back into his charming alter-ego, but it wasn't near as effective anymore, kinda like the wizard being revealed in *The Wizard of Oz*: once you saw behind the curtain, there was no going back to the holographics and illusions.

"You know what, Stephen?" Chassidy said, "I believe you." She leaned forward and put one elbow on the back of my chair and the other hand on the back of my neck, scratching gently the back of my head with her fingernails. "I think Mitchell here could probably hold his own against almost anyone." She ran her hand across my neck and cupped my chin, meeting my eyes with her eyes. "That sound about right?"

For a brief second, the entire world completely came to a halt. The roof of the auditorium flew off up into the air, like a tornado had flung it with little thought. Fireworks exploded around over our heads, the sparks so close that we could practically touch them. There was music playing, floating thought the air, almost like soap bubbles, not coming from the band on the stage, but from an organ somewhere, the kind that you hear playing in the background on a carousel at an amusement park. A sparkling disco ball seemed to float in the air, shimmering its reflection everywhere you looked.

I looked into Chassidy's eyes, and she looked into mine. Her smile, bearing perfectly white straight teeth, glowed with unearthly radiance. Everyone in the theater disappeared. The seats disappeared, the bands, the stage - all gone. It was me and Chassidy standing there, her hand on my face, her other hand holding mine.

Then, just as quickly as time stopped, it started back up again, and the moment was over. There was no fireworks, nor disco ball. The roof of the auditorium was still intact, as were the seats and everything else in the auditorium. The conversation had moved on to Chassidy asking Julie and Katherine about when they had to report to the smaller theater for their second performance. Chassidy's hand had drifted from my face, to touching my hand on the seat, to back into her lap. Lauren, uncomfortable with the situation that Chassidy had created, had her arms crossed over her chest and was staring to the right of us, out at another band, trying to keep her eyes away.

I could feel the heat rushing back to my head, the pulse of my body pounding in my ears. The waves in the ground were back, moving throughout the room like the tide coming in at the ocean.

"Dude, you're blushing." Stephen whispered to me, like I hadn't noticed.

The colors of the room began to swirl. Stephen's face began to melt into his shirt, and the girls, all dressed in identical white shirts and black pants, blended together like a crushed Oreo. A boiling started at the bottom of my stomach, and began to rise at a rapid pace.

"I'll be right back." I jumped up and walked with persuasive force towards the lobby and the closest restroom.

Have you ever been in the ocean and feel the tide start to pull you out? You can swim and swim and swim, but sometimes, you just can't fight the current. When I entered the lobby, I walked right into another band entering the auditorium; it was an entire army of band kids stopping me from reaching my destination. I tried to fight my way through the crowd, but it seemed futile. No matter where I turned, or how I maneuvered, there were kids standing in my way, pushing me back or away from my desired destination.

'Please let me make it,' I thought to myself in an internal panic. 'Please let me make it. Please let me make it. Please let me make it. Please let me make it.'

Finally, I saw my chance, a break in the crowd that would allow me a path to the nearest bathroom. I bumped my way through the crowd, elbowing my way across the current of fellow band students. I burst into the bathroom, ran straight into a stall, and, just like clockwork, got sick, again.

For those of you keeping track at home, the magic number is three; three times I had gotten sick since arriving at Snowfield. Could this day get any worse?

Yep, I know; the day will get worse now.

You can't say stuff like that and not expect the day to get worse. That's a little slice of *Murphy's Law* that you can always count on to kick you when you think you've already been kicked enough. You know the saying, 'What can go wrong will go wrong', or something like that. Well, it's about to go really wrong.

See, when I elbowed my way through the crowd, I was paying attention, but not really paying attention. I went through the restroom door and locked myself in a stall to get sick, but it was after I got sick that I really started to panic. I mean, I was panicking before because I didn't want to get sick in front of anyone, but this was a whole different level of panic that I was experiencing.

Why? As I finished watching what was left of my stomach go down the drain of the toilet, I heard two people talking. I didn't see anyone in the restroom as I entered, so they must have been in some of the other stalls. The problem with that: the voices of these two people were not male; they were girls.

'Why would girls be in the boys' restroom?' one might ask yourself.

Well, it wasn't that there was girls in the boys' restroom; it was that this was the moment that I realized that I was the outsider in this scenario.

Yes, you're catching on now.

In the midst of my panic to not get sick in front of anyone, I may have sorta kinda totally gone into the wrong restroom, and now I was stuck, locked in a stall with no way out. The longer I sat there, the more voices I heard, all belonging to the opposite sex, and all apparently oblivious to the fact that I was in the restroom with them.

Don't ever think that the day couldn't get any worse, because the answer will always be 'yes'.

DECEMBER - 10TH GRADE

I should have known Stephen's house would be crowded with people for his birthday. Stephen had never met a stranger a day in his life, but it was still a little shocking to walk in the front door to Stephen's house and be greeted by Frank Michaels, the 17-year-old high school freshmen, sporting his signature green mohawk, shoving brownies down his throat faster than Stephen's mom could put new brownies out on the kitchen table that was already covered with a variety of sweets, veggies, cheeses, and chips. Beside him, keeping track of how many brownies Frank consumed, was Martin Tant, the kid that got kicked out of Northern Kent on the 2nd day of school back in August when he set the dumpster behind the cafeteria on fire. Standing by the steps leading to Stephen's basement was Anna Koolete, also known as Anna Kool-Aid, and her clique of clueless blonds. Down in the basement was a group of seniors from Northern Kent, mostly football players and cheerleaders, all playing pool on Stephen's dad's pool table. By the television were three couches, each one filled to capacity with girls, all freshmen, all laughing, giggling and talking over each other. By the back porch off the basement sat another spread of food; most people were getting their snacks from this table, each person probably silently hoping Frank Michaels stayed upstairs and did not discover the second layout of food that everyone else could enjoy. A radio blasting rap music played in the basement, requiring every person to almost yell in order to have a discussion.

Hanging out on the back porch was the majority of the band, except Phillip, who was socially oblivious; while he told Stephen 'happy birthday' earlier in the day, Phillip had no plans to make an appearance at Stephen's party.

Phillip was the kind of guy that, if it wasn't for the yearbook, you'd probably completely forget that he had ever existed. Odds are, you probably know someone just like that. Don't believe me? Look through your school's yearbook and then try to tell me I'm wrong.

"Oh, good, Mitchell's here," Kirby said, "he can clarify for me."

"Clarify what?"

"We're debating something," Kirby said. "This is vitally important. Think carefully before you answer my question, ok?"

"Sure," I shrugged my shoulders and shoved a cookie into my mouth.

Kirby took a deep breath, looked me in the eye, and then asked, "Do you promise to tell the absolute truth to my question? No second-guessing yourself."

"Sure, yeah, whatever. What do you need to know?"

Kirby relaxed his shoulders, held his finger up to the rest of the band signifying to stay quiet, and then asked, "Which of the turtles is the absolute best Teenage Mutant Ninja Turtle?"

"Dude, that's not even a question," I responded. "It's obvious: Raphael."

Kirby slumped his shoulders and a look of disappointment crept onto his face while Kevin threw his hands up in the air out of shock. David patted me on the back and yelled out "Thank you! See? This man knows his ninja turtles!" Justin also nodded with approval.

"How?" Kirby finally stammered out. "I mean, how could you possibly pick Raphael when it's clearly Leonardo! Leonardo is the leader! He's got swords!"

"Katanas," I corrected him. "Leonardo uses katanas, not 'swords', so first, know the character that you're defending, and second, anyone that has ever read a *Teenage Mutant Ninja Turtle* comic knows that Raphael may not be the leader, but overall, he's the greatest ninja turtle."

Kirby shook his head back and forth in disagreement. "Leonardo. Leonardo always trumps Raphael. Always."

"Leonardo leads," I said, "but Raphael is a warrior. He's fierce and brutal, although hot-headed."

"And that hot-headedness is his downfall! He's too emotional, but Leonardo? He's always in check with his inner self," Kirby said. "Leonardo is the greatest ninja turtle. Hands down."

"Kirby, Kirby, Kirby," I replied, "let me set up a scenario for you: you're in a dark alley. You're surrounded by 50 members of the Foot Clan, all armed and very dangerous highly skilled ninjas, and their one mission is to bring your head back to the Shredder. Who do you want protecting you: a good leader, or a relentless monster of a warrior?

Kirby hesitated before he answered, obviously giving the matter some thought.

I looked at the rest of the band. 'Did you see that? He hesitated. Kirby hesitated!" I turned back to Kirby, connecting with his eyes. "He hesitated because he knows that his answer wasn't going to be Leonardo."

Kirby, looking guilty, replied, "You can't prove that."

"I don't have to prove it, because you and I and everyone here knows that your answer to that question is Raphael."

“No it’s not,” Kirby shot back, half mad, half grinning.

“Ok, then prove it. Tell me that if you were surrounded by 50 members of the Foot Clan all wanting to kill you that you would pick Leonardo to protect you over Raphael. Say it. Let’s hear you say you’d want Leonardo protecting you in that situation.”

Kirby hesitated again, almost like he was trying to force out the words, but just couldn’t do it.

I threw my hands up in the air. “Ladies and gentlemen of the jury: I rest my case.”

Yeah, yeah, yeah,” Kirby said, shooing me off at his defeat. “Turtle schmurtle. I give.” He then disappeared into the crowd.

Stephen, the social butterfly, bounced from person to person all night. When I finally caught up with him, he was sitting in the middle of one of the couches that was occupied with the seemingly endless number of freshmen girls, both his arms spread out around the shoulders of two girls, one on each side, boasting about our upcoming trip to New York City.

“Are you guys playing at Radio City Music Hall?” one of the girls asked.

Stephen shrugged his shoulders, laughed, and responded “The heck do I know? I just know we’re going to New York Frickin’ City!” He then leaned his head back and sang out, “I wanna to wake up, in a city that doesn't sleep! And find I'm king of the hill / top of the heap!”

The girls laughed. Stephen, once awkward and strange, had grown into this suave, appealing guy that most people couldn’t help but find themselves drawn to his quirky personality full of one-liners and fart jokes.

“Hey! Yo! Mitchell!” Stephen yelled out, “come join us!” He motioned me to sit on a couch, and, like Moses parting the Red Sea, the girls sitting on one of the adjacent coaches split apart, allowing just enough space for me to sit down, my butt barely on a cushion, the rest of me hanging off.

“Ladies, this here is Mitchell, trombone player extraordinaire, fellow band member, the wing man of all wing mans, lover of fine wines and movie trivia. A friend of Stephen, jazz connoisseur, is a friend of Mitchell.”

The girls, all of them, almost unanimously, all waved, batted their eyes out of courtesy, and then returned their gazes to Stephen.

“So when you guys go to New York City, will you all be on MTV? Is that why you’re going?” a girl asked.

I started to roll my eyes at the stupidity of the question, and Stephen, equally sensing the lack of logic in the girl’s common sense, again shrugged, smiled, and replied, “MTV? MTV has nothing on us. I’ll tell you who needs to watch out for us though: them darn New York Yankees.”

One of the girls blinked cluelessly. “The Yankees? Are they a band on MTV? I’ve never heard of them.”

Stephen, initially unsure of what to say to that, again smiled, forever the smooth talker, and replied, “Yes. Absolutely. Definitely check them out.”

The girl beside me smirked a little, obviously trying to hold her laughter in. I turned my head and smiled. “I assume you know who the Yankees are.”

"My dad's a die hard Mets fan, so yeah, I know the Yankees aren't a band."

I nodded in approval, unsure of what to say next. It was one of those moments where I wished I had a black eye to make talking to a girl a whole lot easier.

"You guys really sounded great out there tonight," the girl finally said.

"Oh, you were at the Christmas tree lighting?"

She shook her head, a slight grin on her face. "Dad is also a diehard believer in family traditions. We never miss the tree lighting ceremony. Dad likes it because it always happens the week of Christmas, so he makes a big deal out of it at the house for my brother and me because it kinda marks the oncoming of Santa."

"Your dad sounds pretty cool."

She raised her cup to take a drink from it. "That he is. Or a big dork, depending on the day."

"I had never been to the lighting ceremony before tonight," I said, "but I thought the fake snow was pretty awesome."

She rolled her eyes, but did it with a grin on her face. "Yeah, the fake snow. Gotta love it." She stared at her cup for a second, then said "Stephen says you all are heading to New York City in the spring. That's pretty neat."

"Yes," I agreed, "it's really awesome. We just found out tonight. Mr. Undergrove told us, but we also have to do some fundraisers in order to get there, so I imagine we'll be doing a car wash here and there."

"Car washes..." the girl said, but let her words drift off. "We had to do one of those at the beginning of the school year for marching band. Mr. Undergrove set it up."

"You're in the marching band?" I asked.

She smiled. "Yeah, I know, marching band geek alert. I'm not sure if I'm a fan of marching band, but it was alright. Always gave me something to do on Friday nights, going to all the football games for free and everything."

"Jazz band is cooler," I said. "Nothing against marching band, but we're just a tad more classy."

I said that, but we were not classy.

"I'm a flute player, but I can also play piano, so ya never know, maybe I'll check out jazz band one day."

"Sounds like whether you do marching band or jazz band, you'd be stuck having to do a car wash either way," I replied.

The girl then grinned. "Oh gosh," she said, her face blushing.

"What?" I asked.

She blushed even more, shaking her head, trying to contain her laughter.

"What? Did I say something?" My eyes got wide with fear. "Did I fart? I didn't let one slip, did I?"

The girl laughed even harder while shaking her head 'No'. "I can't say it. I can't. It's too embarrassing." She then let out an even louder laugh, almost like her soul was being tickled and an uncontrollable laughter had taken over her body. She slapped her leg with one hand while trying to cover her face at the same time out of embarrassment.

"You gotta tell me. You can't just laugh that hard and then not deliver. What's so funny?"

The girl wiped a tear from her eye that had formed from her excessive laughing; her face blushed with embarrassment and laughter. "Oh, you really don't want to know. There's no going back once you hear it."

"I can handle it. Tell me!"

The girl, still giggling said, "I was just thinking that last year, when my brother was a senior, the baseball team raised money for new uniforms by doing a car wash. They were all out there at the gas station on Derry Place in their bathing suits and no shirts on, which was helping bring in traffic to the car wash if you catch my drift."

I nodded, symbolizing that I was indeed catching her drift.

"Coach Perry, the baseball coach, thought it'd be funny if he joined in on the fun, so, right there in the gas station parking lot, he strips down to nothing but a purple bathing suit, like the kind guys wore in the 70s - the kind that are incredibly short. Almost like underwear. And he just went to work, washing cars in it."

"Coach Perry did that?"

"Yes," she said, still giggling at the memory of the sight of it. "The rest of the baseball players didn't know what to do; they were so mortified by it. There they are, a bunch of skinny high school guys, and then there's Coach Perry, a 50-year-old man with a gut hanging over his super small bathing suit, soaping up a car without a worry in the world." She wiped her eye again. "Honestly though, my brother said that in the one hour Coach Perry stood out there, too tight bathing suit and all, the amount of tips they received tripled. Maybe you can convince Mr. Undergrove to help you guys out with something like that if you do a car wash."

I laughed at the thought of Coach Perry wearing his super tight purple bathing suit while washing cars, and then we both laughed even harder at the thought of Mr. Undergrove doing the same thing.

"How do you recommend me suggesting that to Mr. Undergrove, because I'm pretty sure he might be weirded out by that request?" I asked. "Especially coming from another dude."

She smiled. "Not my problem. I'm not the one trying to go to New York City."

The crowd began to thin out as the night got later. At 11:30 a mass exodus of kids left as parents began to line the street in their cars, all tired and wondering why it was so important for their children to have social lives. The kids that could drive all left, one car after another, leaving tire marks in the grass beside the driveway.

The wave of freshmen girls also left as well, one carload at a time, leaving the couches empty. "So, Mitchell," the girl beside me said as she was preparing to leave with the last group of freshmen girls, "will I see you at school after Christmas break?"

I could feel a giant wave of heat overtake my face as I nodded and said "Yes."

"Good. Let me know if you guys decide to have a car wash."

"Can you drive? I thought you were a freshman?"

"I am a freshman, but maybe I can convince my dad that the car is so dirty that it needs to be cleaned up by some band geeks trying to make some money."

"Gotcha. That'd be great. I'll keep you updated."

The girl turned to go up the basement stairs when I realized I was missing something pretty important.

"Hey," I called out, "I never got your name."

She walked back over to the couch, picked a pen up off the coffee table, and said "Let me see your forearm." I put my arm out for her, allowing her to write on it. When she finished, her name and phone number was cascading down my arm from my wrist down to my elbow.

"Veronica?" I asked. "Like Veronica as in *Archie Comics* Veronica?"

Veronica rolled her eyes. "Yeah, that's my dad's sense of humor shining through again."

"Your dad really sounds awesome."

"Every parent is awesome except your own parent. Trust me." With that comment, Veronica was gone.

Christmas vacation had officially started and school was out for the next two weeks. My parents had agreed to let me spend the night with Stephen, which meant I had to help him straighten his house back up by picking up crushed cups, dirty napkins, and used plates that had been left here and there throughout the basement and kitchen. By midnight, we were back in the basement, sleeping bags rolled out on the couches.

"Who would've thought turning 16 would be so frickin' epic?" Stephen asked, his arms reaching out to the sky, half stretching them, half soaking in the events of the day. "New York. Like THE New York. Holy Marshmallow Man!"

Stephen then sat up, "What if we get to New York City and the second coming of Gozer happens?"

"Like Gozer, as in *Ghostbusters* Gozer?" I asked. "With hell hounds, dark clouds, scary ominous voices and everything?"

"That's the one," he said. "We'd be doomed."

"No we wouldn't," I replied. "If we're in New York during the second coming of Gozer, then we strap on our big boy underwear and go out and find the Ghostbusters, Spider-Man, Daredevil, the Teenage Mutant Ninja Turtles, the Fantastic Four, and every other superhero that is stationed in New York and hope they can save us," I said with a yawn.

"Good answer," Stephen said, "but I was looking for 'run like hell' for $500."

"Close," I said, struggling to keep my eyes open, "so close."

"I didn't think about the fact that the Teenage Mutant Ninja Turtles are in New York," Stephen added.

I then sat up from my couch. "Hey, question time, but you gotta answer honestly."

"Shoot." Stephen said.

"The best ninja turtle is....?"

"Oh, dude, I thought you were going to ask me some deep theological question. This is easy. It's Ralph, hands down."

"Thank you!" I said. "Kirby and Kevin were trying to debate that tonight. David, Justin, and I all went with Raphael."

"Duh," Stephen said. "Ralph is the obvious choice."

"Kirby didn't agree."

"Let me guess: Kirby thinks Leonardo is the best ninja turtle."

"Bingo," I replied.

"When are people going to realize that just because Leonardo is the leader it doesn't mean he's the best? Look at the X-Men. The best X-Men team member is...." Stephen glanced at me to finish his sentence.

"Wolverine."

"Exactly," Stephen responded, "but he's not the leader. Cyclops is. But honestly, if you were surrounded by an army of baddies, who would you want protecting you: Wolverine or Cyclops?"

I laughed, more on the inside than anything else, at the irony of Stephen's words.

"Wolverine."

"Everyone would pick Wolverine. Even my dad, who doesn't know anything about anything, would pick Wolverine just based on his name." Stephen then projected his hands into the air, like he was plastering the name across the sky; "Wolverine!" he said with emphasis.

Stephen sat back up again. “Oh man! I completely forgot to show everyone this tonight.” He jumped off his couch, picked a remote control off the coffee table, and then pointed it at the ceiling. “I put these up last weekend, and I can’t believe I didn’t have them on during the party.” He pressed a button on the remote and the room lit up with multicolored Christmas lights bordering the ceiling of the basement. Stephen raised a hand; “wait for it’ he said. The lights began to sparkle, fading in and out, glistening brighter before dulling their glow in an off-beat pattern. He just stood there for a moment, basking in the magic aura of the lights.

“When we get to New York, do you think Mr. Undergrove will give us free time to find us some out-of-state beauties?” Stephen asked as he crawled back into his sleeping bag on his couch.

“I don’t know,” I answered. “I guess it depends on how long we will be in the city, how involved and invasive this band competition is going to be, and whether or not that whole ‘second coming of Gozer’ thing comes to pass.”

“Good point,” Stephen said.

We sat there in silence for a moment, staring up at the twinkling Christmas lights on the ceiling, soaking in our own thoughts on the day’s passing. The stillness reminded us both of our sleepiness.

“Hey, Mitchell,” Stephen said.

“Yeah.”

“I love jazz band.”

“Me too.”

"A lot of people will do marching band for like a year when they're freshmen and then abandon it because they get too cool or whatever, but man, I love jazz band. I could do this forever."

"Forever?" I asked.

Stephen adjusted his pillow. "Forever."

Playing jazz for a live crowd. Fake snow. Taco Bell. Hot chocolate. Stephen's birthday. Christmas lights. New York City. Veronica.

Yeah, I thought to myself as I drifted asleep, I could do this forever.

MAY - 8TH GRADE

Have you ever been stuck between a rock and a hard place? I'm sure you have. We all have. It's part of the 'growing up' process; finding ourselves in a 'lose-lose' or a 'maybe win - but most likely to lose' scenario is never fun, but it's how you learn leadership skills and how to adult and all that other crap.

Now, take that whole 'stuck between a rock and a hard place' stuff and throw it away.

I wasn't stuck between a rock and a hard place; I was stuck in a stall of a freakin' girls' restroom.

Cue Freddy Krueger, because this had to be a horror movie.

I sat in the stall completely silent. Every time I thought the traffic in the restroom was dying down, more girls came in. The only way out of this was if I bit the bullet and left the stall and made a break for the restroom door, but then every girl that was in the restroom would see me; that would be social suicide. It would only be a matter of time before word got around the competition that King's Hollow brought a perverted freak with them.

Have you ever just felt like crying for no reason?

Only the Lord knows how long I sat in the stall, panicking, my brain racing on how I could potentially get out of this mess.

But then, it got quiet.

Was there no one was in the restroom? "Hello?" I said out loud.

Nothing.

I unlocked the hatch of my stall and had just started to push it ajar when the main door to the restroom burst open. I pulled the door back fast enough where I wasn't noticed, and quickly relatched my stall. 'So close,' I thought.

"They're both cute, but I'm not digging Stephen like I thought I would. He talks too much. Monsters and stupid stuff."

I froze. I knew that voice.

"Are you sure it's not because he told you that you were full of yourself?" Another familiar voice said.

"'No, that's got nothing to do with it." And then, "well, maybe a little, but it's healthy to be a little full of yourself, right? It's called self-confidence."

Oh no, I thought, that's......that's.....

"I mean, girls need to be aware of their self-worth, so if that means I'm 'full of myself', then oh well, that's the guy's problem, not mine."

That's Chassidy. That's Chassidy's voice! I put my face in my hands; I was scared to breathe.

"So, Lauren, what's the deal with you and the cutie with the black eye? I mean, are you digging him?"

I pulled my face out of my hands. Cutie with a black eye? Is that me that they're referring to? Gotta be me, right?

"I don't know." There was a hesitation; it was Lauren's voice, though. The hesitation went on for an uncomfortable amount of time. "I think it's kinda obvious how you feel about him, so....."

“Well, I like him. I’m just going to get it out there.” Chassidy’s declaration was followed by awkward silence.

“Why did you even bring up Gabe? That wasn’t...” Lauren’s voice hesitated again. “That’s not....” The words couldn’t seem to come out.

“I brought up Gabe because that boy needed to know. What do you think Gabe is going to do when he finds out you’ve been flirting with some other guy you just met here at this competition? Do you not remember last week?

There was a pause, and then Lauren mumbled, “Yeah, yeah, yeah, it seems like no one is willing to let me forget last week.”

Chassidy’s voice continued. “Let me remind you, just in case you forgot about last week. The two of you broke up, that’s what. I’m not saying Gabe didn’t have it coming, as possessive and angry as he was all the time, but, good golly, Gabe broke that boy’s rib in weight training class after Gabe body slammed him just because that boy asked you for your phone number.” There was a pause. “Body slammed him, Lauren! Gabe is not exactly emotionally stable, and here you are being all lovey dovey with someone else from another school.”

“That’s not my fault that Gabe is a butthead,” the Lauren voice said.

“No, it’s not,” the Chassidy voice said back, “but I think it’s your responsibility to protect that boy out there from the butthead that you used to date.”

More awkward silence, maybe even enough to give someone a heart attack, particularly me.

“Look, it’s not just that I like him too, but I’m worried for this boy’s well-being. He’s cute, funny, obviously super protective, but I don't think you should be testing Gabe quite yet. Maybe after some time has passed...." Chassidy's words lingered. There was a pause that seemed to suck all the air out of the room, and then Lauren responded.

"Yeah, whatever, Chassidy. You want him for yourself? Take him." There was an edge to Lauren's voice that gave me the chills. "I saw how he looked at you, all spaced out. He's just some guy, all into you because you're so pretty, and then, just like all the other guys you date for a week or two, you'll start to get bored with him and then move on to somebody different."

"Lauren, don't act like that. Don't try to turn this..."

Lauren cut her off. "Turn this into what? You're throwing Gabe in my face because he's a psychopath, the exact reason why I broke up with him, and now some mystery guys walk into our lives at a band competition and you just get to lay claim to them because my ex-boyfriend doesn't know how to deal with his emotions. What exactly, Chassidy, am I turning this in to?" There was a cocktail of hurt, anger, rage, and frustration in Lauren's voice, all while she tried her best to stay calm.

"Lauren, don't make this...'

Lauren cut her off again. "Don't make this about me? Is that what you were going to say? Don't make this about me? Jeez, Chassidy, I'm just like everyone else here; I'm just trying to make it through the day, and if flirting with a stranger with a black eye makes me feel a little bit better about everything, then so be it." Lauren's voice cracked a little, and she immediately shook it off and added a new layer of sarcasm. "But that's ok, Chassidy, you don't need to worry about me. I won't make any of this about me. You can have Mitchell, or Stephen, or whomever we may meet and I'll stay out of your way. It's no big deal. I'd hate to make anything about me."

There was a pause, and it felt like 500 pounds of dead weight had descended into the room. Lauren's words, hard, angry, and emotional, felt like a sharp blade zinging through the air.

"Lauren, how could you..."

"Leave me alone. Just give me a few minutes to myself."

"Lauren...."

"Just give me a minute. I'll be fine, but I need a moment."

Chassidy didn't respond. I heard the restroom door open and then close.

The stall beside me opened, and then shut. I still had my hands over my mouth, trying my best not to breathe. What had I gotten myself into? That conversation or argument or whatever you want to call it between Chassidy and Lauren was not meant for anyone else's ears, let alone mine. I felt like some type of explosion had gone off and I was the only survivor, and that survival made me feel overwhelmed with guilt, from the top of my head to the bottom of my toes.

Lauren took a deep breath, and then all the emotions she had been trying to contain came pouring out. She let out a sob, and it was followed by tears.

'Now's your chance to get out of here,' I thought. 'Go now, while she's occupied and the restroom is empty.' I put my hand on the latch of the stall.

"You can go now," Lauren's voice said. I froze, my arm stiffened on the stall's latch. Lauren's voice then added, "I know you've been in there this whole time. I know you've heard everything, so why don't you just come on out and leave me alone."

She knew I was in here? How did she know? Did she have X-ray vision?

I still had one hand covering my mouth, trying to keep my breathing quiet; my arm, still squeezing the latch, began to tremble. What do I do? Do I run? Do I speak? Do I stay out of fear of what will happen to me if anyone sees me leaving the restroom? What if Lauren tells someone that I'm like a pervert or something?

"Fine. Stay if you want. It's whatever. I don't even know who you are in there, and odds are you don't know me either, so just stay in there for all I care." Lauren sniffled a few times. She then added, 'Sorry you had to hear all that stuff. It's......it's just....I don't even know."

Look, before you condemn me for not speaking up and trying to make the girl feel better, please remember that I am a guy, a dude, a bro, not a girl, trapped in the stall of a girl's restroom. You just can't reveal yourself in that type of situation and think it's all going to turn out ok.

"Chassidy is....she's.....I can't even explain it," Lauren continued. "She's supposed to be my friend, and she is, at least I tell people that she is, but she's not always a good friend to me." Lauren's tone began to shift her words to where it began to sound more like a confessional. "She's got it all: the looks, the clothes, the smile, and everyone likes her. The guys do at least." Her words drifted off again. She sniffed a few times, allowing the silence to hold the moment.

"There's some guy out there that I kinda like. And of course, Chassidy has to like him too." Lauren readjusted her legs, tapped her left foot twice, and then slid it back and forth on the restroom floor. "That's the kind of stuff that always happens in the movies and TV shows, but you never think it actually happens in real life." She then punched her stall door. The entire row of stalls shook. The latch of my stall's door jiggled and placed my hand over it to keep it still. "Chassidy likes him. Chassidy likes him. Chassidy has just got to like him, doesn't she?" She punched her stall door again, and then muttered out "Ouch'. I heard a light thud on the wall of the stall, almost like Lauren was leaning on it. Lauren didn't speak.

Several minutes went by, me sitting in my stall in silence, Lauren sitting in her stall beside me, equally silent. I didn't dare move a muscle.

"You know, I can hear you breathing. You breathe like a rhinoceros." Lauren giggled a slightly hysterical laugh and then apologized. "I'm sorry; I shouldn't have said that. It's just that you're sitting in there obviously trying not to be heard, and I'm over here being all moody, bustin' up my hand on a stall door. It's just funny, ya know?"

Lauren readjusted her legs again. "I know you're not talking, but you might as well hear me out. Chassidy is right about Gabe, my ex-boyfriend. He's just some overgrown caveman with anger management issues." She paused. "I broke up with him because he threatened to beat up my lab partner in science for calling me and asking me a question on our homework. Gabe was so jealous he just lost his mind and we argued and argued about it, and that was it; that was the last time I thought I'd ever have to deal with his crap." She took a deep breath. "After we broke up, some sophomore guy asked me for my phone number, and I gave it to him, because why not? Gabe didn't like that, so when he got wind of it, he used the opportunity presented to him in gym class to rough the boy up." Lauren paused again, sniffed, and then added, "He hurt the guy, like legit hurt him. What kind of a maniac does that?" Lauren took in another deep breath, almost as if a weight had been lifted off her soul.

"And now there's this guy out there and he's completely adorable with this black eye, and Chassidy wants to throw Gabe out there as a reason why she should get him. I mean, I'm not crazy, right? Chassidy is being ridiculous, right?"

I didn't respond. I wasn't going to respond. All I could do is hope she didn't know it was me. I was a tad concerned that I apparently breathe like a rhinoceros. I thought that I had been breathing quietly, but there went that thought.

"Oh geez...what a mess," Lauren muttered. She sighed. It was a sigh that sounded like it didn't come from Lauren's chest, but her very soul, the kind of sigh that felt like it had some weight to it.

"Why does growing up have to be so weird?"

It was a question, but it felt like it was slightly more than just a question. It was one of those questions that had no correct answer, no way to argue for or against it, no charts or evidence to support it, no 'yes' or 'no' answer or any array of multiple choice answers that could lead you to the correct path.

It was just a simple question, but entirely more than just a question.

"Look," Lauren said, "I gotta get out of here. This....this is all too much for me to process, but it's the hand I've been dealt. I gotta go out there and deal with Chassidy, deal with this boy, potentially deal with Gabe. I don't know." She sighed again. "I can't sit here and avoid all my problems. Sometimes you just have to face them head on and hope for the best." She tapped her feet together a few more times, took another deep breath, sniffed twice, and added, "You ever seen the movie *The Crow*? It's a movie from a few years ago. Some crazy superhero zombie movie. A guy returns from the dead to get revenge on the people that killed him. It's stupid, but not stupid at the same time."

"There's a line, though," she continued, "where the guy, the crow, he says 'It can't rain all the time'. He says it kinda like a reminder to that the day can always be worse than what it is. I don't know, I just like that idea when things are going bad. Can't rain all the time. It's simple, you know?"

My silence was my affirmation.

"Thank you for listening. I know you didn't have to sit here for all that. You're obviously doing the same thing I'm doing: avoiding someone or something."

Avoiding someone right now sounded great; anything except being stuck in a restroom.

"Whatever you're dealing with that's scaring you or stressing you out, just don't forget that it can't rain all the time. Ok?"

There was another moment of silence, seemingly longer than the other previous moments.

Lauren unlatched her stall, washed her hands in the sink, and then left the restroom.

I unlatched my stall and stood up. Now was my chance to escape. I was getting the hell out of there.

I opened the stall door when I realized I was walking into a trap. What if Lauren was waiting just outside the restroom door to see who her mystery listener was? What would she do when she saw it was me that listened to her every word within the confines of the neighboring stall?

I sat back down, closed my stall door, and put my head back into my hands.

I needed a miracle to get me out of this situation.

JANUARY - 10TH GRADE

It was the first day back from Christmas break when Mr. Undergrove dropped the plan on us.

What was 'the plan' you ask?

'The plan' was a giant packet filled with everything we needed to know about our quest to get to the National Miles Davis Youth Jazz Competition in New York City, including music to every song we needed to learn and perfect, dates of every extra after school practice, and a timeline of every fundraiser that we were going to execute between January and March to ensure that the trip would actually occur.

"Dude, four car washes?" Stephen asked. "Four? Are peoples' cars that dirty?"

"Car washes are easy money," Mr. Undergrove responded. "If you notice, each car wash is on a different Saturday in a different location too, so while some of our clientele will be similar, we will hopefully hit a different group of people at each spot."

"Ah, selling our souls for money," Brooks said. "It figures."

"Um, Brooks?" Mr. Undergrove shot back, "how else do you think we're going to get to New York City? The school is covering a very, very small portion of the trip, and you all have earned some of the money through your gigs, but the last time I checked, money isn't exactly falling from the sky, so yeah, we're going to put in some work to cover the bills. If you want to call it 'selling out', I'm ok with that, because if 'selling out' will get us to New York City, then sign me up."

When we all nodded in agreement, Brooks' face grew red. "Oh, ok, whatever."

"What is this, this gig on a Friday in March?" Josh asked. "It says it's in the cafeteria?"

"That, Josh, is going to be a day where we will be set-up in the school's courtyard and play during all three lunches, kinda like we did this past fall, but the difference this time is that we're going to have a tip bucket."

"Nice. That's what every high schooler wants to do: tip the neighborhood jazz band with their lunch change." Stephen grinned at his comment.

"Do you have a better idea?" Mr. Undergrove asked.

"If auctioning me off to a crowd of hot women isn't an option, then no, I don't," Stephen answered.

"That's not going to happen," Mr. Undergrove said, "but I appreciate you volunteering yourself."

"We're working the concession stand at two basketball games?" David asked.

"Yep, and we're getting 50% of the profit from the sales of those two games." Mr. Undergrove put his packet down and rubbed his face with his hands. "Look, guys, I know none of these fundraisers are 100% fun, but they're better than going door-to-door selling wrapping paper or plastic containers. These fundraisers are relatively quick, painless, and produce cash flow that will help us get to New York City. I know they're not easy, and they may interfere with your social lives, so if you want out, you don't have to be involved, and you won't be a part of the trip in April."

Mr. Undergrove's eyes shot across the room. No one said a word.

"I take your silence as an agreement to join in on the entire process: the fundraisers, the extra practices, the hard work that may be uncomfortable at times. We're good, but it's going to take effort to make us worthy of the bands we're going to face at this competition. Does everyone agree with that?"

We all looked around the room at each other, and then turned our attention back to Mr. Undergrove. We all nodded our heads, united.

So we did the fundraisers. The following two Friday nights saw us working the concession stand at the basketball games, from 4:30 in the afternoon through 10:00 at night, as we endured two JV basketball games and two varsity basketball games for both the boys' and girls' basketball programs. We quickly realized that, as a band, we didn't all fit in the concession stand, so we took shifts between working the concession stands and watching the basketball games. Kirby, in order to make even more room inside the concession stand, and also being smart and quick-witted, ran down to the art room, borrowed a handful of washable paints and brushes, and set up a table near the concession stand to paint faces. Josh, realizing that a large number of freshmen girls were lining up for Kirby's face painting skills, left the concession stand and began assisting the face-painting station. "You see that?" Mr. Undergrove asked in between concession stand customers, pointing at Kirby and Josh's face painting station. "That's entrepreneurial motivation right there. That's the kind of drive that is going to get us to New York City."

One week later, the fall semester wrapped up. While we had all pledged to stick around to see the spring semester and our trip to New York City all the way through, the band's lineup experienced some changes. On the last day of the fall semester, Justin, our secondary drummer and sole freshman of the group, changed his schedule to take Spanish. "Sorry, guys," he told us, "but band just isn't for me."

"What about New York?" I asked.

Justin shrugged his shoulders. "It's just that this jazz band thing isn't my cup of tea. I'm not into all this like the rest of you are."

"What are you into?" Stephen asked.

"I don't know," Justin said back. "I'm not even sure." Justin put his book bag on his back. "It's just not this."

And just like that, Justin was gone, out of the band.

"People come and go, guys," Mr. Undergrove said that day during class. "Anytime you're a part of a team, a group, or something special, you'll have people that fail to see that they're a part of something big. No matter how hard you try to make them happy, some people just can't find joy." Mr. Undergrove readjusted the papers on his music stand; he put down his baton on the stand, picked it back up again, rotated his hand a few times, then put the baton back down on the stand. "You never know; Justin may come back some day."

"But he's going to miss out on New York," I said.

Mr. Undergrove sighed, letting his shoulders seemingly sink a little lower than normal. "Yes, yes he will. That's his decision though."

"I think that's the hardest part of Justin deciding to leave what we have going on," Stephen said. "He doesn't understand what he's walking away from. We still have Kirby, so it's not like we're going to be without a drummer, but still, Justin was a part of this band, and it just sucks that we're going to continue the journey without him."

Mr. Undergrove nodded his head. "That was a very adult-thing to say, Stephen. Very good observation about the internal dynamics of a band."

"Plus, let's be honest, with Justin gone, that leaves more women for the rest of us if we ever meet up with an all-girl high school jazz band."

Mr. Undergrove rolled his eyes. "I knew your maturity on something like this was too good to be true."

While Justin was gone, the start of the spring semester brought a handful of new faces into the band. There was Marcellus and Antwan, both saxophone players, which, counting Kevin, brought the saxophone section to a total of three. Joining Josh, Brooks, and Stephen on trumpet was Tim, a senior foreign exchange student that smiled excessively and spent all of his free time reading the money section of *USA Today*. Assisting Kirby on drums was Moose, whose real name wasn't Moose but went by Moose because he was embarrassed by his real name, Mervis. Moose, much to his dismay, did not get called Moose by us, but instead was nicknamed 'Second Justin'.

And then, there was the newest addition to the group: a piano player, which brought a new layer of energy to the melody section of the group. The only swerve was that the new piano player was a freshman.

Also, the piano player was a girl.

Also, the piano player was Veronica.

Yes, the same Veronica from Stephen's birthday party.

That Veronica.

"Hey," I said with a smile on my face as I set up my sheet music and trombone for practice.

Veronica looked up from her keyboard, adjusted her glasses, and replied, "Oh, it's you, the boy who can't work a phone.

Yes, the Veronica from Stephen's birthday party that was now in jazz band was also the same Veronica that gave me her phone number back in December and I never called her. Not once.

"Oh," I sputtered out, "yeah, I, uh, um, well....I..." I was clueless on what to say.

"Well, that sounded like a completely logical explanation as to why you never called me," Veronica said, adjusting her seat. "I'm glad we had this talk."

Look, I never called Veronica because, well, two reasons. 1) I was terrified to talk to her again. You know how it is sometimes: you meet a beautiful girl, the two of you hit it off, she gives you her number, and then the thought of calling her and making a bad impression is so terrifying that you simply don't because it's easier to ignore a girl than it is to actually take a chance and put yourself out there.

That was one reason. The second reason? It's kinda sorta mostly the main reason I didn't call her.

I had forgotten about Veronica's number being on my arm until after I had gotten in the shower the next morning and was washing my body, causing the numbers to vanish with the water and soap running over my body. When I realized what was going on, it was too late and the majority of the numbers were gone. Only the slight remains of '43' and what looked like the bottom half of a 0 or an 8 existed.

“So, how did you get into jazz band?” I asked. “I thought you did marching band?”

“Well, Captain center-of-the-universe, you and your friends don’t have an exclusive claim to jazz.” She cracked her knuckles and rolled out a few notes on the keyboard. “Honestly, I enjoy playing piano more than I do the flute, and Mr. Undergrove told me that this was an exciting opportunity for the jazz band to have a piano player to assist the bass and guitar players.”

I looked down at my shoes. The rest of the band was trickling into the room for practice.

“So you’re done talking to me?”

I looked up. “Huh?”

“You looked down at your feet and didn’t say anything else, so I’m just verifying that you’re done talking to me.” Veronica looked annoyed. Her arms were crossed across her chest.

“I......I, um, it’s just that.....well....I, uh.” Why couldn’t I just talk to her? I didn’t have any problems talking to her at Stephen’s birthday party.

“You’re a man of many words.” She shook her head then stood up to move her book bag away from the practice area.

“Female trouble?” Stephen asked as I sat back down.

“Maybe.”

“That’s always fun.”

“I think your definition of ‘fun’ and my definition of ‘fun’ are drastically different.”

Stephen shrugged his shoulders as he pulled his trumpet out of his case. "If she had a crush on you, it looks like she doesn't anymore."

"Yeah," I agreed, "I think so too."

"What'd you do?"

"She gave me her number at your birthday party. I never called her."

Stephen's eyes widened and then he nodded. "Nice. I've done that before. Never ever works out well, especially if you're the one with the crush waiting for the phone to ring." He adjusted his music on his stand and then slapped me on the shoulder. "But that's why they call them crushes. If they were easy, they'd call 'em something else."

Mr. Undergrove brought the class to attention. He introduced the newest members of the band to the rest of us, and then he passed out music, Miles Davis' 'Bye Bye Blackbird'.

"If we're doing this New York thing, then there's only one way to do it: with a little bit of Miles Davis." Mr. Undergrove raised his baton. "From the top everyone. We will do a cold-play through just to see what happens and go from there. I believe in every single one of you." He winked his left eye, smiled, counted to four, and, just like that, the sound of jazz music filled the band room.

MAY - 8TH GRADE

I wasn't stuck. I was stuckeded.

It's something my dad used to say when you were a tad more than stuck. He used to say that about having to go to work on Saturdays whenever an emergency came up and he was needed. He was stuckeded.

Man, I was stuckeded.

Lauren liked me. Chassidy liked me. Chassidy made it clear that she was willing to throw Lauren under a metaphorical bus in order to 'win' me over. Lauren had spilled her guts about her real feelings about her friendship with Chassidy without knowing that she was spilling her guts to me. And me? Mr. Middle schooler that had the luck of wooing two high school girls at the same time? I was stuckeded in a girls' restroom.

Oh, yeah, one last detail: Lauren's ex-boyfriend was a bit psychotic with a history of anger management issues, and also just happened to be at the same band competition.

Great.

So this is how it ends for Mitchell Williams: alone and distraught in a girls' restroom stall.

I hung my head in my hands. I know my parents always told me not to cry, because as long as someone's not dying, there's nothing to cry about. But man, if there ever was a time to cry, this was it.

Then, it happened. A ringing, slightly faint in the distance, but got louder and louder.

Yes, it definitely happened. I wasn't imagining it.

I could hear it. The one thing that could save me from all this misery.

It was practically music to my ears.

The fire alarm. My savior.

I burst out of the stall, and then threw open the door to the restroom to the view of hundreds and hundreds of kids stampeding through the auditorium lobby towards the parking lot. Before anyone could notice me, a guy, leaving the girls' restroom, I slipped in with the crowd and followed along towards the outdoors.

Free at last. Free at last. Thank God, the almighty, that I was free at last.

The visiting bands swarmed over all of the auditorium's parking lot, while the rest of Snowfield High's student population surrounded the rest of the school. There were kids as far as the eye could see. I looped in and out of crowds of kids, all chattering and buzzing from the excitement of a fire alarm, trying to scan the crowd for my fellow band members, but when every single person in the band crowd is wearing black dress pants and a white top, it made it hard to single people out.

Eventually, after circling through the parking lot in several attempts to locate someone from King's Hollow, I spotted Mr. Undergrove standing on a bench on the sidewalk leading away from the auditorium doors, both hands covering his forehead to shield his eyes from the brightness of the sun, engrossed in looking out over the crowd, probably looking for stray kids like me. Behind him was an entire crowd of recognizable King's Hollow faces.

"Crazy day, huh?" I said as I walked up.

"Where have you been?" he asked, an angry yet concerned tone in his voice. "You disappeared when we were standing in the auditorium and no one could find you!"

"I....I uh, well, I was I in the restroom." I said.

"We checked every bathroom in the auditorium; we couldn't find you."

"You didn't check every restroom," I said back.

Mr. Undergrove looked me in the eye. "You ok?"

I shrugged my shoulders. "I'm a free man, ya know? What once was lost now is found."

"What are you talking about?" he asked, a confused look on his face.

"I wish I knew," I responded. "I'm just feeling all the emotions right now. I mean, we're alive, we're at a band competition, and we now know that the fire alarms work. Safety first, Mr. Undergrove. Safety first."

Mr. Undergrove scrunched his face up. "What?"

"If I knew, I'd tell you." I patted him on the back and joined my classmates.

I had never been more happy to see them.

MARCH - 10TH GRADE

Four car washes, two basketball concession stand stints, a t-shirt sale, a doughnut sale, and a 'tips encouraged' lunch concert later, we were approaching the end of March and the final weeks before departing for New York City.

"This is actually happening," Kevin said. "This is actually happening. This is actually happening. This is actually happening." He sounded like a broken record.

"Dude, this is actually happening," Stephen said.

"I knew Mr. Undergrove said we were going to go, and I knew Mr. Undergrove had a plan and that we were doing all this fundraising for a reason, but this is it: this is actually happening."

"Yeah," Stephen said, "things tend to happen when you put in the work to make them happen. For example, I put gas in my car, and then my car can move and go all sorts of different places." Stephen moved his hands back and forth in front of him, his hands cupped as if he was holding some imaginary toy cars and making them move throughout the air.

"Don't be a smart ass," Kevin shot back.

"I have no idea if my ass is smart or not," Stephen replied, "I've never had a conversation with it. All these years, and not a single one-on-one talk. It probably feels neglected."

Kevin rolled his eyes.

Stephen leaned forward towards Kevin, whispering, "Hey, Kevin?"

"What?"

"This is actually happening."

Kevin turned his back on Stephen; Stephen then looked at me and said, "That actually happened."

Veronica sat down at her keyboard and placed her music out on her stand in front of her. She cracked her knuckles, sighed a sigh that radiated complete calmness, and then, with the amp to the keyboard turned down low, rolled out several scales, each one on a slightly higher octave than the one before it, and then moving back down the keyboard to the lower scales. I found myself transfixed by the beauty of the scales, each note transcending into the next note perfectly, as if there were no exposed seams or wrinkles in her composure. The keyboard echoed with an exposed peace that seemed to blossom out of the amp and across the floor, like a flowered vine.

"Earth to Mitchell. Earth to Mitchell."

Stephen's voice made me realize I had been staring at Veronica playing. I looked away and picked up my trombone out of its case.

"Starting to wish you'd picked up that phone and called her, huh?"

"That's.....I don't.....it's whatever. Really."

"Girls come and go, man. Odds are that she's not the one." Stephen nudged me in my side. "You know, 'the one' - probably not her. She's just a freshman, and you're just a sophomore, and it's high school, it's not forever. So, you can't be sad and stuff because you still got the rest of your life ahead of you."

I looked over at Stephen, scrunched my face up, and shot back, "You got all that from me watching her play piano?"

"Hey man, I can get deep at times."

"You're getting soft. Normally, you'd tell me to man-up and go talk to her."

"Hey, Mitchell?"

"Yeah?"

"Man-up. Go talk to her. And if she tries to bite you, stake her in the heart."

"I doubt she's a vampire," I said.

"But do you know for a fact that she's not a vampire?" Stephen asked.

"Pretty sure of it."

Stephen shrugged his shoulders. "Suit yourself. When she bites you, you're the one that's going to turn into the undead, not me."

"You're so weird." I placed my trombone on its case and walked over to Veronica, still playing the scales on the piano.

I approached the piano; Veronica, never looking up, transitioned from a scale into 'Linus & Lucy'. I stood there, watching her, her eyes focused on the keyboard, never seeming to notice that I was standing in front of her.

'Linus & Lucy' came to an end. "That was really, really cool." I said.

"I try. Were you waiting for me to acknowledge you standing there?"

"Huh?" She caught me off guard. "Oh, um, see I um, I came over here and..."

"I was trying to ignore you, but you managed to momentarily grab my attention with your compliment. Maybe you can help me. I have a dilemma."

“Oh, yeah, sure, what can I help with?” I blattered out, trying to set aside her ‘ignore you’ comment.

Veronica leaned forward towards me. “Well, here’s my issue,” she lowered her voice to almost a whisper, “I really don’t want to talk to you, even in passing, unless I can help it, but right now I feel like I’m stuck in an obligation to converse since you’re standing at the keyboard, practically breathing on me. Could you do me a favor and walk away?”

My ears and forehead grew hot with embarrassment. I didn’t say a word as I turned my back on Veronica and shuffled back to my seat. When I sat down, Veronica made eye contact with me and gave me a sarcastic thumbs up, pulling her hands up to her face, holding her thumbs up on both sides of her cheeks and winking her left eye with immense satisfaction.

Stephen leaned towards me. “Strike out?”

“Struck out,” I confirmed.

“Do you want that talk again about how girls come and go and odds are that she’s not the one?”

“No.”

“Ok.” Stephen leaned back, scratched his nose, and then leaned back towards me. “Hey, Mitchell?”

“Yeah?”

“Girls come and go, man. Odds are that she’s not the one.”

I rolled my eyes. “Thanks, man, I needed that.”

"I know." He then added, "You know who doesn't have to worry about girls?"

"Who?" I asked.

"The Monster Squad. They never have to worry about girls. Ever. You want to know why?"

"Why's that?"

"Because they're the freakin' Monster Squad. They hunt and destroy monsters. No girl would be able to resist that. They'd naturally get all the girls."

"Every single one of them?"

"Every single one of them," Stephen confirmed. "Every single one."

I looked at Veronica at her keyboard, back to rolling out odd versions of scales, every note played with grace.

"Every single one," I said. "Even the vampire ones."

"Definitely the vampire ones," Stephen added. "Most definitely the vampire ones."

Mr. Undergrove, now ready to begin practice, approached his podium, addressed the band, raised his baton, and on the count of four, brought forth jazz music into the room.

MAY - 8TH GRADE

The fire alarm ended. No building devastation, no flames, no smoke, just a pulled fire alarm switch in the main lobby of the auditorium.

"Stupid pranksters," Mr. Undergrove mumbled under his breath when word got around what had caused the evacuation. "This is just further evidence that sometimes, no matter how hard you try, some people just want to watch the world burn."

"Technically," Stephen said as we filed back into the building, "whoever pulled the alarm was trying to protect everyone from burning."

"It's a metaphor, Stephen," Mr. Undergrove said, "I'm implying that some people just like to cause chaos, no matter how hard everyone else is obviously working to make sure everyone has a good time."

"I don't want to watch the world burn. I just want tacos." Stephen stretched his hands into the air and then yawned. "I could also use a nap."

"Performance first. Then we can get out of here and go to the Snowfield mall to get lunch in the food court, and then you can nap on the way home," Mr. Undergrove said. "But first, we've got to rock our second round with the other set of judges."

Every band had to enter the building and get situated in the auditorium all over again, including the judges. Hundreds of kids had to relocate their instruments, which can be difficult when practically every single instrument case tends to be black, and find their way back to the seats. Eventually, a sense of normalcy returned and order settled back into the auditorium.

Stephen and I returned to our seats, noticing the row behind us once occupied by our lady friends from Trenton was now empty.

"You were gone forever, man," Stephen said. "The girls went to the bathroom not long after you did, and when they came back, Lauren wasn't with them. When Lauren did come back, they didn't hang around long before they had to head to the back for their second round. But, then the fire alarm rang, and, well, here we are." He looked around the auditorium several times, probably scanning the crowd for other potential girls to talk to. "Where were you, man? You were like gone gone, like off the face of the planet gone."

What do I say to that? The truth? 'Yeah, Stephen about that. I was in the girls' restroom getting sick. I know that's weird and creepy, but hey, that's my happy place.' No, I couldn't say that. No one would believe me if I told them I accidentally wound up in the girls' restroom, so I wasn't about to tell Stephen.

"Dude, the restroom," I said. "I already went over this with Undergrove. Sometimes nature calls and, trust me, it was calling."

Fun fact: that wasn't a complete lie.

Stephen looked at me, like he wasn't sure what to say. A grin slowly began to blossom on his face, and he said, 'Hey, man, sometimes when you gotta poop, you gotta poop."

"Yeah," I nodded, "yeah, I guess."

"Probably had nothing to do with these freak out spasms that you've been having all morning."

I shot Stephen a look. Stephen shrugged his shoulders, his face still brandishing a grin.

Mr. Undergrove gathered the band and we headed back to the large hall that connected to the back of the auditorium. He gave us another pep talk, more of the 'you can do this, continue to strive for greatness, I believe in you' stuff. I heard him, but on the opposite side of the hall, an adjacent door to the auditorium where we had spent the majority of the morning opened up, pouring out band students into the large hall. The band? Trenton.

I froze; here came Chassidy. No Lauren in sight.

"Hey, Mitchell!" she said, all excited. She reached arms up, as to hug me, but, remembering the conversation from earlier when she tried to make Lauren look bad, I stopped Chassidy from getting her arm around my neck by grabbing her hand and shaking it. I could still be polite, just not too polite.

"How'd you guys do?" I asked, still a sense to maintain politeness grasping at my lips.

"Oh, we rocked. That's not anything new, though." Chassidy continued to talk as Katherine and Julie approached the conversation, along with Stephen coming up beside me. Their lips moved, but their words didn't seem important, just faded out noises that I could ignore. Small talk. Chassidy continued to brag, interposing Katherine and Julie's confirmations of their superiority to validate her claims. Blah blah blah.

A face caught my eye in the final wave of band students exiting the smaller auditorium. Lauren. I moved.

My feet seemed to be weighted down with rocks. The people throughout the large hall all moved in slow motion, but then began to fade to blurs in the background.

Wait. Wait. Here it comes. It's actually happening, just like in the movies. A light seemed to shine from all around Lauren, highlighting and illuminating her. Her hair seemed to blow over her shoulder as she looked up from her music folder that was tucked tightly against her arm. Starting out as a low muffled background sound, a song grew louder and louder until I realized it was 'This Magic Moment' by The Drifters that was playing, once seemingly placed in the background of the moment but now shifted so the song enchantingly surrounded Lauren. Time completely slowed to a halt. It was just me and her, no one else around.

"I heard you all did awesome," I said with enthusiasm.

She smiled at me, but kept walking. "Yep," she said, and continued down the hall. She didn't even slow down.

I spun around and came up behind her. "Lauren?" I said, but she seemed to speed up her pace. I was still trying to catch up behind her when she walked past Chassidy, Julie, Katherine and Stephen; she didn't say a word to the group, but simply smiled, lowered her head and kept walking.

"Uh, good talk," I said.

"It's ok," Chassidy said, turning her attention and body back to me. "She's just mad about something from earlier. She'll get over it. She always does. These little spells are just something that she does sometimes."

I didn't respond to Chassidy. Mr. Undergrove began to motion us to enter the smaller auditorium for our second round.

"Good luck," Chassidy said, a sly smile on her face. "I'm sure you guys will sound amazing." She reached out to hug me again; I stepped back, said, "thanks," and joined my band mates filing into the doors that led to our 2nd round.

We took our seats. This auditorium was significantly smaller; the seating in this area probably seated a quarter of the large auditorium where we performed for our first round. Our chairs on the stage were as close as they could possibly be, the music stands a tad closer, the lighting slightly dimmer. It was clear that this auditorium was designed for more intimate performances, not big concerts.

Mr. Undergrove , like our last performance, bowed to the judges sitting in the fifth row of the seating area, turned back to us, and again closed his eyes, took a deep breath, and when he opened his eyes, Mr. Undergrove raised his arms to his shoulders. We followed in suit by raising our instruments to our mouths, and waited for his cue. "I believe in you," he said, and then with his arms, counted to four; the sound of jazz engulfed the small auditorium.

APRIL - 10TH GRADE

"Are you absolutely certain you have everything you need?" my mom asked. "Plenty of socks? Your dress attire for the competition? Comfortable shoes? A hat in case it rains? Some spare quarters if you get a chance to call us? Enough underwear in the event of an emergency?"

I nodded. "Yes, I have everything that Mr. Undergrove put on the packing list."

"What about sunglasses? Ya know, in case it's sunny while you're there?"

"I packed my sunglasses," I lied.

"What about your pillow? You may want to take a nap on the bus on the way up there?"

"Right here," I patted my pillow sitting beside my bag.

"Does your hotel have a swimming pool? Maybe you should take your swimming trunks in case you guys have some free time at the hotel?"

"Oh, jeez, will you leave the boy alone?" my dad interjected. "Lighten up a little, will ya? They're going to New York City, the big apple. They're not gonna have time for the pool. They're gonna be busy, sun up to sun down, doing the whole band thing." He patted me on the back, and then placed his hand on my neck. "The only thing you need to do is watch yourself at all times, and watch out for your band too. No straying. You all stick together, you got that?" I nodded my head. My dad smiled, and then added, "See? He's a smart kid. Let him go have some fun. He's packed, and if he forgot something, well, he'll be learning an important lesson in paying attention in the future to what he packs." My dad then pulled out his money clip from his back pocket, slipped three $20 bills out, and placed them in my hand. "I know you guys have been working hard to get the whole band to New York, and we're really proud of the effort you as an individual put into it, and while I know Mom gave you some money, and you've got your own money that you've been saving up from mowing the lawn, but that's a little extra, just to ensure you have a good time. If you see something you want, you get it, ok?" I nodded my head again. "The odds of you getting to ever go to New York City ever again aren't big, so you live it up a little. Buy you a souvenir or two."

I hugged my dad and then my mom. "You're certain you have everything?" Mom asked again.

"Yes, Mom, I promise I do. I'm just going to New York City for a couple of days, not Australia for five years."

My mom wrapped her arms back around and squeezed again. "To you it may be a couple of days, but to me, it is five years." I let her hug me until she was satisfied. There was no fighting it.

Sometimes, parents need to hug you, and sometimes, you need to just let them.

We pulled into the Northern Kent parking lot at 4:30 AM. The sun wasn't even trying to peak its way into the world yet. A small bus sat beside the curb of the door closest to the band room, its back door open as members of the band carried equipment from the band room to the bus.

"This may work better than expected," Mr. Undergrove said as he supervised the moving of our instruments and luggage onto the bus to ensure all the space that was offered for storage was utilized efficiently. With the competition being such a big excursion for so many bands, universal drum sets were being provided at the competition for the percussionists to use, opening up a huge amount of the room we needed on the bus for just the drums. With amplifiers and speakers also being provided at the competition, we mainly just needed our instruments and our luggage. The ark, as insisted by Mr. Undergrove, was the first piece of equipment packed. "I'm not going all the way to New York City to discover that we forgot all our music because Kirby was telling a story about a ghost, so the ark goes on the bus first."

You gotta admit that he had a point.

Mr. Undergrove took roll call, thanked all our parents for their support since August, and then it was time to go; we hugged our parents one more time, loaded the bus, and, with great anticipation, rejoiced as the bus lurched forward out of the parking lot.

We were on our way to New York City.

Our bus was a charter bus, but not exactly one of those fancy charter buses. You know, the kind that have fancy televisions and lights in the aisle and seats that recline? Yeah, this one wasn't one of those.

Our bus? Some of the seats reclined, but it was because the seats were broken and didn't sit up anymore. Every time we passed over a bump in the road, two things would happen: two windows on the left side of the bus would each slide down a couple of inches, and the bathroom door at the back of the bus would flap open, regardless of whether the person in the bathroom had locked the door or not. The floor of the bus seemed to constantly vibrate.

An hour into the trip, Stephen leaned across the aisle. "Do your feet feel fuzzy?"

"What?"

"Do your feet feel fuzzy? The floor of the bus is vibrating so much, it makes my feet feel fuzzy."

"My feet feel like feet."

"Hmph," Stephen muttered. "Well, I'm not crazy. My feet feel weird. I think it's the shocks on this bus. Makes them feel fuzzy." He then leaned back towards me. "We aren't exactly living the high life on this bus."

"I think this bus is about all we could afford on our shoe-string budget," I said. "It's getting us there, right?"

"I would have gladly done one more car wash if it was the difference between a charter bus and whatever this is."

We drove through the remainder of the dark morning, passing small sleepy town after small sleepy town on the interstate as the sun finally broke into the sky and the world began to wake. As we approached Washington, D.C., traffic picked up with other travelers sharing the cement highway, slunking along in unison along the dotted lines.

After two brief stops for food and quality bathrooms where the doors don't fly open when you're using them, we were within 30 minutes of the city. It was almost 2:00 in the afternoon.

"Tonight is going to be about checking in to the hotel to get situated for the next couple of days, and then we're going to head into the city to find some food. Plus, I've got a surprise for all of you."

"Mr. Undergrove," Stephen asked, "if I get scared while we're walking around New York, will you hold my hand?"

Mr. Undergrove rolled his eyes and sat back down in his seat. "We will be at the hotel in just a few minutes."

New York City is a sprawling metropolis of skyscrapers and lights, but New Jersey, where we were staying? Not quite so much. New Jersey looks like if every tree, grassy field, or any hint of nature was replaced with a fountain of cement. Cement is everywhere; it covers the roads, the sidewalks, the parking lots, the buildings. Everything. It's like a town was built, and then cement rained down from the sky.

We checked into our motel, which divided the 17 of us up, counting Mr. Undergrove, into six rooms. Mr. Undergrove, being our fearless leader, naturally got his own room. Veronica, being our sole girl, also got her own room; since Veronica was only 15 years old and the only girl on the trip, Veronica's mom got to come with us as a chaperone and stay with Veronica. The rest of us guys were divided up between four rooms.

We found our rooms, unpacked, and then met back in the hotel lobby 30 minutes later. It was April, and even though it was almost spring, the temperature was in the 30's, with the weather forecast calling for a small chance of snow flurries later on in the evening.

"Doesn't seem right, being so cold in April and all," Kevin said. "I don't think I've ever had to wear my winter jacket in April before."

"You might even say that you can't believe this is happening?" Stephen asked.

"Yeah," Kevin said in deep reflection. "I guess. You can say that I can't believe that this is happening."

Stephen momentarily laughed, but after looking around the lobby and realizing that no one else was catching on to his rib at Kevin, he dropped the laughter and went back to looking at vacation and tourist pamphlets.

“Friendly reminder,” Mr. Undergrove said once we were all accounted for, “we’re going to stay together. No one wanders off by themselves. No one. Not even Kirby or Josh.” We laughed nervously.

Mr. Undergrove continued. “New York City is its own beast, its own corner of the universe. We are going to be safe, and we’re going to stay together, no matter what. This is not up for debate. We’re going to keep our eyes peeled on each other, and we’re going to constantly be paying attention. While New York is something different than any of us have seen before, we’re going to be just fine, do you understand?”

We nodded like we understood, but c’mon, it’s New York City - we had no clue what we were walking into.

“First, we’re walking to the subway station to board the Path train and ride it all the way into New York, right into the heart of the World Trade Center district. From there, we’re going to do a little sight-seeing, and then we’re walking to Chinatown.”

“Chinatown?” I asked. “Like an entire town designed to look like China?”

“Kinda, but not really. Chinatown and Little Italy are largely Chinese and Italian-centered neighborhoods. They’re right beside each other. It’s one of those ‘New York City bucket list’ things. We’re going to head that direction to explore, and then, as promised, I have a surprise.”

“If by ‘surprise’ you mean tickets to *Cats*, I think I’m going to take a hard pass,” Stephen said.

Mr. Undergrove rolled his eyes and motioned for us to follow him. We left the hotel and walked four blocks over to the Newark-Penn Station subway station. After purchasing tickets, we descended several stairwells down into a dimly lit skinny cement loading area, where both sides of the loading dock were boxed in by sunken train tracks leading into darkened tunnels. A smell floated in the air, strong enough to smell but not exactly distinguish. "You smell urine?" Kevin asked. I nodded. "Yeah, I thought so. Me too," he confirmed.

"Make sure everyone is behind the yellow line," Mr. Undergrove announced. "The last thing I want is to have to scrape someone's remains off the track."

"What happens if you cross the yellow line?" Kevin asked, but before Mr. Undergrove, or anyone really, could answer, a subway train came whooshing out of one the tunnels and sped by us at what seemed like 200 miles per hour. In the blink of an eye, the train was gone. "Never mind," Kevin said, wide-eyed.

Minutes later, another train came screeching out of the darkness and came to a stop in front of us at the docking bay; its doors opened, and a swarm of people exited the train. Mr. Undergrove yelled, "This is us! Move!" And we moved, quickly boarding the train and finding seats next to each other. Within seconds of boarding, the doors shut tight and the train lunged forward into the darkness of the tunnel.

"Mr. Undergrove, is there a bathroom on these trains?" Kevin asked.

"No," Mr. Undergrove answered, "I told you all to use the bathroom before we left."

"I don't need to go. I was just wondering."

Mr. Undergrove's face scrunched up. "Odd question."

"I'm just asking in case we get stuck down here. I was mentally preparing myself."

"We're not going to get stuck down here," Mr. Undergrove assured him.

"Don't say that," Kevin responded. "That's how it always happens. Saying stuff like that will get us stuck."

"That's a great idea for a movie," Stephen said. "Only with zombies."

"Zombies?" Kevin asked.

"Yeah, zombies. Like a bunch of people get stuck on the subway underground, and one of them has the zombie virus and then starts to turn. Chaos ensues. I'd watch the heck out of that movie."

Kevin stared at Stephen wide-eyed, looked around the subway, then looked back at Stephen. "Let's not talk about this kinda stuff," Kevin said. "It's freaking me out a little."

Stephen leaned closer to Kevin. "Scared you'll be first to go if there was a zombie on this train?"

"Dude, no, just don't talk about that kind of stuff."

Stephen sat back up straight. "That's my golden idea. I wanna write that story." Stephen put his hands in the air like he was imagining the marquee to a movie theater. "Zombie Train! Coming soon to a theater near you!"

With every stop, more passengers got on the train as some of the passengers got off, like the train was playing a game of catch with an unseen force, but instead of a ball, it concerned humans. At one stop, the train would feel like it was at peak capacity, seemingly on the verge of bursting, and at the next stop, the train would momentarily empty itself of all its insides and move on with barely a crowd within.

“Next stop, we move,” Mr. Undergrove said. The train slowed to a halt, the doors opened with a sound of a burst of air, and we were on the move again, pickling along with the crowd. “Stay close,” Mr. Undergrove said, counting our heads as we shifted in and out of a swarm of faces of the subway station. Up a flight of steps we went, followed by another, and then, boom, there we were: in a concrete jungle of buildings, sidewalks, streets, cars, signs, crosswalks, and people, people, and people, all seemingly walking with and against each other all at the same time. Without hesitating, Mr. Undergrove continued to move, never seemingly fazed by the sight of the scenery around us. We followed him with intent and purpose, for none of us wanted to get lost in the organized and understood chaos of the city.

We maneuvered through the crowds, through the jungle that was the city. The buildings stretched toward the sky and seemed to keep stretching, like there was no end to how far up they were willing to go, a concoction of glass and metal, glued together by concrete. The crowds moved about the city, each seemingly following an unspoken formality, but each formality with its own unique identity.

We turned the street corner, and there they were: the World Trade Center towers, standing side by side, hovering over the city, like protective identical twins towering over their own personal playground.

“Gosh, that’s high up.”

I looked at Stephen, his eyes peeled up at the towers. “It is,” I confirmed. “I’d give anything to be Spider-Man right now.”

“I’d give up girls, movies, and jazz band to be Spider-Man right now.”

"Can you imagine?" I asked. "Just getting to swing around the entire city? Nothing holding you back up there. Just you, and all of this as your playground."

"You think Spider-Man wears a cup?" Stephen asked.

"Huh?"

"You know, like in the event a bad guy tries to hit him below the belt? He'd need to wear a cup to protect himself, right?"

I shrugged as we crossed the street. "I've never thought about that before. I mean, I guess he would need to."

"I would," Stephen said. "I definitely would wear one. I bet a lot of heroes need to, especially on the street level. Maybe not so much with the superheroes with magnificent powers, like Dr. Strange, or Professor X, but the hand-to-hand combat heroes, like Spider-Man, Daredevil, or Luke Cage. Those guys."

"Doesn't Luke Cage have super strength and unbreakable skin?"

Stephen shot me a look of disbelief. "Super strength and unbreakable skin doesn't mean it doesn't hurt when you get hit in the nards. Especially if it's by somebody like the Thing or Rhino."

"Eh. Good point."

We passed tall building after tall building, people weaving in and out like ants sewing an unseen tapestry. We passed over crosswalks, by hot dog vendors and by men selling sunglasses out of book bags. We passed homeless people lining the street, each with a sign pleading for help for a variety of reasons, ranging from needing food to needing drugs; some yelled vulgarities at us as we passed. We passed police officers on horseback, just like in the movies; we waved as we passed by them, and they waved, again, just like in the movies. And then, with little build up or suspense, the sidewalks widened and the streets became twice as crowded. The buildings turned from glass and cement structures to storefront after storefront of stuff: shirts, shoes, hats, purses, scarfs, jackets, and snow globes.

We turned down a street, and then another, and then another, and then Mr. Undergrove stopped and turned around. "I assume all of you are hungry, right?" he asked. We didn't have to answer because our eyes were wide and our stomachs were alive with the smell of Italian food waffling through the street, awakening a hunger that we didn't know had existed. There was a united jeer from all of us as we followed Mr. Undergrove into a small restaurant, Pablo's Pizzeria.

Tables were pushed together to accommodate us, our group essentially taking up almost the entirety of the inside seating area of the restaurant. The lighting was dim and the menus were faded.

Kevin leaned across the table. "Are we going to die here?"

Mr. Undergrove laughed. "No, this place is awesome. Pablo's Pizzeria is one of the best places to eat in this neighborhood. It's going to be ok. I promise." When the waitress took our drink order, Mr. Undergrove ordered seven pizzas, each with a different topping. "My treat everyone; dinner is on me tonight. Let's live it up a little, because tomorrow the work starts and we have to be on point at all times. We're going to be butting heads with some of the best bands in the nation."

The food arrived, and it was at this moment that I discovered that the frozen pizzas and the $7 pizzas that my parents had always picked up from Pizza Hut didn't hold a candle to the pizza that was placed in front of us. This pizza swelled with cooked bread and cheese and tomato sauce and pepperoni and bacon and sausage and garlic and love and temptation and beginnings and endings and blood and release and dreams and power and charisma and fireworks exploding in my mind. We all reached in, cutting and slinging pieces of hot pizza love onto our plates, devouring them without hesitation, letting the grease and gooey bread slide down our throats to our stomachs as we reached in for more, tearing piece after piece and then eating it with the same raw, carnivorous action, like it was the first meal we'd ever been formally introduced to and we, as an entire band, had never properly learned our manners.

Mr. Undergrove was correct: this place, Pablo Pizza's, was awesome.

We stumbled out of the restaurant, our stomachs full with the unanimously decided best pizza we had ever experienced. Chinatown and Little Italy awaited us, with its cheap t-shirts and knockoff watches. Mr. Undergrove's only advice: "Stay close to each other, and never take the first price on anything that any of these people are selling on the street."

We walked through fish markets, raw chum sitting out, reeking of the exact smell that one would imagine a smelly fish would smell like sitting out by the street in New York City. We ventured through gift shops, each displaying the same exact ten 'I Love New York' shirts. We paraded by restaurants and local dining destinations, each, like Pablo's Pizzeria, appearing to be no bigger than a small room, but still bursting with people either eating or waiting to eat.

"It's time," Mr. Undergrove said. "I promised you all a surprise, and we're only two blocks away." We followed him, edging step by step into the unknown of what could possibly be our surprise.

We passed several more streets, crossed a street, and, as the sun began to set on the buildings that surrounded us, we saw it.

Something so simple, and so everyday, but so momentous and epic that it could not be ignored.

There it was. A surprise for sure, just like Mr. Undergrove promised.

We all smiled, pointed, and immediately pulled out our cameras. There, in front of us, was the Hook & Ladder Company 8 firehouse.

"What am I looking at?" Josh asked, slightly confused.

We all turned to look at him in disbelief. Even Brooks looked at Josh in disbelief.

"Dude! What are you looking at? You're looking at a piece of history, that's what you're looking at!" Stephen's eyes were wide with discomfort and doubt. "Are you hearing this?" he asked me. "Josh doesn't know what this is! He doesn't know what we're doing here!" Stephen turned back to Josh. "Please. Please tell me that you're messing with us." Stephen put his hands together like he was praying. "Please tell me this is your idea of a joke."

Josh, confused, responded, "I got no clue. Honestly. It looks like just some building."

"Some building?" Stephen said, then, for emphasis, he said it again. "Some building? This isn't just some building in New York. This isn't just some random firehouse. This is probably one of the most important landmarks in all of history." He raised his hand and pressed his fingers together as he articulated his next words, "Most. Important."

Josh looked unimpressed; he crossed his arms in front of his chest. "Are you guys gonna tell me or what?"

"You seriously don't know?" I asked.

"I seriously don't know," Josh responded.

"Josh, so help me," Stephen said, "how do you not recognize the headquarters of the *Ghostbusters*? How? Did you have no childhood?"

"Oh," Josh replied, and then "Oh! I see it now. That's from the movie. Ok, cool." Josh smiled a little, ignoring Stephen's question, and then pulled out his disposable camera from his pocket and took a picture.

Stephen let his hands fall to his side. "I just wish he was excited about what he is looking at as I am."

Kevin leaned his head back, and sang out "When there's something strange in your neighborhood, who ya gonna call?"

We all sang out together, "Ghostbusters!"

"Everyone! Let's cross the street!" On Mr. Undergrove's command, we followed the crosswalk, and we were right there at the firehouse, looking up at its nostalgic majesty.

I leaned over to Stephen. "Aren't you half expecting to look up and see all sorts of ghosts bursting out the top of the building?"

"Nah," he replied, "there's no sign of any criminal violations of the Environmental Protection Act."

"Alright everyone: group picture time!" Mr. Undergrove's announcement was met with groans and moans from us, but he quickly followed it up with, "All I want is a group picture of the band in front of the *Ghostbusters* headquarters. Is that too much to ask?" Being that he had a good point, the band gathered around him, all of us, trumpets in front, saxophones to the right of Mr. Undergrove, trombones to the left; the back row was the percussion and rhythm sections. Veronica's mom stood back about 15 feet, held up her camera, instructed us to say *Ghostbusters* on three, counted to three, and then captured the moment: a teacher with his students standing in front of a firehouse in the heart of New York City.

It was one of those moments where there's a photograph to remember it by, but honestly, none of us needed a photograph to remember it.

The ride back to New Jersey on the subway that night wasn't quite as thrilling as it had been earlier that day, for the shock of being in New York City, although still powerful, had faded a little. We were tired, excited, exhausted, and running on adrenaline all at the same time. Tomorrow morning, the competition would begin, but for right now, we were just a bunch of teenagers on the way out of the city after an afternoon and evening of fun.

On the train, I was sitting beside an older man; when the man got up and left the train at the next stop, Veronica rose up from the other side of the train and sat down beside me.

This was the same Veronica that had potentially liked me months earlier, but also the same Veronica that made it very clear to me that she didn't appreciate me not calling her when she expected me to.

"Did you have fun today?" I asked.

Veronica took a deep breath, letting it slowly in a sigh. "I did. I really did. Fun times." She reached into the plastic bag she was holding and pulled out a black shirt with a yellow Batman logo on it; under the logo were the words 'NEW YORK CITY' also in yellow. "I got this for Dad. It's incredibly cheesy, but I think he'll like it."

"It's not cheesy," I said. "It's awesome, and I know he'll like it. It's got Batman on it. What's not to like?"

Veronica smiled then put the shirt back in her bag. "Are you nervous about the next couple of days?"

"Nervous? Me? Never!" I smiled, then added, "Yeah, it's a little terrifying to actually be here. We're a good band though. At least I think we are."

She looked at me, but seemed to be looking past me at the same time. Veronica then looked back down at her feet, tapped them together twice, then looked back up at me.

"I'm glad you're here," I said. "I'm glad that you're a part of all this."

"Yeah," she said, a smile escaping the corners of her mouth. "I am too." It was the first time I had seen Veronica smile towards me since that night at Stephen's house, the night of the town Christmas tree lighting, the night we learned that we were on a path to New York City.

We sat there, smiling, riding the train from the city back to New Jersey. Tomorrow would come tomorrow, but for right now, tonight was enough to make me happy.

And tomorrow did come, but not the way we'd all hoped it would. At 5:45 AM, all of our hotel phones began to ring, for Mr. Undergrove had arranged for all of us to receive wake up calls from the front desk.

By 7:00 AM, dressed in our performance clothes and armed with our instruments, we loaded the bus and made the trek into the city. By 8:00 AM we were deposited in front of a large theater and conference center swarming with other high school jazz bands, all dressed to the nines and carrying their instrument cases. By 8:30 AM we were being guided to a large conference room that seemed to be bursting at the seams with hundreds of other band kids. Some adult with the competition picked up a microphone and welcomed us, and then lectured everyone for close to 30 minutes on what the word 'respect' meant and that we would all learn the meaning of the word on a personal level over the next couple of days. His speech was then followed up by a different man that gave the same lecture, but this time it was on the meaning of the word 'excellence'; he also promised us that we would learn the meaning of that word on a personal level over the next several days.

Stephen leaned in close to me. "I think they both found the script for their speeches in *Motivation for Dummies*."

The National Miles Davis Youth Jazz Band Competition began its Day 1 activities and classes. From 9:00 to 10:00, we had solo and improvisation class. From 10:00 to 11:00, we were lectured in a theater by an old lady on the history of jazz. From 11:00 to noon, we were divided by our instruments and worked with designated instructors on how to effectively enhance our personal ability to perform. At noon, we were walked a block over from the theater and building that housed the competition to a hotel that had a large enough area to feed all the participants a catered lunch of hot dogs, potato chips and oatmeal cookies.

"Who the heck serves oatmeal cookies to a bunch of high school kids?" Kevin asked as we sat down to eat. "Oatmeal cookies aren't really cookies; they taste like wet sand and betrayal."

"I'll take your cookie!" Brooks piped up. "Oatmeal cookies are amazing."

"Of course you would," Mr. Undergrove said. "Oatmeal cookies are the Sonic Youth of the dessert world."

After lunch, we were entertained by a performance given by some of the instructors of covers of some Miles Davis songs. From 2:00

to 3:00, we reunited as a band and played a set of three songs for an instructor who then gave us tips, advice, and critiques on our performance, ranging from our percussion section to 'play like you really mean it' to our trumpet section to 'loosen up' a little when they improvise because, as stated by our instructor, 'your trumpet solos are all boring'. From 3:00 to 4:00, we returned to our individual instrument classes for more direct instruction. From 4:00 to 5:00, we were placed back together for a cold reading of a song we had never played before; it was considered 'cold' because the instructors wanted to see how we were able to do playing a song that we hadn't heard and had no preconceived knowledge of going into the song, which is kinda like making someone play basketball for the first time when they're never seen a basketball before. At 5:00, we reconvened in the main theater to watch a 45 minute documentary on the life of Miles Davis, and then returned to the hotel up the street to eat dinner in the conference center. While we ate, we were lectured again, this time by two different instructors, on how we would learn the meaning of the words 'respect' and 'excellence'.

The ride back to the hotel on the bus was quiet, for while we weren't physically tired, we were mentally wrecked and exhausted from the day's instruction, the musical notes we had never seen or attempted to play before, the bands that had more members in their brass section than we had in our entire band, the schools that had matching jackets, matching shoes, matching ties, and matching instrument cases, the musicians that could pick up on a song within seconds of reading the notes on the page without having heard the actual music, and the instructors with the volcanic intensity that we had never experienced. All these factors were ingredients to an overwhelming concoction of what felt like the recipe for drowning.

The lights of the city reflected on your eyes, but they didn't seem to faze us with excitement like they had the day before.

When we got back to the hotel lobby, Mr. Undergrove had us gather around him for a quick meeting.

"How'd that feel today?" he asked.

We didn't respond. We didn't know how to respond. We just sat there, wide-eyed and dazed. It had been an incredibly long day, and we all had the same look on our faces that could be read a mile away; we were clearly in over our heads on the competition.

"Well," I spoke up, "I don't think it was the worst day ever."

"I don't think it was the worst day either," Mr. Undergrove confirmed. "There are some incredibly talented bands and musicians at this competition."

"Dude, some of those kids are just so awesome!" Brooks blurted out. "They're doing things on the trumpet that Stephen, Josh, and I can't do! It's so overwhelming to sit there knowing they're the ones that we're going up against."

Various side conversations opened up; each one confirmed that we were surrounded by all-around better musicians.

Mr. Undergrove sat there, listening, nodding along, taking in our thoughts and opinions. He looked stressed, maybe sad, maybe feeling a tad lost like we were. When our sidebar conversations began to die down, Mr. Undergrove spoke.

"I know exactly what you all are feeling. I'm feeling it myself. A lot of these bands have been playing together for years. A lot of these bands come from schools that have established jazz band programs that have been around for decades. A lot of these bands are coming from incredibly wealthy foundations, so they've had the luxury of having personal instructors and have been to large band competitions in the past. They all have experience and skill that we don't have." Mr. Undergrove swallowed. "We don't fit in with these people. We're just a bunch of teenagers from Northern Kent High School, just some small school in the middle of nowhere next to not much at all. We come from a small community with small community values and a small community way of life. We aren't like these people." Mr. Undergrove sat up straight, readjusting his shoulders. "But it's not going to stop us. If anything, they are all reasons why we're going to have to work twice as hard as every single band and musician at this competition."

Mr. Undergrove pulled out an agenda from his back pocket, unfolded it, and then continued to address us. "Today was kinda like a tryout day, or a practice. It was designed to give us a feel for the expectations and quality of performance that the competition is looking for, and to get the instructors familiar with the bands. Tomorrow is when things get real." Mr. Undergrove scanned the document one more time. "Our first performance is in the morning at 10:00; it'll be in front of five of the instructors, and we get to pick three selections to play for them."

"We get to pick our songs? Like any three songs that we do well?" I asked.

"Three songs, all our choice, which is nice because it lets us start the competition on a strong leg."

We were all collectively relieved by that confirmation.

"At 11:30, we play again, this time for three judges and it'll be a cold reading."

"So we'll be walking into that one completely blind?" I knew the answer to my question, but I had to ask it, just to reassure myself of what I already knew. Weird, right?

"We're going in completely blind. I don't even know what they're going to throw at us. But, we're going to do our best. That's all we can do."

"What if our best is just mediocre compared to the other bands?" Stephen had asked the very thing that was sitting on all our brains, like a cat on a fence.

"Well," Mr. Undergrove said, "we're going to be the very best mediocre jazz band here." He put the agenda down on his lap. "Guys," Mr. Undergrove looked at Veronica, "and ladies, I don't care how good everyone is or appears to be. We are a great band, and I know it, your parents know it, and most of all, you know it. Don't tell yourself anything different." He paused. "Pardon my French, but, oh my gosh, we busted our asses to get here by putting in the practice and rehearsal hours, doing fundraiser after fundraiser, playing gig after gig, and I don't care what any of these instructors or fancy schools think or look like, we are a great band!"

Stephen raised his hand. "Yes, Stephen, go ahead," Mr. Undergrove said.

"Great words, man, but I need to correct you on something."

"What do you need to correct me on?"

"The word 'ass' isn't the least bit French."

Mr. Undergrove put his hands on his face and began to laugh. "You're right. It isn't French at all, is it?" We all laughed. Mr. Undergrove leaned back and let out a bellowing laughter, his face a bright red. He rubbed his eyes as he continued to chuckle, wiping a tear away. Stephen's joke was funny, but it was just as funny watching Mr. Undergrove lose it. "You can either laugh or cry; you might as well laugh."

"So, we play twice in the morning," I said, trying to get us all back on focus on what tomorrow would look like. "What about the afternoon?"

Mr. Undergrove glanced back over the agenda. "After we eat lunch, we go into our third round at 2:00; that'll be with another five instructors judging us, and it'll be with another set of three songs that we get to select again. At 4:00, we play for a panel of ten instructors, and that's the one where we will have to play one Miles Davis song of our choice."

"Oh," I said, "that's not so bad."

Mr. Undergrove nodded. "It's not so bad."

"What comes after those four rounds?" Brooks asked.

"After those four rounds? We pray."

"We pray?" Brooks asked.

"We pray," Mr. Undergrove confirmed. "The scores from those four rounds will determine if we get to move on to day three."

"What?" We all asked in unison.

"The scores from day two determine who gets to stick around for day three; day three determines who gets to stick around for day four, and day four decides the winner."

"If we don't rock tomorrow then," Stephen started.

"Hasta la vista, baby," Mr. Undergrove finished.

"Judgement day," Stephen said.

MAY - 8TH GRADE

We finished our second round with the judges in the smaller auditorium. Mr. Undergrove seemed confident in our performance as we headed out to the large back hall, a smile bursting through his face when he clearly was trying to keep his poker face in control. We took apart our instruments, placed them in their cases, and reconvened in the large auditorium. Several bands had left; several new bands had arrived. I looked around the theater, but no sign of our Trenton friends.

Mr. Undergrove directed us to a set of empty rows. Stephen reappeared at my side, who was also visually scanning the theater, presumably with the same purpose as me. "Any sign of the girls?" I asked.

"Nah, no sign." He looked around the theater again and then down at his knuckles as he cracked them. "They're from Trenton, which is God knows how far away from where we live, and we're just some guys still in middle school. How far did we really think it was going to go before reality kicked in?"

I nodded. He had a point. After a moment, I added "Stephen, you're right; odds are it wasn't going to work out, but I got to correct you on one thing."

"What's that?"

"We're not just 'some guys still in middle school'. We go to King's Hollow. We're more than middle schoolers; we're survivors."

Stephen laughed. "You're right,' he agreed. "King's freakin' Hollow. People like us are one of a kind."

A man in a suit with a smile on his face approached Mr. Undergrove, handed him an envelope, shook his hand, and then walked away. Mr. Undergrove quickly tore into the envelope and read the letter inside. He leaned his head back, appeared to close his eyes for a moment, and shook his head. He arose from his seat, and then instructed us to quickly and quietly grab all of our stuff and head out to the bus.

"Ladies and gentlemen," Mr. Undergrove said as he stood at the front of the bus, a poker face resting on his face, so stern and unemotional it was like someone plastered his face in cement. "Today was a long time coming. I told you all about this competition back in January, and since then, you've given me your time, energy, and a countless amount of your patience. Today was basically a giant test." Mr. Undergrove pulled the same envelope that was handed to him just moments earlier from his suit jacket. "Here are the results from this test." He opened the letter and then took a deep breath, almost for dramatic effect to pull us all in and make the moment last a big longer.

"We were rated on both of our performances, each by a different set of judges. Our first performance, given on the stage in the large auditorium, was rated, on a scale of 1-5, with 1 being 'Superior', and 5 being 'Poor', was a 2, 'excellent'.

We looked around each other on the bus, not really sure if 'excellent' was a compliment or not.

"This is where you clap and feel good about yourselves because that's a great score!" Mr. Undergrove said.

We all started clapping with a sense of relief from Mr. Undergrove's reassurance.

When our clapping died down, Mr. Undergrove resumed. "The score of our second performance in the smaller auditorium, again on a scale of 1-5, with 1 being 'Superior', and 5 being 'Poor", was a..." Mr. Undergrove put the paper against his chest. "You guys know that whatever this score says isn't a true reflection of how proud I am of you all."

Our excitement couldn't hold us back. "Read the score," someone yelled.

"Yeah, read the score," someone else agreed.

"Read it! Read it! Read it!"

A chant broke out across the bus.

Mr. Undergrove raised his hand, "Ok, ok, ok, I'll read it. Everyone sit down." We settled back into our seats; Mr. Undergrove cleared his throat. "As I was saying, the score of our second performance in the smaller auditorium, again on a scale of 1-5, with 1 being 'Superior', and 5 being 'Poor", was a...". Mr. Undergrove stopped again, his paper still held up in front of him for reading purposes but his eyes on us. "Drum roll." We looked at him blankly. "Drum roll, please," he repeated. The drummers, picking up on the cue, began a drum roll, hitting the seats in front of them, and soon the entire band was participating, a loud drum roll echoing throughout the bus.

Mr. Undergrove cleared his throat, raised the paper back to reading level, and then placed his hand in the air, signaling the drum roll to halt. "King's Hollow Middle School Band, congratulations; your second performance, on a scale of 1-5, was a 1. 'Superior'.

The bus erupted with cheers as kids were jumping out of their seats.

It was one of those moments, ya know. Like a feel-good movie moment. Here we were, just a bunch of kids from King's Hollow, a not-so-great school from a not-so-great-neighborhood in a not-so-great town, and we had done something. Not something earth-shattering, like won a gold medal or got on TV or something like that. But something. Something probably no one thought we could ever do.

Excellent and superior. That was us. Maybe not to everyone, but man alive, those two words labeled our band in a way we never imagined that we would be.

The bus shook. We hugged, high-fived, and, as my grandma would have said, raised a ruckus. And it felt great.

Mr. Undergrove was all smiles as he stood at the front of the bus. He kept talking about how proud he was of all of us, but we knew that already. We could have been rated 'Poor' and he would have told us that he was proud of us. That's just how he was. I'm proud of you, I believe in you, yada yada yada.

Mr. Undergrove - what a teacher.

Our activity bus rolled out of the Snowfield High School parking lot. The bus was loud and rowdy, kids still clapping, cheering for each other, for our own victory. Mr. Undergrove sat at the front of the bus, a smile gleaming on his face. I don't think anything could possibly erase that smile, not even, well, anything.

But somehow, I did.

APRIL - 10TH GRADE

"Not 'Georgia on my mind'. It's too obvious. Too 'basic'. Too easy to pull off and make it look like you know what you're doing. I'm betting one out of every three bands will throw it into one of their sets this week. We can do better," Mr. Undergrove said.

We were on the bus on the way into the city strategizing which three songs we would play for the judges in our first round of the National Miles Davis Youth Jazz Band Competition.

"What about 'Fly me to the moon'?" David asked.

"Sinatra? In New York?" Mr. Undergrove said. "Falls in the 'too obvious' category. We do a great job executing that song, but I'm on the fence on that one. We won't rule it out, but let's keep brainstorming to see what else we can drum up." Mr. Undergrove looked at Kirby. "No pun intended."

"I say we play 'Hold on, I'm comin'," I said. "It's technically more of a rock song, so it'll have the 'whoa' factor when we play it, but we also do a great job on that song, so maybe that will get us some brownie points in the eyes of the judges for going with something that will grab their attention that's still executed with some grace."

Stephen pointed at me. "Mitchell has a point. We could get those judges on our side by opening up with that."

Mr. Undergrove rubbed his chin in deep thought. "Ok, I'm willing to entertain that idea if you can tell me what we would follow it up with? We come out loud and strong like that, it makes it hard to slow down and ease the pace, so if we start loud and upbeat, we have to stay loud and upbeat. I'm not sure how the judges are going to feel about that."

“Birdland?” Stephen asked.

“Birdland?” Mr. Undergrove repeated. “Birdland.” He entered this deep state of meditation as he mulled over the suggestion. His eyes seemed to roll to the back of his head and then back around to us. “Birdland. We’ll do it. But we’re going to switch it around: ‘Birdland’, then ‘Hold on, I’m comin’, then here’s my suggestion: we wrap it up with ‘Hey Jude’.”

We sat in silence for a moment, letting Mr. Undergrove’s suggestion soak in.

“Close with a 10 minute song? We always drag ‘Hey Jude’ out way too long,” Brooks spoke up. “Besides, we’ve only played that song publically once, and when we did, you stepped in to play the double high C part. None of us can hit that note. Not me, nor Josh, nor Stephen. This is a stupid decision.”

“He has a point,” Josh agreed reluctantly. “I don’t think I’d be able to pull off the note.”

Mr. Undergrove nodded. “Ok, we need a song that we’re all comfortable with, so what else do we think we could use as our closer?”

“‘Hey Jude’ is a good choice,” I said. “Couldn’t we improvise a little when it comes to hitting the double high C?”

“Well, yes, that’s a good point. Whichever trumpet player takes the lead in the finale could, in theory, just play high C and we can make it work.”

Brooks shook his head. “No,” he said, “It’s not going to work. This is a bad idea. Does nobody else see this except me and Josh?” Josh nodded along in agreement.

"I like the idea of us playing 'Hey Jude,'" Kevin said.

Brooks snapped around at Kevin. "Dude, it's not happening. Josh and I are united on this. We can't play the note required for the song. We'll go out there and look like idiots if-"

"Jesus, I'll do it," Stephen interrupted. "I'll play the note. I got this." Stephen's eyes turned to Mr. Undergrove 's. "Give me the chance. I can do it." Skeptically, Mr. Undergrove's eyes met Stephen's; Mr. Undergrove hesitated.

"We most certainly should not play a song that we're not 100% on board with," Mr. Undergrove said. "If Josh and Brooks don't think it's a good idea, and the trumpet section is doing most of the heavy lifting in that number..."

"I can do the solo," Stephen repeated.

Mr. Undergrove took a deep breath. "No," he said, "I think Josh and Brooks have a good point. We did come all this way for this competition. The fundraising. The long hours. We got to consider all of that with our music selection, and we do have a plethora of songs to choose from." He cleared his throat. "I think 'Birdland' and 'Hold on, I'm comin' are strong selections for us, and I do think we do an excellent job on 'Hey Jude', but it's too much to risk in this situation."

Everyone got quiet. Awkwardly quiet.

"So," Mr. Undergrove broke the silence, "who else has an idea for our third number for this morning's performance?"

We all looked around at each other, our brains raking ideas for other songs but also what to say or do with the obvious tension that had drifted into the bus. "What about 'New York, New York'?" Josh asked. "I mean, I know it's obvious, but maybe it would work?"

"Yeah," Brooks added. "'New York, New York' is one of our stronger pieces, and quite honestly, doing something that everyone expects you to do is sometimes a shock." Brooks' voice, usually full of confidence, seemed sad and weak.

Mr. Undergrove let out a sigh, almost defeated-like. "Well, the thing about Sinatra is, with us being in New York and all, is that the judges-"

"Oh this is complete crap!" Stephen blurted out. "Complete crap!" Stephen turned to face Mr. Undergrove. "You're all the time telling us that you freakin' believe in us, and this," Stephen pointed his finger down at the floor of the bus, "this is one of those moments. We came all the way to New York freakin' City to play in this competition, and now, here we are, a moment where the fate of the band hangs in the balance, and you want us to risk it on 'Hey Jude', but you're not willing to give me a shot because you got two other trumpet players that are whimpering in the corner because they don't have the balls to man up!" Stephen turned to Veronica and her mom sitting across the bus aisle. "No offense, ladies."

"Oh, none taken," Veronica said back, her eyes wide with amusement.

"Look, Mr. Undergrove ," Stephen's voice softened but maintained passionate and charged, "I know I'm a slacker at times, and I know I'm not always 100% focused, and I'm by far not the smartest guy on this bus, but damn, I love this band. I love this band so much. This is a chance for me to show and prove it." Stephen straightened his back and ran his hand across the back of his head. "You gotta give me this chance. You picked 'Hey Jude', and someone has to have the guts to play the solo."

"Hey, that's not fair!" Brooks yelled out. "I could do the solo if I wanted to!"

"Oh shut up, Brooks," Stephen said without a flinch. "You thought playing 'Hey Jude' was a stupid idea. Had you had any..." Stephen hesitated, glanced over at Veronica and her mom again, and then continued, "male genitals, then you would have volunteered to do the solo, but you didn't."

Stephen turned back to Mr. Undergrove. "We can do it. Let us play 'Hey Jude'; let me play the solo. If I'm wrong, then you can bench me the rest of the competition. You'll hear no complaints from me."

The air was heavy with astriction. Mr. Undergrove, eyes wide with astoundment, sat in his seat speechless, his mind visibly running in about 20 different directions.

"I'm with Stephen." I said, breaking the tension. Collectively, the eyes of the band turned to me. "We all should be with Stephen on this. "Think about it: we're only as strong as our belief in our weakest player." Stephen shot me a look, but didn't interrupt me. "We don't have a weak player here. We've proven time and time again that we are an awesome band. Most of us have been playing together since King's Hollow." I rose up in my seat. "I mean, this is not a crazy decision; we all know we can rock 'Hey Jude', so that shouldn't be up for debate or discussion. On top of that, we shouldn't doubt Stephen. He believes he can do it," I put my hand on Stephen's shoulder, "and I do too. I'm not doubting him, because this is it, this is one of those moments that Mr. Undergrove always talks about."

All eyes shifted from me back to Mr. Undergrove; Mr. Undergrove's eyes met mine and held them. "What moment?" Kevin asked.

"The moment of no return," Mr. Undergrove said. "All the good movies have them. All the great songs have them too." A smile seemed to bud on Mr. Undergrove's face as he also rose up out of his seat until he was eye level with Stephen. "Jazz is about letting go of your fear. That's what we need to do: let go of our fear." The confidence in Mr. Undergrove's eyes seemed to swell. "Stephen, do you believe that you can do this solo? Honestly?"

Stephen took a gulp of air, rolled his shoulders back, and, without a flinch of doubt in his voice, he answered, "I know I can do the solo."

Mr. Undergrove nodded in approval. "Then you got it. We close with 'Hey Jude.'" Mr. Undergrove looked around at the rest of the band. "Do we need to vote on this, or are we all in approval?" Mr. Undergrove's eyes rested on Brooks and Josh. "Fellow trumpeters: what say you?"

Josh and Brooks looked at each other. Brooks rolled his eyes as Josh turned back to Mr. Undergrove and responded, "We're with Stephen."

"Everyone else?" Mr. Undergrove asked.

An overwhelming loud 'YES" filled the bus.

"It's settled then," Mr. Undergrove said, a gleam of pride in his eyes, "we're together on this. Today is our moment of no return, and the day we let jazz show us how to let go of our fear."

MAY - 8TH GRADE

The activity bus rolled into the Snowfield Mall parking lot. Mr. Undergrove glanced at his watch, instructed us to be back on the bus by 1:20 PM, to be safe, and to stay in groups. "No one wanders off alone," Mr. Undergrove said, "even if they're weird," and then added, "looking at you, Brent."

"Hey!" Brent yelled out from the back of the bus.

"He's got a point," Kevin piped up.

"Yeah," Brent resigned himself.

We filed off the bus, excitement tingling under our skin. Yeah, yeah, yeah, we came to the band competition for Mr. Undergrove, and we practiced, practiced, practiced because we knew he believed in us, but really, all you got to do to get a bunch of teenagers to do anything is mention getting the opportunity to go to the mall while they should be in school, and just like that, they'll do it, no questions asked. The band competition was over, our hard work complete; now, we were going to take advantage of the fruits of our labor and spend roughly an hour and ten minutes at the Snowfield mall.

"Food court first, or we check out the stores and then circle back to food?" Stephen asked.

"Food. Always food," I responded.

We entered the mall like a pack of hungry wolves chasing deer, eyes wide with excitement. The girls split into groups and headed for the various department stores. The guys, the majority of them, headed for the food court.

You know what you never see anywhere except in a mall? Sbarro. Go ahead and think about it. How often do you see a Sbarro standing on its own? Yep, never. But walk into a mall, any mall in America, and what do you immediately find in the food court? Sbarro. Sbarro is like the McDonalds of the food court industry; you find one every time you turn around.

So, naturally, because teenagers like pizza, Stephen and I selected Sbarro for our day off from school lunch enjoyment. Stephen got all sorts of weird stuff on his pizza, like mushrooms and green peppers and sausage and stuff; he claims it's because his parents never get that type of pizza, which is why he wants it even more, but that seems all very psychological and I don't know much about that kind of stuff.

When we sat down, things got real.

I mean, things were real before; this is all a very real story, but things got real in a sense that you could feel gravity shifting a little in a way that made the day feel a little different. Like that type of real.

Sitting not but a few tables over from Stephen and me in the food court were Chassidy, Katherine, Julie, and Lauren all carrying on conversations and socializing together at the same table.

"Stephen, look to your left."

Stephen's eyes grew wide. "Dude!"

"Dude, indeed."

"Ok," Stephen hunkered down to the table as he began to inhale his pizza at a rapid pace.

"What are you doing?" I asked. "You're eating that like you're in a race."

"We are. Do they see us yet?"

I glanced back at the girls; they were still at their table, oblivious to our presence.

"We're undetected still, although this food court isn't but so big so it's only a matter of-"

"Ahh!" Stephen blurted out. "This pizza is so frickin' hot! Burnt my tongue!" Stephen grabbed the drink cup closest to him and began guzzling it.

"Two things:" I said, "1) that's my Sprite." Stephen looked at the cup in his hand in surprise.

"Whoops. Want it back?" He held out the cup to me but I shook my head.

"No, no, it's fine; you can have it." I grabbed Stephen's cup. "I'll take yours."

"It's Mountain Dew," he said.

"Ah, the nectar of lime diesel fuel. Never mind. You take both drinks. I didn't want my Sprite anyways."

"What's the other thing?" Stephen asked.

"What?"

"You said 'Two things' and then only said one thing."

"Oh," I replied, "right. 2) What's the purpose of you eating your food so fast?"

"I figured if we ate our food real fast, we could mosey on over to the girls' table and speak to them before they got up."

I rolled my eyes. "I think we can do better than that. Follow my lead," I got up from our table, my tray of food in hand. Stephen's eyes grew wide again as he stuffed another bit of pizza into his mouth.

What was I doing? 'Follow my lead'. This isn't like me. But it's also not like me to accidentally go into a girls' restroom and sit in silence while some girl that I just met spilled her metaphorical guts to me without a clue of who I was, so today has been full of surprises.

I walked up to the girls' table. "Hey everyone! Small world, right?" Wow. I said that without my voice shaking or feeling nauseous. The girls all looked up from their conversation; they smiled, but it wasn't Julie or Katherine or Chassidy that I was focused on, it was Lauren. Her eyes sparkled for a moment.

But did they? That's one of those stupid movie cliques. Maybe I imagined it. Who knows?

Stephen came fumbling up beside me, pizza crammed into his mouth. "Lhhoks five fairs from fat fis fable for few for," he gasped out his mouth, "Find ffi fe foil you?"

Chassidy looked at Stephen confused. "What?"

Before Stephen could answer with more gibberish, I translated for him. "I believe what my buddy was trying to say is that we noticed that there is room for two more at this table and we were wondering if we could join all of you for lunch."

Stephen nodded his head, still trying to chew the pizza crammed in his mouth. "Fats fut if was fryin' to fay."

We joined the girls, me sitting directly across from Lauren. I was trying my absolute best not to blush, and honestly, my best wasn't good enough; my ears were burning and I could feel my neck radiating heat, but unlike earlier, the anxiety wasn't flushing to my stomach, causing me to evacuate the scene to go to the bathroom. I had had my fill of bathrooms for the day and I had no plans to visit one anymore. Well, at least until after I got home. I don't want to commit to refusing to use the bathroom when, well, what if I need to pee? You catch my drift, right?

Lauren sat across from me, kinda fluttered up too. I could tell she had that same level of nervousness racing through her that I had racing through me. She kept looking at me, probably getting a good look at my black eye in the natural light. My shiner was huge, but hey, if it made me better looking, then so be it.

"So," Chassidy spoke up, "how long is your school going to be at the mall? We've managed to convince our director that we need to be here until 1:15."

"We're here until 1:20," Stephen replied.

"Lucky us then," Chassidy said. "Don't you want to take us all shopping and buy us anything and everything we desire?" She grinned a sly grin, slightly devilish yet charming at the same time. Stephen's eyes opened wide; it didn't take a genius to see that he was heavily considering Chassidy's proposal.

"Or you guys can just hang out with us and we can make the most out of the time we have together," Lauren piped in.

Chassidy jokingly rolled her eyes and smiled, "Yeah, I guess that'd be fine too." She then wrapped her arm around Stephen's arm and laid her head on Stephen's shoulder. 'But if you want to take me shopping, I'm ok with that."

"Stephen, ignore her," Lauren said, "she's lovely to look at, and charming to listen to, but she'll drain that wallet of yours in a heartbeat."

"Oh, stop! Don't scare him away before he buys me something!" Chassidy said with a laugh.

"How did you all rate in your performances?" Stephen asked,

"I'm not even sure you needed to ask that question because we always achieve 'Superior,'" Chassidy said. She then looked at Stephen in the eye. "Always." Julie and Katherine giggled.

"You two have been around us long enough to know Chassidy isn't the most humble person around," Lauren said to me.

"Hey, we've got a record that speaks for itself," Chassidy said. "It's ok to be a little cocky when history is on your side." That same devilish-yet-charming grin flashed across her face as she gazed at Stephen. A few hours ago, Chassidy seemed annoyed with Stephen, but here we were at the food court in a mall, and all of a sudden it looked like the girl had a change of heart.

Lauren leaned forward towards me. "I'm sorry for being weird earlier today. It's nothing personal against you, I was just....just...."

"Dealing with stuff," I said, finishing her sentence.

"Yeah," Lauren said, nodding her head, "that's accurate."

"Sometimes we all deal with stuff. Sometimes it's good, and sometimes it sucks."

"Yeah," Lauren agreed, nodding her head again, 'sometimes it sucks. Like really, really sucks." Her eyes met mine for a moment and just seemed to linger there.

“I understand,” I said. “Is there anything I can do to help?” Lauren slid her hand across the table and squeezed my hand.

“Thank you. I was just having a hard time with-” Lauren hesitated as her eyes drifted over to Chassidy who was busy flirting with Stephen. “Girl stuff, you know? Just crazy girl drama. I just needed a few moments away from everyone to get myself straight.”

“Believe me, I understand.” I smiled, not really by choice, but because I was still blushing after all this time.

“You know, I have no clue where King’s Hollow is,” Lauren responded. “Is it a big high school, or just a small one? If it’s small, that’s probably why none of us have ever heard of it; we typically only encounter bands from larger schools at competitions.”

“King’s Hollow? It’s....uh....it’s,” I looked to Stephen for help but he was drawn into a different conversation with Chassidy and the other girls. “Small. It’s a super small high school. Not well known or anything.”

Add ‘lying to a beautiful girl’ to my list of achievements.

“Oh, well, that explains it,” Lauren said with a smile. “Maybe we will start seeing you guys on a regular basis at these competitions. They’re pretty fun.”

“Yeah, definitely fun.” Know what’s not fun? Lying to a high school girl about not being in middle school.

We finished our lunches, and then, exactly as Stephen and I had planned, we were invited to join the girls as they walked around the mall, but first, collectively, the four girls went to the bathroom, giving Stephen and me a chance to talk strategy.

"Dude!" I said, grabbing Stephen by the arm and turning him around away from the girls, "Lauren asked about King's Hollow."

Stephen's eyes grew wide. "Did you tell her that we're still in middle school?"

"No, she asked how big of a high school King's Hollow was since she had never heard of it. I went along with King's Hollow being a high school because I didn't have the guts to tell her we were just 8th graders. Obviously they didn't hear or pay attention to the announcement in the auditorium that we were a middle school"

Stephen nodded. "Nice. We're legit now."

"What do you mean we're legit now? I lied to Lauren! That's bad, right?"

Stephen cracked his knuckles. "Could be, but like I said back in the auditorium, how far do we think this is actually going to go? I mean, odds are, after today, we're not going to see them again. Maybe talk on the phone, but we can't drive, so I don't see us making the trek to Trenton to see them on a regular basis." Stephen checked his watch. "We've got less than an hour to make the best of this situation. We can keep up the lie for a little while longer, and then, after that, we're in the clear. No reason to cross the streams and tell them that we're middle schoolers."

"Cross the streams?"

Stephen rolled his eyes. "*Ghostbusters*, man, keep up."

The girls rejoined us and off we went into the mall. But something strange occurred. Something that had never happened to me before. As we progressed out of the food court, I felt something at my side, and when I looked down, I saw that my hand was interwoven with

Lauren's. She smiled at me, leaned into my side a little, and even though I continued to walk and try to act normal, fireworks were going off in my head. I couldn't help but smile.

We went to all sorts of stores I had never been into before. You know, like girl stores. Stores that sold make-up. Stores that sold hair clips. Stores that sold purses. Stores that sold perfume. Stores that only carry stuff that girls are interested in. But then we got to the music store; the only problem: the girls didn't seem interested in going into the music store, but being that Lauren was still holding my hand, it didn't bother me, and we just kept walking onto a different girl-oriented store.

Then, we stumbled upon something I hadn't expected: a comic book store, situated right between a luggage store and a place to get your hair cut. Stephen and I tried to mask our excitement, but I guess Lauren sensed my hidden joy by the way my fingers were twitching in her hand.

"If you guys want to go in there, that's fine," Lauren said. She then added, "I'll go with you." I glanced at Stephen; Stephen nodded in approval. You would think a girl wanting to go with you into a comic book store would be a great idea, right? I mean, you'd think we would take advantage of this situation, right?

"Gross," Chassidy blurted out. "I'm not going in there. Comic books are for weirdos." Stephen looked back at Chassidy, a look of disgust on her face, and then looked at me, the internal conflict writhing in his eyes.

"Oh, come on, Chassidy, it's ok for a couple of minutes." Lauren squeezed my hand and we kept walking towards the store's entrance. Stephen was half frozen, his legs pointed to follow us, but his body turned towards Chassidy.

"We will meet you at the bus then," Chassidy said, pointing to her watch. "We don't have long." She reached out, grabbed Stephen by his wrist, and said, "C'mon, you're with us. There's a store over here you need to take me to." I watched as Stephen walked off with Chassidy, Julie and Katherine, confused, yet content to follow.

"Well, I guess it's just us then," Lauren said.

We entered the comic book store. Lauren's eyes grew wide and she tightened her grip on my hand; I'm guessing that she felt the same way about the comic book store that I had felt about every other store that we went into since lunch. The walls were covered in all sorts of colorful posters of various heroes, all clad in a plethora of bright colors and accented muscles. "Who's that guy?" Lauren asked, pointing to a poster.

"Oh, that's Green Lantern," I said. "He's a member of the Green Lantern Corp that protects the universe using their power rings that were gifted to them by the Guardians of the Universe on the planet Oa."

"Right." Lauren's grip seemed to tighten even more.

Let me take a moment to address something: guys, if you're ever on a date with a girl, don't take her into a comic book store, even if she says it's ok. If she's not into comic books and superheroes, then walking into a comic book store with her is just going to make her really not be into comic books and superheroes. It's kinda like jumping into the deep end of a pool if you hate swimming; it's just going to do is make you hate swimming even more.

Lauren never said it, but I could tell that the comic book store was not the place she wanted to spend her last moments with me, so we left, going out on our own into the mall instead of rendezvousing with the rest of the group.

As we walked through the parking lot to Lauren's school's bus, I could feel Lauren's grip start to squeeze my hand again. "Look, I got to tell you something." She stopped walking and pulled me a bit closer to her. I could feel the heat rushing to my cheeks again, but no spinning or nausea followed, which, I gotta admit, was progress. "I don't know when I'm going to see you again, and today so far has had its ups and downs."

"You can say that again," I said, having flashbacks to the joy of getting on the bus this morning to being trapped in the girls' restroom back at the competition.

Lauren looked at me a little puzzled, but then continued. "Meeting you has been a definite up. Probably the best up."

"What was the down?" I asked, knowing what the answer was.

"I let some stuff bother me earlier today that I shouldn't have. Personal stuff. Girl stuff."

"Chassidy?" I asked, again knowing the answer.

Lauren looked at me, reading my eyes. "You're good at picking up on things, huh?" Both my hands were intertwined with both of her hands. "Yeah, Chassidy and I had some words back at the competition. See, well," she hesitated. "It's just really complicated. Can we leave it at that?"

I wrapped my arms around Lauren's shoulders, hugging her. "Yeah, we can leave it at that."

"I need your number. Ya know? Just in case...." Her words drifted off. "Can I call you? Like, whenever?"

"Yeah, sure," I answered. Lauren ripped a piece of paper out of a small notebook from her pocketbook and handed it to me along with a pen. She then scribbled something in the notebook, tore it out, and then folded it up, placing it in the front pocket of my dress shirt.

“Don’t look at it right now, ok? Promise me you’ll look at it later, ya know, like afterwards...” Lauren’s voice drifted off.

I placed the piece of paper with my phone number in her hand. “You can call me anytime, but I want to warn you: my mom asks a lot of questions. She’s very nosey.” Lauren giggled and then hugged me.

I know it’s cheesy, but if only time would slow down at the parts that you want to keep tucked away in your memory.

“Your black eye, it’ll probably be long gone the next time I see you.” She put her hand against my face, looked me in my eyes, and then wrapped her arms around my waist to hug me again.

“Can I walk you all the way to your bus? I do get to stay here a whole five minutes longer than you and it looks like my bus isn’t but a hop, skip, and a jump away from your bus.”

Lauren hesitated; her arms tightened up. “I’m not sure if it’s such a good idea. I don’t want you to be late getting to your bus.”

“Oh, why not? It’s an entire extra minute more that I get to hold your hand.” I began walking, Lauren walking with me, but almost like she wished she wasn’t walking with me, like she didn’t want to be seen with me. You know what I’m talking about? Like, the same feeling you get when you’re somewhere with your parents and you see your friends in the distance and you don’t want them to know that you’re hanging out with your parents and you feel like hiding. That’s the feeling that I was getting from Lauren.

“Mitchell, really, you don’t have to walk me over there. Really.”

“It’s not a problem.”

She squeezed my hand harder this time, jolting me to a stop. We were only 20 yards away from the Trenton bus. "It will be a problem if we go any further near that bus and my ex-boyfriend sees you holding my hand. He's got some serious issues."

"Gabe? The one that body slammed the kid in weight training class?"

Lauren looked at me confused. "What?"

"Gabe, your ex-boyfriend. The one with the issues. He body slammed a boy last week when Gabe found out he asked you for your number."

Yeah, Mitchell, keep talking about stuff that you're not supposed to know about. That'd be great.

"How did you know that? Did Chassidy tell you that?" Lauren's eyes looked into mine with confusion, shock, and anger all mixed together.

Yeah, I probably shouldn't have mentioned all that. See, Chassidy had mentioned Gabe's name in the auditorium, but stupid me forgot that the whole finding that Gabe had anger management issues happened when I overheard Chassidy and Lauren talking in the girls' restroom.

(Insert foot into mouth here.)

"Um..." I stumbled out. "I thought you mentioned that?"

"No, I never mentioned it." There was a moment of awkward silence, us standing together, me holding Lauren's hand but Lauren not necessarily holding my hand.

"Answer the question, Mitchell. Did Chassidy tell you about Gabe?"

Now, in this scenario, you normally wouldn't want to lie, especially to a girl that you really, really like, but I've been getting quite good at lying. I mean, I went along with Stephen's lie about my black eye. I also have been going along with the understanding that Lauren and the rest of the girls thought that Stephen and I were in high school. So, would lying at this point be so terrible?

"Chassidy didn't tell me about Gabe," I stammered out.

"She didn't?"

"Yes, I mean no. I mean, yes, she didn't."

"Then how do you know about Gabe?"

Stop. Freeze time. Seriously. Freeze it. Pull the camera back. Look at this moment.

There's a boy holding a girl's hand in the parking lot of a mall. Twenty yards away rests several school buses. Just outside one of those buses stands a rather large 17 year old teenager. Muscles. Square jaw line. Crew cut. Narrow, dark eyes. Tan skin. He looks like he could play football, or wrestle, or throw discus. Large. You know the type. He rests his arms folded against each other as he watches from a distance the girl, one that he favors, speak to the other boy, a stranger. This girl, this beautiful, lovely girl, captures the stranger's attention in a way that the large, muscular boy wishes he could. He looks around; no one seems to notice him. He takes one step forward, and then another, and then another. In the muscular boy's mind, he will get the girl's attention; he has had her attention in the past, and he knows exactly how to get her attention now.

And pull the camera back down to Lauren and me. Action.

"Mitchell, who told you about Gabe? It wasn't me." Lauren pulled her hand out of mine. A look of slight tension rested upon her face. "Be honest with me."

I sighed. "Honesty, huh?"

"Yes."

No. Don't do this, Mitchell. Don't you dare do this. Think for a second, man! Think about the repercussions of telling Lauren the truth! Don't go down that path! Just play it cool for a few more seconds and you'll be free!

"I overheard you and Chassidy talking in the bathroom back at the competition."

And you did it. Great. You told the truth. Oh jeez.

Lauren stood there, looking at me in disbelief. "What?"

I took a deep breath. "At the competition. You and Chassidy had that argument in the bathroom. I heard it."

Lauren's ears and neck began to grow red. Her eyes almost seemed to look like they were bulging. "How on God's green earth would you know what happened between me and Chassidy? Were you in the bathroom? The women's bathroom?" Then, Lauren covered her mouth in shock, for she internally answered her own question. "No."

I stood there in silence. My heart felt like it stopped beating. I could feel the pavement beneath my feet begin to grow wavy.

"No. No, no, no, no, no." Lauren's bottom lip began to tremble. "No, no, no. This isn't happening."

"Look," I said, "it's not what you think-"

"Then what is it, Mitchell?" Lauren yelled, cutting me off. "What exactly is it? Because, right now, I'm thinking a lot of things!"

"I....I..." I was stammering. "I was....I was just..."

Lauren cut me off again. "You were just what? Spying on me?"

Ya know, I'd try to argue with her, but looking at it from her point of view, there's nothing I could say that could fix this situation. Man.

I just stood there, choking on my own words, no clue on how to form a sentence. And then, well, things took another turn for the worse.

"This guy botherin' ya, babe?" boomed a voice. Behind Lauren rose the shape of the large, muscular teenager.

"Gabe!" Lauren wrapped her arms around his waist and buried her face into his shirt.

"Oh, so you're Gabe," I said, looking up, up, up to Gabe's height.

Lauren looked back at me, the hurt in her eyes boiling over; she was crying. Yeah, I made a girl cry. That gets me the 'Tough Guy' award, right?

"Yes," Lauren said, looking at me and then up at Gabe. "He's bothering me. I want him to go away."

"You got it, babe," Gabe's voice boomed again. And then he moved toward me.

APRIL - 10TH GRADE

"Birdland. Hold on, I'm comin'. Hey Jude. Birdland. Hold on, I'm comin'. Hey Jude. Birdland. Hold on, I'm comin'. Hey Jude. Birdland. Hold on, I'm comin'. Hey Jude." Stephen paced back and forth outside of the assigned room where our first evaluation of the National Miles Davis Youth Jazz Competition would take place at 10:00 AM. It was currently 9:57 AM. "Birdland. Hold on, I'm comin'. Hey Jude."

"Yep, that's the line-up," I said. "Are you expecting it to change?"

Stephen shook his head. He pulled his trumpet up to his lips, took a deep breath, put his lips to his mouthpiece, and then made a quiet, high-pitched toot with his trumpet. He pulled his trumpet back down to his side, took another deep breath, and then whispered to himself, "I got this." Brooks eyed him, half glaring with either anger or jealousy. Stephen continued to pace, reciting the three song line-up.

Mr. Undergrove was pacing as well. Shoot, we were all pacing, whether physically or mentally. This was it: the thing we all had wanted since Mr. Undergrove first told us back before the tree-lighting gig in December. We were here, in New York City, the end-all be-all city in the world, to play in this competition. And, man, it was stressful. Maybe had we not seen or heard some of the competing bands the day before we'd probably feel more confident in ourselves? We knew we were Northern Kent good, but were we New York City good?

Mr. Undergrove patted Stephen on the back. "Stephen, I know you know this, but I believe in you. I believe in all of you, but you showing leadership back there on the bus and wanting to take this opportunity to-"

Stephen cut him off. "Save it for later today. Let's get through these three songs, and then our three other performances, and then we can start shaking hands and feeling proud of ourselves." He then added, "No offense," and then "sir."

Mr. Undergrove halfway smiled, shook his head in agreement, and said, "I'm with you. No harm done."

The door to our assigned performance room opened and a small, frail balding man stepped out with a clipboard in hand. "Northern Kent?

We filed in, music in one hand, instruments in the other. Mr. Undergrove approached a panel of five older men all sitting at a long, wide table situated about 15 feet back from the designated performance area. All five men, including the frail, balding man, wore the same spectacle reading glasses pulled down to the tip of their noses. They talked briefly and quietly to Mr. Undergrove while drums, amplifiers, and music stands were adjusted to fit our needs. We quickly completed a 10 second scale to signal that we were warmed up and ready to perform. "Birdland. Hold on, I'm comin'. Hey Jude." Mr. Undergrove said to us quietly, mimicking Stephen from just a few minutes earlier. "I believe in all of you. Let's make these judges believe." He raised his hands into the air; we raised our instruments, and as Mr. Undergrove's right hand dropped, the sound of jazz filled the air.

MAY - 8TH GRADE

Gabe's first punch connected with my stomach. His second punch connected with the left side of my head. I staggered backwards, forcing Gabe's third punch to just barely clip my left side of my chin. Gabe twisted his right arm down across his chest; the wild swing wasn't so much meant to connect but to keep me at a distance. He twirled his left arm back around and took another full force swing at my head, which I was able to jump back to avoid. Again, with his left arm crossed across his chest, Gabe sent his right arm out with a wild punch trying to keep me from driving in towards him. Smart. I took three more steps back as Gabe squared himself back up, fists in front of his chest.

"Hey man, I got no beef with-" Gabe's fist cut me off, catching me in the ribs. I went down, rolled to the right, and then popped up with my hands upward into Gabe's chest, pushing him back. A crowd of kids that I assume were from Trenton had gathered around us. Lauren stuck out from the crowd, her arms crossed across her chest, a torn look on her face. Another left-handed swing came my way. I dropped my head to avoid my face getting knocked off, and then stepped back to avoid the right fist that followed.

"You don't upset my girl!" Gabe yelled out. He dropped his shoulder and charged at me, knocking me square in the chest, resulting in me hitting the ground. A collective "Oh!" rose up amongst the crowd. I rolled backwards, flipping my feet over my head and rose up from one knee as Gabe lurched over me, fist cocked backed for ignition; my right hand caught him square in the chest. Gabe stepped back, my punch only slightly fazing him, and then let loose his left arm, this time straight towards my face, connecting with my eye.

I went down, rolled again over to the right, and, as I came up, I received another solid punch to the same eye. Double whammy.

Now, hold on a second. You don't have to worry but so much. Gabe didn't connect with the eye that was already black from the locker room incident a few days earlier. No no. He connected with my other eye, and after two direct hits to it, my eye lid was swollen shut. Ever been half blind in a fight before? Yeah, me neither.

I tried to stand, but Gabe delivered a stiff kick to my side, knocking me back down. Kids were pointing and laughing. Another kick to my side. More laughter. I was able to get a glimpse of Lauren; her hand was over her mouth. Gabe circled back around me, arms up in the air, paying more attention to the crowd of his peers than to me, his target, rolling on the gravel of the parking lot. "You wanna see me beat this punk up a little more?" Gabe asked. A decisive roar from the crowd affirmed this statement. I staggered to my feet. Boom - my ribs were burning as another punch sunk into them. I was back down on one knee. A fist came raining down towards my head, but I was able to get my forearm up to absorb the blow just in time to avoid another hit to my cranium. Gabe sent another sloppy right hand in my direction, but I was able to avoid it. I had a half of a second opening to make a move. Not enough time to throw a punch, so I improvised: I head butted Gabe right in the nose. Blood splattered. Again, another lusty "Oh!" from the crowd.

Gabe staggered backwards holding his face. "You dip brain!" He yelled. When he moved his hands away from his face, myself and the rest of the crowd got a head-on view of Gabe's crooked nose. Blood ran down his cheeks and chin onto his white shirt. I put my hands into the air in the form of surrender but Gabe had already put his fists back up and was pacing towards me again.

He swung twice, left then right, both missing my head. I pushed his right arm down and then snapped my head forward again, delivering another head butt to the side of Gabe's head. Gabe took two steps back; I again began to put my hands in the air, trying to signal to him that I did not want to fight. Gabe took advantage of my hesitation and backhanded me right across the face. "Screw you," he said, drew his left arm back, and slapped me in the face again with the back of his hand, hard enough for me to hit the ground again.

I pushed myself up; there was blood on my hands, my pants, and my shirt. I wasn't sure if it was my blood or Gabe's. Gabe was back to trying to rouse the crowd in his favor. Lauren's eyes met mine, angry, sad, full of tears. Gabe turned back to me, dropped his shoulder, and rammed me again to the gravel.

Yes, ladies and gentlemen, I was getting my butt handed to me. And it was embarrassing because it was happening In front of Lauren. And a lot of other people. But mostly Lauren. I mean, I know she was technically the person that directly caused the beat down at the hands of Gabe, but still. Well, maybe I was the cause. Let's not debate this matter right now.

"Mitchell! Mitchell!" It was Stephen's voice, but it was kinda swirly sounding. I know 'swirly sounding' doesn't explain much, but trust me, his voice was swirly sounding. "Dude! You look terrible!" He was at my level, kneeling down to the gravel. "What the hell, man?"

I motioned my head behind me. "It's Gabe," I said. "Lauren's ex-boyfriend."

Stephen's eyes grew wide. "Is she making you fight her ex-boyfriend in order to earn the right to be betrothed to her in the future?"

"What? No, just gimme some help up." Gabe, for a third time, was egging the crowd in his favor to continue the fight. Stephen grabbed my arm and helped me to my feet. "Any advice?"

"You could run, but the giant Wolfman over there will most likely be able to run you down."

"Gabe," I said, "not a Wolfman. He's mortal."

Stephen shot me a look. "Well, he looks like a Wolfman compared to you."

At that moment, lightning struck my brain. I mean not literally struck my brain, that would have killed me, but I got an idea.

I shrugged Stephen's hand off of my shoulder and took my first step forward towards reapproaching Gabe. "Hey Wolfman!" I yelled.

Gabe cocked his left arm back as I got close, releasing it as I got within striking distance, his fist coursing towards my face.

And that's when I let go. My left leg went up in a kick, hitting Gabe right between his legs. Gabe's eyes went wide, like all the wind in his chest left him all at once, and then he went down, hitting the asphalt of the parking lot, and stayed down, holding his stomach with one arm and the other, well, you know, protecting himself 'down there'.

A gasp erupted amongst the crowd of teenagers that were watching my beating at the hands of Gabe. The crowd went quiet. This wasn't supposed to happen: Gabe had this fight in the bag. How had this happened? Their Trenton hero had fallen.

I looked up and saw all the eyes of Trenton and King's Hollow students looking at me; I could feel my heartbeat thumping in my head. Gabe made a moaning sound as he tried to sit up and then fell back to the ground. "Only one way to kill a werewolf," I mumbled to myself.

I looked over at Stephen, who offered me a thumbs up that seemed to beam with pride.

People started shouting angrily, and then people started running. An older man broke through the crowd and grabbed me. "You're not going anywhere," he rasped, and then, with one hand locked on my arm, he knelt down to check on Gabe.

Then Mr. Undergrove came through the crowd. He looked at me in shock, and then down at Gabe, still on the parking lot gravel. "What did you do?" Before I could answer, several police officers weaved through the crowd of kids scrambling to get back to their buses.

"Nobody move!" one of the officers yelled.

And that's when I realized I had really, really messed up.

APRIL - 10TH GRADE

Double C. Double freakin' C. Like, the granddaddy of notes. I mean, it's not THE granddaddy of notes, but ya know, it's up there. Especially for a high schooler to be able to hit it.

We nailed 'Birdland'. Maybe not 'nailed it', but we were as close to 'nailing it' as one could possibly get to 'nailing it'. Then 'Hold on, I'm comin'. We can rock that song in our sleep. That may be an exaggeration. But still, good. Great even. And then came 'Hey Jude'. The look on Mr. Undergrove's face moved from confident to concern. He was just as nervous about this number as we were, but he was trying not to show it. I glanced back at Stephen; the nervous sweat that was on his forehead earlier was now gone. He was calm, collected, and cool. 'He's got this,' I thought to myself.

And he did. Stephen's double C never wavered while he played. It was one of those moments that we all almost wanted to collectively stop playing to watch and listen to Stephen play the solo at the conclusion of 'Hey Jude'. He didn't sound like Maynard Ferguson (no one sounds like Maynard Ferguson except Maynard Ferguson), but it was a close second. A very close second. Well. Yeah, close second. We'll give that honor to him. When the song finished, Mr. Undergrove's face was bright red from trying to keep his excitement at bay. He kept his poker face going and his arms up in the air, signifying to us to all do the same and not break out of our 'performance mode' in front of the judges.

When we got outside, we all lost our minds, yelling, rejoicing, and hugging, kinda like a team that just won some huge playoff game and Stephen had been our star player. Mr. Undergrove reined us back in, getting us to regroup and head out and away from the other bands waiting for their turn to get evaluated.

"Holy St. Francis! How did you pull that off? Double C? Crap!" Kevin gave Stephen a playful punch in the arm. Stephen smiled a sly smile, and shrugged his shoulders while casually holding his trumpet at his side.

"Before we get too excited about our performance back there," Mr. Undergrove said, "we cannot forget that we have three more performances today. Three more chances to go above and beyond. Three more performances that can either keep us here at the competition another day, or eliminate us. So, while we all did a fantastic job back there," Mr. Undergrove put his hand on Stephen's shoulder, "especially Stephen, we need to stay focused. In less than an hour, we have to complete a cold reading, which means we have zero clue what piece they're going to throw at us." Mr. Undergrove then leaned in towards all of us. "We must steady our emotions, and stay focused. Every note counts. Every one of them."

For almost an hour we waited. Our adrenaline was still gushing when we made our way into a small performance room that was located in the basement area of one of the theaters. Again, we were directed towards a performance area of the room and instructed to set up our instruments. Meanwhile, Mr. Undergrove talked to several of the judges, was handed a large brown envelope, and then Mr. Undergrove shook their hands and returned to where we were situated.

"Cold reading time guys," Mr. Undergrove said, holding up the envelope in the air. "This contains the sheet music for our next performance. Once I open and distribute the music within, we will have exactly ten minutes to prepare our performance for the judges over there." He pointed to the table on the opposite side of the room where three older men sat, each one with peppered gray-and-black hair. "Ten minutes, that's it. So we must read and respond accordingly. Questions?" We nodded our heads, Mr. Undergrove opened the envelope, pulled out the music, half-grinned, and then distributed the music as quickly as he could.

"Your time starts now," one of the judges said.

"'In The Mood'? Really?" Stephen said. "Like, Glenn Miller's 'In The Mood'? We know this."

Mr. Undergrove's eyes flashed with excitement, but still maintained his composure as he immediately began to walk us through the piece, pointing out areas that could cause concern, assigning solos to Kevin and Brooks, and stressing the articulation of notes at certain areas. You know, kinda like he was teaching like it was any other day.

'In The Mood' is a basic staple to any jazz band. It's kinda like the song that most jazz bands learn first. Well, not first, but it's pretty basic. I mean, we'd been playing that song all year long. Our collective confidence instantly rose 10 points.

Wait. That came out weird. Does anyone measure their confidence in points? I mean, I don't. What I am trying to imply is that we felt good about ourselves going into 'In The Mood'.

And so we played it. Pretty flawlessly too. When it comes to 'In The Mood', we don't make mistakes.

We finished, Mr. Undergrove's hands hanging in the air, almost soaking in the moment, like he could feel it too, ya know? The intensity. The perfection of our performance. We landed it. The judges scribbled stuff into their notebooks, all looking very intense. We collected our instruments, thanked the judges for their time, and departed while Mr. Undergrove shook their hands. Again, we rejoiced in our ability to rock our performance, exchanging high fives and hugs as we applauded ourselves in our job well done. Like before, Mr. Undergrove was all like 'we can't forget about the rest of our performances, yada yada yada." I know Mr. Undergrove was trying to keep us focused, but, man, c'mon, let us enjoy the moment.

We traveled next door to the conference center for our lunch, which was pizza. Gobs and gobs of pizza. Not near as good as the pizza we had devoured in Little Italy either, but it was still strides ahead of what we were used to. Way better than any of the franchise stuff we have back at home. Like, you could actually taste the flavor of the sauce and the cheese. Bold. Nothing bland about it.

Stephen leaned over. "When we get back home, I don't think I'll be able to eat pizza ever again. This stuff is amazing. Makes me want to move to New York City, start a jazz band, and eat pizza every day."

Our next performance at 2:00 PM required us to select another three songs. Mr. Undergrove, hoping to avoid the rift that happened earlier when we were selecting songs, announced that he had already put some thought into our playlist. "We did a good job at being loud, so I think for the next round, we're going to slow it down a little." His choices: Oliver Nelson's 'Stolen Moments', Cannonball Adderley's 'Mercy Mercy Mercy', and then Herbie Hancock's 'Watermelon Man'.

Slow. Like slow jazz. Slow. Which was something we could do, it's just playing loud and fast is a lot more fun. Someone pointed that out, but Mr. Undergrove just shook his head. "We gotta show we can do everything, that we've got a wide range. If we're always loud and fast, it may leave a bad taste in the judges' mouth."

I looked at Stephen. "Satisfying these judges is worse than trying to make a girl happy."

"Don't I know it," he said, and then we bumped fists.

"You guys know that I'm right here, right?" Veronica said. "I can hear you."

"Guys are terrible creatures. You know that already," I said.

Veronica rolled her eyes, nodded, and then smiled. "Don't I know it indeed."

The nerves from this morning were fading. After experiencing what we thought were two back-to-back successful performances, we were growing numb to the overcast of the intimidation of the competition. I mean, it was still there, but not like it had been earlier when we were arguing on the bus. We were back to our normal selves, fully aware of what we could accomplish. The way we handled 'Hey Jude' and 'In The Mood' made us feel powerful. Sure, there were other schools here that we were sure could give us a run for our money, but we were on a roll.

And we rolled on through into our 2:00 PM performance, playing for a different set of judges that we had not seen before. We were smooth, accurate, hit all the accents that we wanted to emphasize, and, like our earlier performances, left that session feeling confident in ourselves. Mr. Undergrove seemed to think so too, a sly smile on his face shining through.

"Look at Mr. Undergrove sitting over there smiling to himself," I said to Stephen as we waited for our last performance of the day. "He's probably feeling really good at how we've been doing. All this does is make him look like an awesome instructor. He's done a great job teaching us and it's paying off."

"He deserves that, ya know? Us doing well, here in New York, swimming with the sharks of the jazz world." Stephen leaned back in his chair and put his hands behind his head. "We could buy that man a Cadillac and it feels like it still wouldn't be enough for everything that he's done for us."

4:00 PM was descending upon us; it was time for our last performance, which would hopefully give us a ticket to move on to the next day. The relaxed and confident smile on Mr. Undergrove's face began to slide back into a stern and serious grimace. We could all feel its weight too. My hands began to get sweaty. Stephen's ears turned pale. David kept scratching the left side of his head, something he only did when he was nervous. Looking around the competition, it looked like we weren't alone in our feelings; all day long, kids had been lurking around the theater and conference center looking zoned-out, half pumped up on adrenaline and half wrecked with nerves. Other bands didn't seem fazed by the pressure of performing in New York City at a national competition. Must be nice.

Mr. Undergrove gathered us around for one final pep talk. "This final performance is another cold reading; the only thing we know about it is that it will be a Miles Davis song. Being the whole 'National Miles Davis Youth Jazz Competition' thing, we know that this is the round where everything we do, every note we play, every mannerism we put into our performance will be under the scrutiny of a microscope. The judges will show no mercy here. We're lucky to be in the position where we're facing this performance at the end of the day and not at the beginning. You all have proven that you can perform well here under pressure and your confidence reflects that. So, remember that going in. Be the unstoppable force that you believe yourself to be." He then added, "I believe in you. You know that. You hear it from me all the time. But hear it one more time: I believe in you."

"You got any idea of what song they're going to throw at us in there?" I asked.

"Good question. I've spoken to several band directors, but nobody is really talking about their experiences. This competition is about as cut-throat as they get. Nobody wants to give any other school an advantage." Mr. Undergrove shrugged his shoulders. "And I can't blame them. All we can do is hope that it's one of the songs we prepared for this competition. If we walk in there and we see 'Freddie Freeloader', 'Blue in Green', or 'Stella by Starlight', then we will feel pretty good about ourselves."

"And what if we don't see any of those songs?" Stephen asked.

Again, Mr. Undergrove shrugged his shoulders. "Well, I guess we're going to have to show the judges some of that famous Northern Kent jazz band magic."

"Crap!" Stephen said, and began to frantically check his pockets, almost panicked.

"What?" I said. "What did you forget?"

Stephen's panicked look turned into a sly grin when he saw he had our attention. "I left my bottle of Northern Kent jazz band magic on the bus."

"Oh my gosh, you're so lame!" Kevin yelled out.

We recollected ourselves and listened to Mr. Undergrove talk some more. Every note counts. I believe in you. Yeah. When you hear the same variation of the same speech over and over and over again, you grow numb to it, ya know? So it's not personal against Mr. Undergrove, but I just think we had had so much success in the first three rounds that this fourth round pep talk was just, I don't know, forgettable.

"Everyone understand?" Mr. Undergrove had finished his speech that I think everyone had largely blanked out on. Mr. Undergrove's face looked concerned.

"Oh, yeah, we got this," Stephen said, sensing the awkward silence. He then added a "Totally."

The fourth round was held in the largest theater within the building, an homage to the weight of the round where each band would be asked to play a song that Miles Davis had once performed and made famous. Miles Davis: the prince of darkness. I think any musician that had the nickname of 'the prince of darkness' would probably get a kick out of a national high school competition being named after them.

The lights on the stage were blinding when we looked out into the audience. A row of judges sat about a third of the way back into the seating of the theater, each one wearing glasses, speckled black and white hair, and sat with their elbow up on the arm rest, their face leaning into the palm of their hand. We adjusted our seating area, warmed up with several scales, and then watched as one of the judges rose from seat, walked down the aisle, greeted Mr. Undergrove at the stage with an envelope, and then walked to the conductor's podium.

"Welcome, friends, to our little competition. We are glad that you are joining us today from," the man's eyes glanced down to a notecard he held in his hand, "Northern Kent High School. I know that this is your first time here." The man adjusted his glasses. "Quite a feat to make it here. No doubt that it included lots of hard work, lots of long hours, lots of pushing yourself to be the best band that you can possibly be. You've probably noticed that there are a lot of bands here, a lot with prestigious titles from all sorts of other national competitions. They don't matter right now; what matters is you and this band. We want to hear what you can do with those instruments. Now, that being said, your conductor," the man looked back down at the notecard in his hand, "Mr. Undergrove, is holding an envelope containing music to a Miles Davis song. Your job is to play that song and play it well." The man then pointed to the audience seating where the rest of the judges sat. "We'll be listening to you with eager ears. Our job is to determine exactly who is the best band at this competition. It's a job with a heavy burden, and it's a job that we don't take carelessly; we are, to put it simple, looking for excellence in performance. Maybe that's this band, right here, a band that can perform with excellence. Maybe this is the best band at this national competition. Maybe this band," he looked back down at his card one more time, "the jazz band from Northern Kent High School, is the band that we place that honor upon. Maybe this band is the band that Miles Davis would want to play with." The man smiled, turned to Mr. Undergrove to shake his hand, and rejoined the other judges in the audience.

Mr. Undergrove opened the envelope. "Same thing as before: ten minutes to prepare, then we play." He reached into the envelope and quickly passed out the sheet music. Our eyes grew wide. Imagine us, just being mystified by our luck.

"Stella By Starlight," someone whispered.

"Well, band, let's take a look at this," Mr. Undergrove said in his teacher voice. You know that voice that a teacher does when they want to sound all business-like? That voice. Like earlier, he guided us through the music, line by line, going along like it was the first time we had seen 'Stella'. Solos were assigned, notes to pay attention to were pointed out, and cues were discussed.

And then we played.

But it wasn't a good play. It was like, oh, well, we played it. Confused, right?

I remember back in 5th grade when Stephen and I would be playing soccer on Saturday mornings. Our team would win and I'd be like 'Yeah, man', but my dad, man, my dad would tell me that I could do better and that I needed to hustle and play better defense and watch out for the long range kicks and stuff, and I'd be sitting there like, 'but we won?' That's how we kinda felt after our 'Stella' performance.

"Crap, man," I said, as we exited the theater. Nobody said anything, not like our earlier rounds. That bedazzle wasn't in our step like it had earlier. No zing. Our eyes were wide and shaken as we put our instruments into our cases and shuffled up the steps leading away from the theater. Mr. Undergrove wasn't smiling; he just had a grim look on his face, like someone had just stole his new bike.

We reached the main lobby of the competition; it was riddled with bands, swarms and swarms of kids all sitting around, all with the same wide-eyed stressed-out look on their faces like ours. It had been a long day, not just for us, but for everyone here. Each band had undergone the same performances we had, just in various orders. I'm sure some kids had experienced the joy we felt after some of their performances, and I know some of the bands probably felt the way we were feeling at the moment: like their neck was resting on a chopping block. Hundreds and hundreds of teenagers, all feeling like their necks were resting on a chopping block, waiting for either the exultation of victory in surviving to compete again tomorrow or losing their head to the cold steel of an ax. Geez.

"What time will we find out?" Kevin asked. "Like, if we get to come back tomorrow, or if, you know, we don't."

Mr. Undergrove checked his watch, sighed, and then replied, "It'll be a while. There's still bands competing in their respective performances. After dinner I'm sure." Mr. Undergrove then covered his face with his hands, and then dragged them downward, pulling the skin on his face down in a way that made him look like a zombie. "Oh wowzers," he mumbled.

"Look, Mr. Undergrove," I said, "when we were in there, in that last performance, I'm not sure what happened, but-"

Veronica cut me off. "I screwed up." She pulled her hands up to her mouth, a look of panic in her eyes. "I screwed up. I screwed up. I played the wrong chord at the chorus, and then I panicked and worried I was going to do it again, then I did it again. It's my fault." Her face grew red and her eyes became wet. "I'm so....I'm so...." her voice choked and tears burst out. Kevin wrapped his arms around her in a hug. "I'm sorry. I'm sorry." She buried her face into Kevin's shirt.

"I played a wrong note too," Stephen said. "Twice. I also panicked. Stupid..." His voice drifted off. "Went from nailing notes to fumbling notes."

Nobody talked. Nobody wanted to talk. We were all speechless, wondering if we had made mistakes or if we should admit our mistakes or keep them silent.

Mr. Undergrove sighed. "No, it wasn't our best performance, but it doesn't take away from what we did earlier today. We performed excellently earlier today. That may be enough to save us." He rubbed his hands through his hair. "We'll be ok. Maybe." Veronica had left Kevin's embrace and was now leaning on my shoulder, wiping tears out of her eyes. "Veronica, Stephen," Mr. Undergrove said, "you two may have made some goofs, but that's what life is about: making goofs and finding a way to build on those goofs." Mr. Undergrove then reached his arms out and hugged both Stephen and Veronica at the same time, and like really hugged them, like he loved them, like they were his own kids. He hugged them like they mattered more than any Miles Davis song in a national competition could ever matter. As we stood there, watching this moment, something magical happened: Kevin joined the hug, and then David, and then Brooks, and then the rest of us, even Veronica's mom. All of us just standing there, just some little jazz band from just some little town, all hugging in a big group hug in the lobby of some fancy theater building in New York City.

The moment lasted for more than a moment. It lingered, felt real, like this was us, a family of kids that loved their leader and loved their bandmates and loved playing jazz together. Jazz. Kids aren't supposed to like jazz. Jazz is for old people, not teenagers. Jazz music is for grandparents. But we loved it because it mattered to us. It mattered. It brought us all the way from King's Hollow to Northern Kent to New York City.

We ate dinner in the conference center. It was hamburgers, but they didn't have taste. Nothing had a taste. Looking around the center and all the other kids, I think the collective nervousness of the competition was ruining the meal for everyone. Stephen leaned over to me. "It's like the last supper up in here. How many bands are going home?"

"Mr. Undergrove said 35 were going home tonight and another 35 tomorrow. Then the remaining bands battle it out for the title on the last day."

Stephen put his elbows up on the table, took a bite out of his hamburger, and nonchalantly replied, "Well, I think we can all agree we're not going to be here on the fourth day, so we can go ahead with our plan of not bringing home the trophy."

"That's brutally honest."

Stephen shrugged his shoulders and then grinned. "My mom says my brutal honesty will one day either take me places or get me fired."

After dinner, the main lobby of the building housing the competition was littered with teenage bodies, as was the conference center and the outside areas of both buildings. Kids just waiting for news from the judges that would either be great or, well, not great. Outside, the moon cut through the lights of the city and seemed to bounce along the wide sidewalks. The leftover winter winds seemed to collaborate with the warm spring air to make a chill that hugged our bodies. Veronica stared off into the big city sky, her arms crossed into each other. "You ok?" I asked.

Veronica closed her eyes, hung her head, and took a deep breath. "I feel like crap. For you guys. For me. Just, crap." She placed a hand on her forehead. "This is not what I thought jazz band was going to be like, all this pressure. You guys make it look so easy. When you guys play, it's just....just....I don't know? Natural? And me? I'm just so...so..."

"Talented?" I replied. Veronica rolled her eyes. "Since you joined us, the band has been able to step up our melody game. Having a piano player that knows what they're doing is part of the reason why we sound so awesome. You know that, right?"

Veronica looked down at her feet. "You're just being nice."

I shook my head. "If Mr. Undergrove has taught us anything, it's that all of us, every single member of the band, matters. The trombones, the trumpets, the piano, everyone. We're individuals, but we play as one. And that means we experience success or failure as one."

Veronica kept her eyes down at her feet, arms still crossed. After an awkward moment of silence, she lifted her head. "I wanted to be a part of this band because I wanted to be a part of something bigger than me. Watching you guys play at the Christmas tree lighting was just so freakin' mesmerizing and incredible that I thought, well, when you told me that you were going to come here to New York City, I was just like, I want to be a part of that. I wanted to be a part of something that I'd be proud to tell people about."

I nodded and then looked down at my feet as well.

"Why didn't you ever call me?" she asked. I looked up; Veronica's eyes peered into mine.

"What?"

"Why didn't you ever call me? After Stephen's party? I gave you my number; I actually wrote it on your freakin' arm. Not once did you even try. Not once. Why?"

"I.....I....." I was tongue-tied. I had no answer.

Her eyes burned into mine. "I liked you. I really liked you." Her eyes narrowed with focus. "Like, I went home that night from Stephen's party and I couldn't sleep. That's what girls do when they like somebody: they think about them and who they are and all the reasons why they like that person. And that night, I did that. I had the butterflies in my stomach and everything. And then I waited for you to call. And I waited. And I waited." I could hear the emotion rising in her voice. "And nothing. Nothing at all. You could have called. You could have picked up the phone and said 'Hey Veronica, we can be friends.' But you didn't." She stopped, took a gulp of air, and added, "You were a jerk. You may not be a jerk right now, but you were a jerk to me then, and you deserve to know that. That's not how you treat people. I hope you realize that."

My mouth was dropped open, partly in shock, and partly because I felt like someone had just punched me in the stomach.

"And it's taking me months to have the courage to say that," Veronica continued. "To say that to your face. And not only do you not ever call me, but then I have to sit at a piano in a jazz band, whether it's at rehearsals or at a gig and look at this guy that I liked and he never bothered to call me." She took in a deep breath, put her hands up to her head and rubbed her hands through her hair. "And now, we're here," she looked around her at the city lights gazing down overhead, "we're here in New York City, the center of the world, and now you know how I've felt all this time, and now we're probably going to be sent home from this Miles Davis thing after all our hard work because of me. So, yeah, tonight has just sucked." Veronica crossed her arms back, shivered, and took in another deep breath.

"I....I...," I repeated. I was still tongue-tied.

"Don't," Veronica said. "There's nothing you can say. Not now. I don't need to hear it, but you needed to know how I feel."

Stephen came bustling out of the theater. "Hey! Results are starting to come in. Undergrove received an envelope, but he's not opening it until we're all together."

Veronica rushed past us into the theater without saying a word. Stephen looked at me confused. "She ok? She looks mad? And you? You look like someone kicked you in the nards?"

"We're fine.....I'm fine....whatever, just come on. Let's go in."

"Ok, boss, whatever you say," Stephen said. We rushed into the lobby to locate the rest of the band. Mr. Undergrove stood in the center of us, his hands trembling a little as he held an envelope with NORTHERN KENT JAZZ BAND printed across the front.

"Whatever this says, just know that I love you, I'm proud of you, and I believe in you." Around us we heard cheers of bands that were finding out that they were staying another day; we also began to notice the disappointment surfacing from bands that were receiving news that they were done at the competition.

"Skip the pleasantries, man," Stephen blurted out. "We love you too! Now, the results, what do they say?" Mr. Undergrove nodded, opened the envelope, pulled out several papers, and we all watched his eyes as they moved back and forth across the page as he quickly read the statement on our fate. The color in his face began to drain.

"Guys...." The words seemed to struggle to leave his throat.

"What? What's it say?" someone asked.

Mr. Undergrove sighed. Not like the kind of sigh like when you're disappointed in someone, like when your parents are mad at you, or the kind of sigh you let out when you're having a bad day, but the kind of sigh like you've just received terrible news and you don't know how to process or deal with it.

Mr. Undergrove looked down at the papers again and then lifted his head to look at us. You could tell he was trying to put on a poker face for us and mask his emotions, but you could see the sadness in his eyes, and that's when we knew, we all just knew instantaneously without him saying a word what the papers inside the envelope stated.

His eyes darted back down to the judges' envelope and then back up to us. "We have been eliminated from the competition."

There was a stunned silence.

"I stand by what I've always told all of you: I am proud of you, and I believe in you.

We stood in a group, an iron curtain of quietness holding us captive, as we listened to other bands rejoice in their success of moving on to the next day. Veronica covered her face with her hands and began to cry. All of us had glazed looks in our eyes, a mixture of exhaustion and defeat.

"C'mon, guys," Mr. Undergrove finally said. "Let's grab our stuff and go load the bus."

MAY - 8TH GRADE

It was a few minutes after 8:00 in the morning; the King's Hollow front office buzzed with a sense of routine that probably happens every morning at every middle school in America: kids checking in late, secretaries reading the announcements over the loudspeaker system, and parents calling to ask questions about lunch menus, sports team early departures, or to complain about a teacher assigning too much homework. And then there are the kids that are sitting on the benches and the chairs outside of the principal's office. It happens all the time; a kid will do something stupid near the end of the day and either the teacher didn't have time to file the discipline referral or the principal didn't have time to deal with it. The result: kids get flagged as they walk into school to report to the front office. I was fresh off my fight with Gabe the day before, so I was told to report to the office first thing in the morning by Mr. Undergrove.

Mr. Undergrove had to plead with the Snowfield Mall security to let me go while Trenton's band director had to do the same for Gabe. In order to release us, assurances were made that: 1) both schools were departing the mall immediately, and 2) both schools would not ever return to the mall's property. Walking back to the bus, Mr. Undergrove didn't say much; he glared at me with a sense of unspoken rage. I struggled to keep up with his brisk, angry pace while holding ice on my new black eye. No, not my old black eye. My new black eye. That's right; I now had not one black eye, but two. If I was a pirate, I'd be Captain Blackeye. Mad props to Gabe, Lauren's, well, whatever he is: boyfriend, ex-boyfriend, body guard? I don't know. He's the one that gave this thing to me.

We loaded the bus; Mr. Undergrove instructed everyone to sit down and gave the thumbs up to the bus driver for us to depart. I didn't have to look up to sense all the eyes on the bus were staring at me. I just knew, ya know?

Kimberly leaned over from across the aisle. "You ok?"

"Yeah," I croaked out.

"Who was that girl that you were holding hands with? She was with you and Stephen and some other girls in the food court and throughout the mall?"

The ice was beginning to burn my eyelid, my forehead, and my hand. I could feel my heart beating in my ribs, and my head was throbbing from the public thrashing I had received at the hands of Gabe.

"Mitchell?"

My front pocket. I removed the ice pack from my head and pulled the note from my shirt pocket. My hands trembled as I unfolded it, parts of the note stained red with either my blood or Gabe's. It read: 'Don't forget how great of a guy you are. I hope to see you soon. 555-4255'.

"Mitchell, are you ok?"

I was back on the bus. Kimberly was looking at me, trying to connect my eyes with her. "That girl, did she get that guy to beat you up? Is that what happened?" I crumbled the note, shoved it into my pants pocket, and placed the ice back on my head.

"I don't know her," I said.

"But...but you were holding hands with her. I saw you. How can you not know her?" Kimberly asked.

"Hey, if my client says he didn't know her, he didn't know her, ya hear me?" Stephen blurted out from the other side of me. "And unless you're charging my client with a crime, then all questions can be directed towards me, his lawyer. Are we clear here?"

Kimberly stared at both of us wide-eyed, and then shifted her body back towards the front of the bus, rolling her eyes in the process. "Geez, you two are just weird."

"Well, that's for the court to decide and not you." Stephen nudged my shoulder and then said to me, "I got your back; don't worry."

But with the memory of Lauren haunting my mind and the reminder of Gabe's fists haunting the soreness of my body, I sat in silence all the way back to King's Hollow.

We arrived back at school, but the rest of the day seemed to pass by in a blur. Mr. Undergrove called my parents, my parents came to get me, my parents talked to Mr. Undergrove , my parents tried talking to me, I got mad and told my parents that I didn't want to talk about it, yada yada yada. After sitting through dinner, which I didn't eat a bite of, my parents excused me to my room; all I wanted to do was wallow in my own pity from the comfort of my own bed. But then, the phone rang.

"Mitchell! The phone is for you!" my mom yelled from downstairs. "It's your teacher!"

My teacher?

I picked up the phone. "Hello?"

"Mitchell, it's Mr. Undergrove. How are you feeling?"

"I'm...I'm.....honestly, everything hurts, but it's nothing I haven't lived through before."

"Crap, you're right," Mr. Undergrove hesitated. "You've got a history of....well....yeah."

"Yeah," I agreed. "Look, about today-"

Mr. Undergrove cut me off. "Today was a long day. As a band, we performed amazing, we earned high marks, and nothing can change that." He cleared his throat, and let the silence hang for a moment. "Look, I'll be honest with you: I had to report the incident to Mr. Cooper. I didn't have a choice. I can't pick and choose who I file a discipline referral on, so I did what was required of me as a teacher. He wants you to report to his office first thing in the morning."

"Yeah," I said, feeling awkwardly accepted yet defeated, "I figured that was bound to happen."

Mr. Undergrove sat on the other end of the line, letting the silence between us be filled with the sound of his breathing. "Tell me about this girl."

"What?"

"The girl. Tell me about her."

"What....girl?" How did he know?

"Don't play dumb. Stephen told me everything."

Dang it.

"Everything?" I asked.

"Maybe."

I sighed. Why was Stephen telling Mr. Undergrove everything about today? "Lauren. Her name was Lauren. We met at the competition."

"And she didn't tell you she had a boyfriend?"

"Well," I hesitated. "I'm not sure if he was her boyfriend."

"Mitchell, trust me, no man goes ballistic and beats up another guy unless there is a female involved," Mr. Undergrove said.

I didn't mention the whole women's bathroom incident; some things are best left unsaid.

"Girls can be mysterious creatures," Mr. Undergrove continued. "I'll never forget my first girlfriend because she dumped me in the middle of the 6th grade school dance and then started going out with some soccer player like ten minutes later. It was humiliating because everyone at the dance knew that she dumped me."

"Why'd she dump you?" I asked.

Mr. Undergrove let out a deep sigh. "I had never danced with a girl before, so when we went to the 6th grade dance together, she expected me to dance with her, and when I didn't, she dumped me. All because I was too scared to try something new."

"Oh, man," I replied, "that sucks."

"Yeah, it sucked bad. And it only happened because I refused to take a risk. Life is about risks. Heck, music is about taking risks. Look at what we did today! Our band saw a form of success we have never experienced before because we took a risk and entered that competition. That's something to be proud of."

"It also led to me getting beat up," I added.

The other end of the phone went quiet. After a moment, Mr. Undergrove spoke up. "Did you like her? This Lauren girl, did you like her?"

"Yes, sir," I answered, "I did."

"Then you took a risk. Granted, it didn't end the way you wanted, you took a risk, and that's something to be proud of."

"You're proud of me? I embarrassed you and the whole band today."

Mr. Undergrove cleared his throat. "Your actions this afternoon, to someone looking in from the outside, were not what I would want associated with the King's Hollow band program. But after discussing the situation with Stephen, and then again right now with you, I see it from a different perspective." He then took in another deep breath. "You fought for something that you believed in. I think that's an honorable thing to do."

Honorable thing to do? After the day I've lived through, Mr. Undergrove was on the phone saying that fighting my crush's meathead ex-boyfriend in the parking lot of a mall was an honorable thing to do? Was I in an episode of *The Twilight Zone*?

"Thanks, Mr. Undergrove, I appreciate it. I'm sorry for causing you grief or stress today. I never intended to hurt anyone-"

Mr. Undergrove cut me off again. "You don't need to apologize to me anymore. I've told you so many times before, but don't forget that I'm always proud of you, and I always believe in you." I couldn't help but smile behind my phone; I got the feeling that Mr. Undergrove was smiling as well.

"Hey, Mr. Undergrove, can I ask you something?"

"Sure. Go ahead."

"What exactly did Stephen tell you?"

Mr. Undergrove hesitated. "He told me enough. Said you were just in the wrong place at the wrong time. Said this Lauren girl pulled you into her crap with her ex-boyfriend. He vouched for you, saying you would never start anything like this on your own. I believe him. Stephen's a good guy."

Not quite the whole truth or even the actual story, but Stephen was obviously trying to cover for me. I grinned. "Yes, sir, Stephen is a good guy. He's a great friend."

"Oh, and he said something weird. What was it? Something about a Wolfman or something weird like that. I assume that means something to you? Like a joke between you two or something? I don't know."

My grin turned into a full blown smile. "Yes, sir, it's just an inside joke. Nothing crazy."

"Alright then. Well, don't forget that you're to report to Mr. Cooper first thing in the morning."

"Yes, sir."

"And, Mitchell?

"Yes, sir?"

"I'm incredibly sorry about today. I mean that. I'm sure there's more to the story than what Stephen offered, but I was a teenager once too, and I know how much of a roller coaster these years can be. And I haven't forgotten what it's like to have a crush on someone, and I've never forgotten how bad a broken heart feels. So just remember that, ok?"

"Yes, sir, I will."

It was 8:05 AM when Mr. Cooper walked into the King's Hollow main office fresh from drop-off duty at the front door of the school. He placed his two way radio on the front desk, put his hands on his hips, and hesitated briefly as he eyed the collection of students that shared the benches outside of his office with me, mainly 6th graders that had started a food fight in the home economics class as school got out the day before. "Ok, ok, I'm going to deal with all of you here momentarily, but let me step inside to make a phone call or two before we get down to business," Mr. Cooper said before entering his office. "No one cause any trouble for at least a minute or two," he added before pulling the door shut behind him.

The 6th graders all eyed me with both fear and respect. I sat there, legs spread out on the bench, one eye black (although fading) from being jumped in the locker room, the other eye freshly black from my tangle with Gabe in the Snowfield parking lot. I had cut on my forehead, a scrape on my chin, and yellow and green discoloration on the bridge of my nose. Various gashes and bruises decorated my arm like random Christmas tree ornaments. I leaned forward and put my forearms on my knees. "You all the food fight kids?" I asked. The 6th graders all nodded their heads in unison, a few bobbing with visual fear in their eyes for it was clearly their first visit to the principal's office, and the rest sat with seasoned confidence for they were repeat offenders when it came to the King's Hollow discipline process.

"Is it true about you," one of the veteran offenders asked, "that you're the dude that got beat up with a football helmet in the locker room a few weeks back?"

"What do you think?" I asked back.

The boy smirked. "I think you look like crap."

"Yeah, well, you can't win over all the critics." I sat up straight and leaned back into the bench, folding my arms across my chest.

"That must have been some beating you got," the boy added, pointing to my face.

"Oh, those doozies," Stephen's voice said, "are not from the locker room incident. The majority of the trophies on my friend here are from yesterday's adventure." The 6th graders heads' all turned as Stephen maneuvered his way by the office benches and sat down beside me. "You guys are going to get exclusive dibs on some juicy news. Mitchell here went toe-for-toe with a 200 lbs. high school linebacker in a fight in a mall parking lot yesterday afternoon. I don't think any of you are qualified to tell my client that his looks are less than favorable." Stephen patted me on the back and winked.

The door to Mr. Cooper's door swung back open; he stepped out and said, "Alright, people, some of you were involved in a food fight yesterday afternoon in Mrs. Campbell's class, correct?" The 6th graders all looked up and nodded with a little hesitation; even the veterans nodded with hesitation. "Good, since we're all in agreement, and it looks like all of you can't fit into my office, I'm going to take half of you now, and then the other half a few minutes later." Mr. Cooper pointed at four of the boys and signaled for them to file into his office first. "The rest of you can think about why you're here for a few more minutes."

"What are you doing?" I whispered to Stephen.

"You think I'm going to let my best client walk into an important meeting without representation? That's bananas."

"Stephen, this isn't some joke. This is serious stuff. Cooper is going to suspend me or expel me or something."

"Then you shouldn't be alone when that happens," Stephen said back. He then looked over at one of the 6th graders still sitting near us and said, "Did you fart? It sounded like you farted? Was that you? Man, that was loud." The 6th grader, eyes wide, quickly got up and moved to a different bench. Stephen turned back towards me. "We're going in there together. Leave no man behind, that kinda thing."

"Dude, you're not going in there!" I said, probably a little louder than I should have.

The office secretary lifted her head, pulled the phone away from her ear, covered the phone's mouthpiece, and shot us an evil stare. "I believe Mr. Cooper instructed all of you to be quiet," she snapped. The door to Mr. Cooper's office swung open and the four 6th graders filed out; Mr. Cooper motioned for the rest of the 6th grade food fighters to enter and then the door shut back.

"You got to go back to class," I whispered. "You have to. What's going to be your reason for being with me when you go into Cooper's office? If you try to pull this crazy 'client' crap, he's going to suspend you too."

"Let me worry about that then," Stephen responded

"This is bonkers! You can't-"

The office secretary cut me off. "Excuse me! I believe I've instructed you to shut your mouth, young man!" Her eyes seemed to glare red.

"Yes, ma'am," I said and put my eyes back down to the floor.

"As your state-appointed attorney, I advise you to trust me," Stephen whispered.

I shook my head back and forth but, as instructed, kept my mouth shut. When I got into Cooper's office, I'd explain Stephen had nothing to do with my fight with Gabe. Stephen will be mad, but he didn't need to go down with me.

Mr. Cooper's door swung back open; the remaining 6th graders emerged with all of their heads hung low, like Mr. Cooper had collectively popped all of their metaphorical confidence balloons with a needle. Mr. Cooper watched with his hands on his hips as they each 6th grader left the office; he turned to the office and secretary and said, "Call Officer Wrenn over the radio and make sure every single one of those boys report to in-school suspension. There's eight of them total." He spun around to rest his eyes on Stephen and me. "Ah, yes, Mr. Mitchell. You look terrible. Let's talk in my office. Mr. Stephen, you too." We rose from the bench, my eyes nervously meeting Stephen's calm demeanor.

Mr. Cooper instructed us to sit down in two of his office chairs as he sat down on the edge of his desk right in front of us. "Alright guys, everyone ok from yesterday?"

I nodded yes, my eyes embarrassingly glued to the floor. This was my third visit to Mr. Cooper's office this school year; he probably thought a whole lot less of me than ever before. Category: bad kid.

"Jesus, Mitchell, you look like you went a few rounds with Rocky," Mr. Cooper said as he leaned in closer to get a good look at my newly-minted black eye. "It hurt?"

I nodded. "Yes, sir."

"Sore?"

"Yes, sir."

"So," Mr. Cooper said, sitting back up and crossing his arms across his chest, "Mr. Undergrove called me at home last night to explain what happened to the two of you yesterday afternoon after the band competition."

"Sir," I spoke up, "about that, it's that-"

Mr. Cooper raised his hand, cutting me off. "No need to try to explain. Mr. Undergrove told me the whole story."

"He did?" I asked.

"I understand there was a tussle in the mall parking lot when you all stopped for lunch with some high school bullies from another school. Some big guys looking to flex their muscles on some middle schoolers. That true?"

I hesitated. I mean, it was true, but it wasn't the whole story. "Well, sir, that's-"

"Yes, sir, that's about right," Stephen responded, cutting me off.

"From what Mr. Undergrove told me, Mitchell, is that you're somewhat of a hero, protecting your buddy Stephen here. You held off this big guy so Stephen could run and get help?"

Stephen started speaking before I could. "I'm not sure if 'hero' sums up this guy's bravery, but it's as close to his actions as we could possibly get." He looked at me, a continued confidence glowing in Stephen's eyes.

"Mitchell, it seems like you've had a string of bad luck this year." Mr. Cooper rose from where he was sitting on his desk and walked around it to sit in his chair behind it. He leaned back and put his hands behind his head. "Mr. Undergrove mentioned something particular, something specific that I cannot really ignore in this matter."

I gulped. Oh boy.

Mr. Cooper took a deep breath and then leaned back forward onto his desk. "Mr. Undergrove mentioned this altercation may have begun over a girl. That true too?"

Stephen sat forward like he was about to say something but I beat him to it. "There was a girl, yes, sir. But-"

Mr. Cooper raised his hand up off his desk to stop me. "No need to explain. I've heard my fair share of fight stories that all started over a guy or a girl. Look, it's not something I would consider making it a habit of. If a girl is a reason to get into an altercation with another person, that girl is probably always going to bring trouble to the table."

I nodded, lowered my head, and then, against my better judgement, lifted my head and said, "I disagree, sir."

"How's that?"

"I don't think the girl, er, uh, Lauren, was bringing trouble to the table."

"That's the girl's name?" Mr. Cooper asked, "Lauren?"

"Yes, sir. She didn't start the trouble. Her ex-boyfriend did."

"I see." Mr. Cooper leaned back in his chair and put his hands together, almost like he was a supervillain contemplating his next move. "So this Lauren girl, she had nothing to do with the fight?"

"Well, sir, she.....she....." My words had left me.

There was Lauren, melting my heart with her eyes in the auditorium at the band competition. There was Lauren, holding my hand in the mall. And then, there was Lauren, standing in the parking lot of the mall, confusion, anger, and hurt blazing from her eyes as she turns to Gabe and says "He's bothering me. I want him to go away."

"I want him to go away." Her words played over and over in my head as I looked at Mr. Cooper. "I want him to go away." Oh jeez. I felt like my throat was closing in on itself. I opened my mouth, but nothing came out. There she was, turning to Gabe, not saying 'beat this guy up", but totally saying 'beat this guy up".

Mr. Cooper leaned forward at his desk. "Mitchell, relationships can be difficult. They're kind of like cars. There could be an absolutely beautiful car sitting on the car lot that's calling your name. Fresh paint job. Shiny rims. Nice tires. But if there's not a good engine under that hood that you can depend on, then that car is destined to break your heart and leave you sitting on the side of the road, wondering how you got into that mess." After an awkward amount of silence, Mr. Cooper asked, "What kind of car was calling your name yesterday?"

"He's bothering me. I want him to go away." Lauren had figured out that I was the one in the restroom stall during the band competition. Who was really the victim here: me, or Lauren?

"Mitchell, you ok? Don't space out on me quite yet; it's too early in the morning."

I jumped back to being in Mr. Cooper's office, Stephen at my side, both of them staring at me. "Sir, I don't even know how to answer that question."

"Do some soul searching over the next couple of days. I'm sure eventually you'll find the answer. May not be one that you like, but it'll be an answer." Mr. Cooper stood up from his desk. "Well, gentlemen, I think we're done here. Both of you may return to class. No need to keep you any longer, right?"

"You don't want to punish me or anything?" I asked with a layer of shock in my voice.

Mr. Cooper shook his head. "Mitchell, you've had a tough couple of weeks. Let's just get you out of 8th grade. What do you say?"

Stephen patted me on the back, speaking before I had a chance to say anything. "Yes, I think that's a grand idea, you know, being that we don't have but a handful of days left in the school year. Let's take that route."

We rose from our seats, each of us shaking Mr. Cooper's hand and headed for his office door. "Oh, shoot," Mr. Cooper said, reaching back for a note on his desk. "Stephen, can you excuse us for a moment?"

Stephen stared at me in the eyes for a brief second, shrugged his shoulders, and responded, "Yes, sir, no problem," before heading out the door.

Mr. Cooper looked back down on his note that he had picked up and said, "Look, Mitchell, I know I said I'd get to the bottom of you being jumped a few weeks back, but honestly, I'm coming up cold on any lead I get. There's one kid though that kinda gave me bad vibes. Nothing he said or anything, just mainly a gut feeling, but I don't have any evidence to prove he did it. Want to see if you even know the kid. He's in your gym class with you."

I knew who Mr. Cooper was going to say before he even had a chance to say it.

"Kid's name is Max. You have a history with him or anything?"

I thought about my dealings with Max, the way he talked to me in the gym after Coach Brier mispronounced my name for the thousandth time, or how he claimed that he head-butted Coach Brier during a fight a few years back.

"I know him, yes, sir. He's..." I hesitated. He's what? A jerk? A butthole? Gotta watch my words with Mr. Cooper. "He stays in trouble with Coach Brier, I know that much."

Mr. Cooper sat back down at his desk. "Yes, he does. Max is never one to shy away from trouble. Like I said, I have no evidence, just a gut feeling. Stay away from him by all means necessary, do you understand? I can't prove anything, so as far as you and me both know, he had nothing to do with you being jumped." Mr. Cooper then hesitated. "Unless there's something you're not telling me."

Not telling him? There's a lot that I'm not telling him. There's a lot he doesn't know. There's a lot that he doesn't need to know, especially about yesterday, but in his words, 'Let's just get you out of 8th grade'. Nope, I'm not falling down this rabbit hole. My lips are sealed.

"I don't know him like that. I just know he's always in trouble," I said.

Walking out of the front office, I felt a wave of mixed emotions. Yeah, yeah, yeah, I had gotten off without getting any additional punishment from Mr. Cooper (my bruises, bumps, and black eye were enough), but that seemed to largely rest in Undergrove's hands and whatever he told him.

APRIL - 10TH GRADE

The ride back into New Jersey didn't quite have the electricity that it had earlier in the day on the ride in. We were tired, upset, and deflated. Mr. Undergrove's head hung a little lower than normal; Stephen's perky side seemed to have vanished in the dark shadows of the bus. The whole band, all of us, sat in the darkness, sulking in shock. We knew going in that we were amongst some tough competition, and we knew we would have to be on our 'A' game, but I don't think any of us ever considered the possibility that we could be one of the bands cut after the first round.

"I never liked Miles Davis that much anyways," Stephen said, the lights of Manhattan passing behind us as we left the city limits.

"Miles Davis is dead, dude," Brooks said. "He had nothing to do with today."

"All the more reason not to like him. Had he heard us, he would have kept us in his stupid competition," Stephen scowled.

No one argued with him. No one had reason to argue with him. Deep down, we all agreed with Stephen, whether Miles Davis was alive or not.

When we got back to the hotel, Mr. Undergrove gathered us in the lobby. He looked defeated, not like we had ever seen him look before; his hands sunk into his pockets, his eyes dark with mental exhaustion, his demeanor like that of not of our leader, but someone trying to hide in the shadows.

"Tonight was..." Mr. Undergrove's voice lingered. "Tonight was....well, it kinda sucked. Today didn't suck. Today was inspiring. Today was fantastic. You all played the best I've ever heard you play.

But tonight, those results," Mr. Undergrove lingered again as he searched for the right words, "it was like playing a basketball game, and we had been winning that basketball game from the start of the first quarter all the way to the final seconds of the fourth quarter, but in the final second of the game, the other team made a three pointer to win the game by one. We know we dominated the entire game, but somehow we lost. We can be mad at the other team for winning, and we can be mad at ourselves for losing, but we still played an awesome game of basketball. Does that make sense?"

"Isn't that similar to the saying that's like 'Don't hate the player; hate the game'?" Stephen asked.

Mr. Undergrove nodded. "Yeah, Stephen, I guess it is. I don't know if that makes it feel any better, but I suppose that's one way to look at it."

"So, like, what happens now?" I asked.

Mr. Undergrove looked down at his shoes, took in a deep breath, and then looked back up at us. "We came to New York not knowing when our opportunity at the competition would end, but, to be honest, I've had a secret plan of what our last day in New York would look like that I've managed to keep from all of you all this time. We're not going home tomorrow. We're here, and we're going to spend our last day enjoying what this city has to offer."

"Wait, what?" someone blurted out.

"Get some sleep tonight," Mr. Undergrove said, "some serious sleep. No tears about today. Today was great. Nothing can take away how great today was; remember that. Today, we went into that competition and put our heart and soul out there, and just because some judges didn't like our heart and soul doesn't mean it's not there. It's within us, it binds us and gives us purpose. You all collectively brought that to this band, not me. Tomorrow, we celebrate, for tomorrow is a new day, a new chance at life, another pitch from the mound, another shot at immortality." Mr. Undergrove's eyes seemed to connect with every single one of us all at the same time. "Tomorrow awaits, and tomorrow isn't going to be about making us better musicians, or solos, or rhythm, but about us: the Northern Kent Jazz Band. Tomorrow will be a celebration of what makes us great, the adventure of a lifetime."

MAY - 8TH GRADE

"Does it hurt?" Brent asked during math class. "It looks like it hurts. It hurts, right? I mean, it's gotta hurt."

"I'm gonna hurt you if you don't leave me alone or get us in trouble with Mrs. Watson again," I snarked back at Brent under my breath.

"Dude, do you know how popular you are right now? Everyone, literally everyone is talking about you. The kid with the two black eyes. Legendary, man."

"Mr. Brent," Mrs. Watson called out, "is there an issue over there?"

"No, ma'am," Brent said back, "just letting my buddy Mitchell here give me some guidance on how to solve this math problem that I'm stumped on."

"Is that true, Mr. Mitchell?" Mrs. Watson asked, her eyes glaring at me, most likely staring at my black eyes.

"Yes, ma'am" I nodded, trying to keep my eyes to the floor. How many more lies was I going to tell?

"You do realize that like every girl in this school would probably go out with you right now just based on the fact that you've proven how tough you are?"

"Getting your ass handed to you not once but twice doesn't make someone tough," I said back, hoping Brent would notice me rolling my eyes.

"Who cares if you got your ass handed to you during the fight if you won the fight? You've got the sympathy votes from all the girls and the rampage votes from the guys. You put King's Hollow on the map, man!"

"Says who?"

Brent began to throw his hands up into the air but stopped himself when he realized it would just draw more attention from Mrs. Watson, which was the last thing he wanted. "Were you not there yesterday?" Brent rasped under his breath, trying not to be loud, but at the same time, trying to be loud. "Do you not remember taking everything that Macho Man wannabe threw at you and then walking away from the fight victorious? Maybe he punched you in the head too many times. Maybe you have a concussion or something that wiped your memory."

Brent had grabbed my interest. "People are talking about yesterday a lot?" I asked.

Brent raised his hand to slap his desk out of excitement, but again caught himself midair before his hand hit to avoid more unwanted attention from the teacher. "Man, are they ever! Nobody wanted to say anything to you yesterday, but good golly, it was all the fuss. I was going to call you last night, but I figured you were grounded from the phone, ya know, being that you got into a fight on a field trip and all."

Mrs. Watson walked by our desks, supervising our progress. Satisfied to see that I was actually helping Brent with some of the assigned problems, and that he seemed to be receptive to my help, she carried on to the next set of students. "So, the fight," Brent said, "is it true that the girl you met at the competition made you fight her ex-boyfriend for permission to date her, kinda like a dowry or something like that?"

I put my pencil down on my desk and rolled my eyes again, really hoping Brent would notice. “No, it’s nothing like that.”

“What was it like then?” I thought for a moment. How could I explain the fight without mentioning the whole girls’ restroom story? Brent put his eyes back on his paper as Mrs. Watson came back around the classroom. “Seems to me like that’s exactly what it was,” Brent said under his breath, loud enough for me to hear.

I didn’t respond. Sometimes there’s just no reason to respond.

APRIL - 10TH GRADE

Our alarms went off at 6:45 AM. The excitement of playing in the National Miles Davis Youth Jazz Competition was now gone, but had been replaced by a different excitement: the excitement of New York City. We congregated in the lobby of our hotel, ravishly consuming the cereals and bagels offered in the continental breakfast area. Mr. Undergrove stood there, clipboard in hand, checking our names off as he saw us, occasionally sipping a cup of coffee, reminding us to eat enough to give us the energy to get to lunch. "Also, make sure you bring your wallets and whatever you need for the day," Mr. Undergrove said. "We won't be back until late tonight."

"Where are we going? What are we doing?" we asked.

Mr. Undergrove just grinned. "It's like I said last night: the adventure of a lifetime, and we're going to start that adventure by giving our bus driver the day off while we ride the subway."

The thrill of loading the subway was still with us as we headed to the city. We were being revisited by the same energy from a few days earlier; everyone's eyes a little wider than normal with a bit of fear and excitement all mixed together, including Mr. Undergrove 's. "Stick together at all costs, just like we have so far," Mr. Undergrove said to us on the train. "Pay attention to me, and pay attention to your band mates."

The train came to a stop and we flooded off along with gobs of other travelers, zigzagging through the crowd, moving together as we climbed stairwell to stairwell until we again resurfaced at street level and began to walk the sidewalks. A block this way, a block over, two more blocks this way, another block over. Mr. Undergrove stopped, read a street sign, asked a bystander a question, and then we resumed moving, our walking set at a brisk pace, our arms swinging collectively, our eyes up and around as we took in the streets and the skyline.

The buildings cleared out as we arrived at our destination: a port with various ferry boats. Mr. Undergrove pulled a wad of tickets from his book bag on his back, made sure each and every one of us received a ticket, and then directed us to follow him as we boarded one of the ferry boats, taking the stairs within that took us to the seating area at the top of the outside the boat. "Is this taking us to somewhere exotic?" Stephen asked.

"No, nothing exotic," Mr. Undergrove replied.

"Good," Stephen said, "I completely forgot to bring my bathing suit or shave my legs."

The ferry left the harbor, giving us a scenic view of the Manhattan skyline. The buildings loomed over us, like giants standing beside each other in a crowd, waiting for a concert to begin. The colors of the different types of glass and steel reflected in the sun, making the city look like a living, breathing kaleidoscope of all the ideas and imagination in the world placed together like puzzle pieces. Stephen leaned in close as we gazed at the city from the boat; "I've never felt smaller," he said.

We coasted along the various port areas. We saw buildings, neighborhoods, and businesses that we had seen and heard about in the movies and television shows our whole lives, but now we were seeing them actually exist in front of us. They had always been there all along in our subconsciousness; our eyes widened as these images emerged as reality.

Mr. Undergrove grabbed our attention and began pointing at the other side of the ship. "Whoa," I said out loud, "look at that!"

Standing there, reaching her arm into the bright morning sky, torch in hand, was the Statue of Liberty. "Before you ask, Stephen," Mr. Undergrove said, "no, Lady Liberty does not move like she did in *Ghostbuster II*, so save your breath."

"Mr. Undergrove, I'm incredibly honored and humbled that you thought to answer my question before I even got the chance to ask," Stephen said back.

The boat took us around the rest of the city's coastline before eventually docking. We followed Mr. Undergrove with eagerness off the boat and back onto the sidewalks of the city.

That eagerness never left us. It stayed with us as we crossed streets amongst traffic, loaded and unloaded subway trains, entered historical churches, strolled through areas of Central Park, waltzed through quiet art and historical museums, meandered through giant libraries, gazed at skyline creations looming on the horizon, listened to street corner musicians, ducked in and out of crowds, and feasted on food carts and vendors throughout the city.

"What's this place called again?" I asked Veronica.

"Grand Central Station," she said back.

"This was in *Home Alone 2*, right?" I asked.

Veronica looked at me all strange like. "Beats me. I guess."

I turned to Stephen. "This place was in *Home Alone 2*, right?"

Stephen mimicked Veronica's look from seconds earlier. "This place? Grand Central? No way."

"Well I've seen it somewhere before," I said, looking around the ballroom that surrounded us. "Are you sure it's not *Home Alone 2*?"

Stephen shook his head, then tapped his forehead with his finger. "Everything movie-related that gets stored in here is accurate. You're thinking of *Superman: The Movie*."

"You guys are odd," Veronica said.

"Odd? Or incredibly adorable?" Stephen asked with a grin on his face.

Veronica looked at Stephen and then at me. "No, just odd."

I looked back at Stephen. "*Superman*? Are you sure it wasn't *Home Alone 2*?"

"Lex Luthor's secret lair was below here, duh."

"Lex Luthor's lair can't be below here because we're in New York City and Lex Luthor lives in Metropolis," I said.

"Lex Luthor is a fictional character," Stephen stated. "He can be anywhere he wants to be."

We boarded the subway late that afternoon, this time riding the D train. "Where are we going now?" we asked, knowing Mr. Undergrove was going to tell us without really telling us.

"The Bronx," he replied, a slight grin resting on his face.

"What's in the Bronx?" I asked.

"You'll see," Mr. Undergrove said.

"What's in the Bronx?" I asked Stephen.

Stephen thought for a moment. "Rappers?"

"I don't think Mr. Undergrove is taking us to a rap concert in the Bronx."

"You're going to feel pretty stupid if he does," Stephen shot back with a grin.

Mr. Undergrove rose to his feet, signaled for all of us to prepare to follow him, and said, "Here we go everyone."

We whisked off the train with the crowds (man, we were getting good at that) and zoomed through the subway station up to the street level.

Our jaws dropped. I mean, they didn't really drop, but they dropped, ya know? Like, we were kinda shocked. I don't know why we say 'our jaws dropped' because that's impossible, right? Anyways, yeah, jaws were dropping.

"We're here," Mr. Undergrove said.

"We're definitely here," someone said.

Before us stood Yankee Stadium. Yeah, THE Yankee Stadium. Sprawling, large, all those words that pretty much mean 'big'.

"Who's up for a little baseball?" Mr. Undergrove asked.

"I don't think 'little' is the right word here," I said.

Have you ever heard that phrase 'sitting in the nosebleed section'? Our seats at the baseball game were definitely in the 'nosebleed' section, like so high up we were practically out of the park. We were in the last row of the stadium up behind center field. If any of us were good at jumping, we could've touched the clouds.

'How did you score these tickets?" Stephen asked Mr. Undergrove as we got comfortable in our seats.

"I made a few phone calls last night. A friend of a friend of a friend type deal."

"Ah," Stephen nodded, "the mafia, huh?"

"Not quite," Mr. Undergrove said with a laugh. "Try the girlfriend of my wife's cousin. She's got a friend that works in the main office here."

Stephen shrugged his shoulders. "Sounds like a total mafia move to me."

"Call it what you want. We're here. Enjoy the game. Not many people will be able to say they attended a Yankees game on a high school field trip." Mr. Undergrove put his sunglasses on and turned his total attention to the diamond on the other end of the field.

The sun was setting in the sky; the lights of the stadium burned brightly, illuminating everything, making it look as bright as day. From our view, the field looked like a miniature set of plastic players come to life, one team fielding the bases while the other frantically tried to get to those bases after each hit.

"I know we're rooting for the Yankees," Stephen said, "but who is the other team?"

"The Cleveland Indians," I answered.

"Cleveland," Stephen said with a smirk.

"What's wrong with Cleveland?" I asked.

"I'm not really sure," Stephen said back, "except it's just a funny name: Cleveland."

Down the aisle, I saw Veronica's mom get out of her seat beside Veronica and disappear towards the concession area. I rose from my seat. "You think about that Cleveland situation for a moment," I said, sliding past Stephen's legs.

"Where are you going," Stephen asked, "and is it Cleveland?"

"Doing some damage control," I said back.

"Damage control?" he asked. "Are we under attack?"

"Just trust me," I said, wiggling past multiple sets of legs, squeezing myself down the aisle until I got to Veronica. "Care if I join you?" I asked.

"My mom was sitting there, but I'm completely ok with her having to sit somewhere else when she comes back."

"That bad?"

Veronica shot a look at me. "Imagine being on a field trip to New York City and your dad gets to go as well because you're the only boy."

I shrugged my shoulders. "My dad beat up my soccer coach once," I said.

"Your dad beat up your soccer coach?" Veronica asked, eyes wide.

"My dad beat up my soccer coach," I repeated, "all because he yelled at me for not being good at soccer."

"Ok, never mind, maybe having your dad would be a good thing."

There was a crack of a bat at home plate; the crowd erupted into cheers as the ball straddled over top of the shortstop's glove, drifting into the outfield. The batter sprinted down the first baseline, circled round the base, took three strides towards 2nd base, and then jumped back to first base. People clapped, music blared over the loudspeakers, and the electronic sign lit up enticing the crowd.

"Can I talk to you about something?" I asked.

Veronica looked at me, rolled her eyes a little, a smile crackling across her face. "Sure."

"Last night was-" I then hesitated, unable to conjure my words of where I was going next.

Veronica cut me off. "I knew you were going to bring up last night." She covered her face with one of her hands. "I knew it! Last night was so embarrassing. I don't want to talk about last night and whatever I said." Veronica looked down at the ground kept her eyes covered.

"Last night was something I had coming."

Veronica lifted her face out of her hands with a look that seemed to want to know more, but also wanted to punch me. "Why's that?" she asked.

"I was a jerk for not calling you at all after Stephen's birthday. A total jerk. You didn't deserve that."

"You're telling me this like I don't already know that."

"Yeah," I nodded, "but maybe it's time you heard it from me." I scratched my chin out of nervousness. "I'm not good at any of this....this relationship stuff. Not good at getting close to girls. I mean, well, I don't know." I scratched my chin again and then the side of my head. "A while back, a few years back actually, I got hurt by a girl, like not physically hurt but like emotionally or something, but kinda physically hurt too."

"I don't follow," Veronica said bluntly.

"Kinda like, well, I liked this one girl, but then like, well, her boyfriend beat me up and I just, kinda, I don't know, just..." my voice trailed off. "I mean, it's complicated. I liked her, she liked me, but then I did something I shouldn't have done, but it wasn't on purpose or anything, it was like an accident, but still I did it and she found out and so her boyfriend or her ex-boyfriend or something like that beat me up, but I guess if you want to get technical I won the fight because I kicked him, well, I kicked him right, well, you know, right in his manhood and he went down." I looked at Veronica, her face blank with what looked like confusion. "That's kinda why I think I have issues. At least I think it's why. I guess."

Veronica sat in silence while I stared down at my hands; after a minute, Veronica broke the silence. "So what you're trying to tell me, and correct me if I'm wrong here, is that you couldn't call me all the way back in December after Stephen's party because some girl's boyfriend beat you up before you ever met me?"

"Ummm...." I couldn't find the words. "I guess, I just don't......I wanted you to know that it wasn't your fault I didn't call you. It was more, like, a personal thing with me."

Veronica looked at me, like really looked at me. I could feel her eyes connecting with mine, and I couldn't blink or look away. I just looked back into her eyes, and then I started to feel uncomfortable because she wasn't looking at me in a good way, but more in a way like she was really angry.

"Bull crap," she said.

"What?"

"You're full of bull crap," Veronica repeated. "Complete bull crap."

Sheesh. I thought I had come down here to smooth things over with Veronica, but it didn't look like I was smoothing anything over. I'm pretty sure I had just made it worse.

"Why am I full of bull crap?"

"Because you just are," Veronica shot back.

"Look," I responded, "I came down here to explain why I never called you, not to be ostracized. I don't think you're being fair."

"I'm not being fair?" Veronica asked loudly. "I'm not being fair? You never called me, and you've got the nerve to say I'm not being fair? Wow!"

"I thought I was trying to apologize!" I snapped back. "Why are you turning this around on me?"

"Because your reason was terrible," Veronica said coldly. "I get that some girl hurt you. I get that. But that was however long ago?"

"Um......" Say 'Two years ago.' Say it. "Uh....." Just say 'Two years ago.' Say something. Anything. "Well......" OH MY GOSH JUST TELL HER FOR CRYING OUT LOUD!

Nothing. I said nothing back.

Veronica rolled her eyes. "And this is a great reason why I really don't want to talk to you right now: you can't even answer a simple question." She turned her body and eyes back to the game, her demeanor becoming cold. The crowd erupted as the runner on first base ran to second. "Please leave. Now isn't the time," she said.

"But," I said; Veronica cut me off.

"Mitchell, just go. You never called. I'm over it. You need to get over it."

Hey guys out there: when a girl gives you her number, call her. Don't wait. Don't try to play it cool. Just call her.

When I moved back down the aisle, Stephen seemed to know my situation without me saying a word. "Strike out?" He asked.

"Struck out. Definitely," I confirmed.

Stephen patted me on the back. "Love hurts, man."

"I'm not in love."

"Dude, we're teenagers; we're always in love. Either falling in love, being in love, or falling out of love. Always. Always in love. Sometimes we know it, and sometimes we can't see it until later on."

"Who died and made you Yoda?" I asked.

Stephen pointed to the side of his head. "I just know things sometimes. Deep meaning stuff."

"Ok," I said, "then why do bad things happen to good people?"

Stephen leaned back in his seat. "Are you implying you're a good person?" And then before I could answer, Stephen added, "Because, let's be honest: you're not."

"What?" I asked. "I'm a good person," I said defensively.

"Dude, you're a teenager. We are all teenagers. Teenagers aren't good people. We're just kids trying to make it to adulthood. That doesn't mean we're good people."

"A teenager can be a good person," I said back.

"You can think you're a good person, but look at this situation you're in: you've got a girl mad at you because you made her feel less than what she is. Would a 'good person' do that?"

Crap. What do I say to that?

"Probably not."

"Yeah, you're not a good person, but neither am I. Or any of us really. Teenagers can't be good people. We're trying to be, but it's just tough. We're learning. We're getting there."

I leaned forward, putting my hands on my head. "When do we get there?" I asked.

"Get where?"

"To the point where we can be 'good people', ya know? To not be so idiotic?"

Stephen patted his knee twice while he thought. "I don't know, man. It's a process. It's different for every person. The 'teenager' phase of life is a good chunk of that journey. One day we'll take all of our experiences and become the kind of person we want to be, or we'll take all of our experiences and become someone completely different."

"Different?" I asked.

"Yeah, different. Not all of us will turn into heroes. Some people are going to fall short."

Stephen?" I asked.

"Yeah?"

"Do you think I'm going to be one of those that fall short? Like, I'm not going to live up to my potential?"

Stephen sat quietly beside me as the crowd erupted again when one of the Yankees' players crossed home plate. Chanting roared through the crowd as people hugged and high-fixed each other. Finally, as the crowd began to return to their seats, Stephen spoke up. "Remember when you got the crap kicked out of you in the locker room a few years back during our time at King's Hollow?"

"Yes, that's kinda hard to forget."

"And then a few weeks later, at that band competition in Snowfield, you got beat up again by the Juggernaut."

"He wasn't the Juggernaut," I said back, "he was a Wolfman."

"That's right," Stephen said, a smile spreading across his face. "Wolfman had nards, just like in *The Monster Squad*. He was after you because of whatsherface, right?"

"Lauren," I said. Man, that name still hurts a little. Not like, 'Oh, I'm in such dramatic metaphorical pain that I cannot say her name without weeping in agony,' but like 'Oh, man, I'm still kinda bitter about that,' type of pain.

"Lauren, right," Stephen said, nodding his head. "I keep forgetting how messed up that was of her to have you fight her ex-boyfriend. That's some stuff straight out of *The Book of Bad Relationships*."

"I didn't have to fight her....." I drifted off because I knew exactly what it looked like. I had heard it enough over the past two years to know no one was going to believe anything different, so I didn't try to correct Stephen. Instead, I rubbed my head with my hands, messing up my hair, and leaned back into my seat. "Yeah, yeah, yeah, go on."

Stephen continued, "My point is this: not once, but twice you were knocked down, physically and metaphorically, on your butt, and not once, but twice, you got back up again. That's not easy, and it's especially not easy when you're in 8th grade. It's really not easy when it happens in front of a whole crowd of people. But, you got back up, even when it was tough. That counts in my book." Stephen leaned toward me. "And look at us now. Look at where we are: New York City! At a Yankees game!" Stephen spread his arms up into the air, seemingly engulfing the atmosphere of the baseball game going on around us into his presence. "We're here with our school's jazz band! Just a bunch of dumb teenagers from who-knows-where Northern Kent High School playing in the Miles Davis Young Intergalactic Jazz Competition for the Gifted!"

"I think you messed the name up," I said.

"Well, if Miles Davis had had any say in the naming of that competition, it would've been the Miles Davis Young Intergalactic Jazz Competition for the Gifted, that's for sure."

A player was hit with the ball. The crowd cheered and booed at the exact same time as the runner took his base. A vendor walked the aisles, yelling loudly that he was selling boxes of Cracker Jacks.

"Whatever is going on with you and Veronica will pass. All things pass, man. Look at what went down with myself and Brooks yesterday. I survived it. He survived it. We as a band survived it." Stephen paused for a moment and then added, "We may not be in the competition anymore, but screw that, man. We're still a band, a kick-ass jazz band at that. We're everything we all need right now."

The runner on first base sprinted towards second, sliding arms first. More cheers. The pitcher from the other team shook his head, looking defeated.

"So yeah, I think as long as you keep that 'get back up' mentality that you've always had, and you learn from your mistakes from time to time, especially when dealing with women, then I think you'll be alright." Stephen patted me on the back. "Hopefully we'll all be ok, but you never know. Everyone and anyone can slip."

"Wait," I said, "you make mistakes with girls all the time. All the time," I emphasized.

"Just because I see the big picture doesn't mean I always know how to get to the big picture," Stephen replied. "Teenagers aren't good people, remember? We're learning. I'm learning." Inside my head, I could hear Mr. Cooper telling me that, just like in *Rocky*, sometimes the hero of the story doesn't always win.

The runner that had been on second base took advantage of wild pitch and sprinted to third. The crowd was beginning to become deafening with excitement.

"I appreciate the advice," I told Stephen, and after a moment, I added, "Someone once told me 'it can't rain all the time'. I guess that applies to this situation."

Stephen shrugged his shoulders nonchalantly. "The fact that you just quoted *The Crow* gives me hope in the universe, and don't expect my advice to be so great all the time. I try to remain true to my idiotic adolescent roots."

Another crack at home plate brought the crowd back to life; the runner on third base dashed down the baseline and crossed home plate while the batter made it safely to first. People stood up and yelled loudly. The electric scoreboard blazed the crowd to continue to be loud. It was a perfectly beautiful evening to be at a baseball game in New York City.

MAY - 8TH GRADE

Mr. Undergrove was ecstatic. I mean, wouldn't you be ecstatic if your middle school band just made awesome scores at a band competition the day before? He was all grins as we walked into the band room, high-fiving every kid as they assembled their instruments. "Ladies & gentlemen," he announced to the class, "I am proud of you, and you should be proud of yourselves too. Everyone did an excellent job yesterday."

"Even Mitchell?" someone from the clarinet section asked loud enough for the whole band room to hear. There was snickering and giggles as some people laughed and others tried to conceal their laughter.

Mr. Undergrove frowned. "That is a personal issue that we're not discussing. What we're going to focus on is getting ready for our spring concert coming up in just three weeks." There was a slight groan that waved over the class. "The good news: we're playing our songs from the competition, so now we're going to focus on perfecting these pieces even more than what we have already." There were some more groans, mostly stretching out of the percussion section. I felt both of my black eyes throb with embarrassment whenever I looked up at Mr. Undergrove. His eyes briefly met mine, he winked, and raised his arms in the air to signal the band into performance.

As band class wrapped up, we began to disassemble our instruments, Mr. Undergrove waved me over to the podium. "You holding up ok?" he asked, his eyes focused on me, but more specifically my fresh black eye. "Kids aren't being too mean to you, are they? I mean, with the exception of the comment made at the beginning of this class."

"Yeah, I'm fine," I answered. "Some of the kids think it's kinda cool to have two black eyes, but I'm not so sure."

Mr. Undergrove nodded rather seriously. "Yeah, yeah, I get that." He put one of his index fingers to his chin. "Everything go ok this morning with Mr. Cooper?"

I glanced into Mr. Undergrove's eyes. "Yeah, things went ok. He's not kicking me out of school or anything." Mr. Undergrove nodded along and half grinned; it was at that point, I knew why he was grinning. "You sent Stephen down to the office!" Upon vocalizing my revelation, Mr. Undergrove's grin grew and his half poker / half concerned face collapsed. "You sent him down there to keep me from telling Mr. Cooper the whole story about why I was in that fight!"

Mr. Undergrove grabbed my arm and quickly ushered me to his office, away from the other students as they prepared for dismissal. "I sent Stephen down there to make sure you didn't say too much and get yourself kicked out," Mr. Undergrove said in a hushed voice. "Stephen was insurance."

"Stephen said he was my attorney."

Mr. Undergrove put his hand over his face, shook his head, and sighed. "Of course he did."

"Why?" I asked.

"Why what?"

"Why did you tell Cooper I was protecting Stephen from a fight?"

Mr. Undergrove relaxed his shoulders, slightly rolled his eyes, and took a deep breath. "I told Mr. Cooper on the phone that I wasn't clear on all the details, which I'm still not, but that Stephen was at the fight, and since the two of you are thick as thieves, it wouldn't shock me if you were protecting Stephen from the other guy." Mr. Undergrove's eyes connected with mine. "Tell me that you wouldn't step in to protect Stephen if a guy of that size at the mall was aimed at fighting him unprovoked."

I put my eyes to the floor. "I would step in, yes."

"See? I'm not wrong. Mr. Cooper jumped to that conclusion by himself."

"He only jumped to that conclusion based on what you told him."

"I gave him what information I had at the time," Mr. Undergrove said back. "I sent Stephen down because I knew he could protect you from getting yourself suspended for good."

I kept my eyes focused on the floor, letting Mr. Undergrove's words sink in. "What if I'm the metaphor you talked about yesterday? What if I'm the one that's subconsciously causing trouble despite how hard everyone else is working?"

Mr. Undergrove sighed. "Mitchell, here's a tidbit of info that I know you already know, but you still need to hear it: you're important to this band. You're a part of it, and that's good enough for me to put my faith in you. I believe you wouldn't ever do anything to put this band's well-being at risk. I believe in you, both as Mitchell the band member, and Mitchell the middle schooler." I looked up and met Mr. Undergrove's eyes. "Sometimes we do things to protect the ones that we have faith in." He then added, "And no, you're not the type of person that would cause trouble or burn the world down just for fun. That's totally a percussionist thing to do."

I shook Mr. Undergrove's hand. Well, then I gave him a hug. "Thanks for always believing in me," I said as I left the band room.

By the time gym class rolled around near the end of the day, you would have thought me getting into a fight with a high schooler and winning was the social event of the season. Kids I didn't know were high-fiving me in the hall. During lunch, Kevin gave everyone at his table a blow-by-blow account of his perspective of the fight. "And it was bloody as hell!" Kevin said loudly. He had been so loud describing the fight that Mrs. Tolbert got up from the teachers' table and circled around the cafeteria towards Kevin's table to see what all the fuss was about, prompting Kevin to lower his voice and not be so rambunctious.

I was the kid. You know, THE kid. Like every kid dreams of being the most liked or most popular kid in school, but very rarely do any of us get to actually live that experience. Well, there I was, two black eyes and all, living the experience. The other students all knew me, even the ones that had previously pretended to ignore me in the hall, and all the teachers now knew me, even the ones who had taught me in 6th and 7th grade who used to pretend that I didn't exist anymore. In some ways it was strange, in some ways it was exhilarating, and in other ways it was terrifying; it was everything and nothing what any 8th grader could wish for.

And then, it was time for me to report to gym class.

Yep, you know you're thinking what I'm thinking: will Coach Brier even notice?

Spoiler: she did.

"Mitchell Waters, what happened to you?" she asked as she was doing attendance.

Ok, she noticed; she still didn't get my last name correct, but she did get at least my first name right, so that counts for something, right?

"Mitchell, I'm waiting." Coach Brier said. "Quit looking so dumb-founded and answer me. What happened to your face?"

"I was in a fight," I said, quite bluntly and matter-of-factly.

Coach Brier shook her head back and forth. "When are you gone learn? Fightin' ain't no way to keep your spot here on this team."

I looked around the gym confused. "Team?" I asked. "This is gym class."

"Don't give me lip. Run three laps and then sit down on the bleachers. I have a class to teach, Marshall." Coach Brier's eyes returned to her clipboard and calling attendance. Instead of arguing (when did that ever work with Coach Brier?), I ran my three laps around the gym, and then took a seat on the bleachers. I mean, if Mr. Cooper didn't punish me for getting into a fight, Coach Brier couldn't do but so much, right? Better to bear her ramblings and move on than to cause more trouble for myself.

"Ay, yo," I heard from behind me. "Both yo eyes got shiny, eh?" I turned around and there was Max, sitting on the top tier of the bleachers. "Yeah, both eyes shiny," he confirmed upon looking at my face. He stood up and stepped down a few tiers until he was sitting parallel with me one row back. "Yeah, you know that talk don't lie."

"What's that supposed to mean?"

Max smacked his lips, rolled his eyes, and then said, "Man, c'mon now, that talk don't lie," he repeated, slapping his knee with joy. "Halls talk, yo. Halls talk."

I turned my body towards him. "Do you constantly make a point to speak in riddles?" I asked. "Just say what you're trying to say. Quit beating around the bush and say it."

Max rested his elbows on his knees and leaned forward towards me. "You done got yo tail beat twice," he said, "and you got the shinys to show it. Shinys don't lie."

Instead of snapping back out of anger (which I wanted to), I took a deep breath, trying to keep myself calm. As much as I wanted to raise my voice and lash back at Max, letting my anger get the best of me again probably would not go over so well with anyone, including Mr. Cooper.

I stood up, looking down on Max still sitting on the bleachers, his elbows still on his knees. "Three things," I said, "Three things I have to say to that." I held up three of my fingers on my left hand to empathize to Max three statements would be made. "1) Yes, I have two black eyes, or 'shinys' or whatever you want to call them, and yes, they both came from two different occasions. I got a few more bruises too. You want to see them too?" I asked. "You want that validation that I have bruises? Maybe take a picture of them? Show them to all your friends?" Max just looked at me, like he wasn't understanding what I was saying to him. "2)," I continued, "I took my beating yesterday, and then I won the fight. And even though I took a beating, at least the guy I fought didn't try to jump me in the bathroom, in the dark, using a football helmet, like some little punk did back here a few weeks back." I felt like I was getting taller and Max was getting smaller, his eyes growing wider and wider with each word. "And 3) if I have learned anything, it's that I can survive. I can survive a beating in the darkness of the locker room by some pansy that can't face me like a man, I can survive a beating by some beefed-up high schooler, I can survive whatever crazy thing Coach Brier can throw at me, I can survive heartbreak, I can survive King's Hollow, and most specifically," I leaned forward towards Max, whose eyes could not get any wider, "I can survive you, Max. I don't need you. I don't need your crap, I don't need you trying to make yourself feel tough by trying to jump me in the locker room, and I don't need you ruining my gym class experience. So why don't you sit here on the bleachers and know that you can't break me, not anymore."

Max, eyes still wide, speechless, sat there. He just sat there. No weird comeback. No trash talk. He just sat there. Silent. Maybe confused. Maybe he didn't understand me. I don't know. I jumped down from the bleachers and called out to Coach Brier. "Coach Brier, I don't think I've learned my lesson," I said. "Maybe I should run a few more laps?"

Coach Brier looked back at me, put her hands on her hips, and responded, "Eight more laps should fix that then. And run them fast, too, Mr. Williamson. Life's too short for any more of this silliness."

So I took to jogging. And Max just sat there on the bleachers watching me. Not saying anything. Just watching me. Eyes still wide, mouth slightly open, just sitting there like he wasn't sure what to think.

I don't know if Max figured out what I was pretty sure what I already knew before Mr. Cooper said it. I don't know why he did it, why I was the one he decided to beat with a football helmet. But he did, and it doesn't change anything. Without Max's actions, I never would have had my black eye at the band competition, and I'm guessing I never would have met Lauren, and without Lauren's actions, I never would have been the lucky recipient of two matching black eyes, cementing my place in history within these walls of King's Hollow Middle School. So, yeah, it's whatever.

Max is probably still sitting on those bleachers. I don't know if he ever got out of 8th grade.

Coach Brier was right; life's too short for any more of this silliness.

APRIL - 10TH GRADE

We loaded the bus the next morning, our eyes still slightly shut with exhaustion from our adventures in the city the day before. All of us were tired except Mr. Undergrove. I don't think he ever gets tired. "Good morning, everyone!" his voice boomed as we climbed aboard the bus, coffee cup in hand. He was met with mostly grunts and groans; I think the only person that cheerfully responded back was Veronica's mom. Maybe it's just an adult thing. I don't know.

The bus hissed and rolled out of the parking lot of our New Jersey hotel, homeward bound. The skyline of the city and concrete and cement that had surrounded us for the past couple of days slowly disappeared from our window views, fading into trees and greenery as we left our city adventures behind and traveled back to the real world of high school, like notes traveling down the keys of a piano. "Miles Davis," I muttered under my breath as I watched the world blur by the window.

"Miles Davis, man" Stephen said from beside me. He fiddled with his CD Walkman for a moment, sighed heavily, readjusted his pillow behind his neck, looked around at the rest of our band mates, all attempting to get comfortable in their seats, and then added, "Jazz, man. Jazz, jazz, jazz." He thumped his Walkman with his fingers, like he was rapping along to an unheard beat.

I smiled and nodded. "Jazz, man."

"Jazz forever," Stephen said.

"Jazz forever," I confirmed.

JUNE - 8TH GRADE

The last day of school had arrived. You know how the last day of school goes, all exciting and nostalgic and everything. Like, you can't wait for summer to start, but at the same time, you kinda wish you had one more day, just to soak it all in. It wasn't just the last day of school, though; it was the last day of middle school. No more King's Hollow. Hello Northern Kent, the high school King's Hollow poured in to.

Really, when you think about it, the last day of school really is a waste. No learning is going on, but for some reason, we're all there. Not even the teachers want to be there with us, but we're all together. One more day. Blah.

Mr. Undergrove had already told us that we didn't have to bring our instruments for the final day, so instead of practicing like we normally did during 8th grade band class, he subjected us to a documentary on Jimi Hendrix. "Hendrix is enlightening," he said.

As class came to an end, Mr. Undergrove turned on the lights, killed the TV, and stood by the band room door. Every teacher gives the same speech during the final minutes of class on the last day, always about how it's been a long year and it's been an honor and blah blah blah. Forgettable. We expected the same from Mr. Undergrove, only maybe something a little more relatable because, well, we actually liked Mr. Undergrove. We all knew we were going to miss him. Shoot, even the percussion kids, as dumb and obnoxious as they could be at times, were going to miss band class with Mr. Undergrove. He had brought out the best in all of us.

"It's the last day of school," Mr. Undergrove said, "and I assume you all want something from me, like a speech about how much you all mean to me, correct?"

We all nodded in unison. That's exactly what we wanted. No one blurted out 'Yes, exactly' but our eyes collectively probably said it for us.

"You all have brought out the best in me and each other," Mr. Undergrove said, a smile on his face, "and I hate that this chapter in our lives is coming to an end. But all things end. Life moves on. This place, King's Hollow, is just a building, a place in your history. One day, you'll drive by here and remember the adventures you had, the adventures we had together in this band room. Or maybe you won't. Maybe you'll leave this town and never come back, so your memory of King's Hollow will stay intact in your mind as long as you allow it. Either way, this chapter comes to an end today. Come the end of school today, we're all going to move on to the next chapter."

Mr. Undergrove then checked his watch, and added, "Oh, all of you should not be sad about leaving me and my wonderful musical guidance, because effective August 1, the county office is moving me from band director here at King's Hollow and reassigning me to Northern Kent, where all of you will be attending high school."

Our eyes grew wide. Mr. Undergrove was going to be coming to Northern Kent with us?

"I've been instructed," Mr. Undergrove added, "that my top priority is to take the success our band has experienced here at King's Hollow and make it happen over at Northern Kent. I find all this so ironic, because, honestly, I'm just a guy waving a baton in the air. It's you all that made the music. You all are the success story. I've just been here for the trip." There were a few collective 'aw's from people (mostly the flute section). Mr. Undergrove began to smile. "So, this isn't 'goodbye', it's 'see you at the end of summer.'" He then opened the door, and added, "I'm proud of you, and I believe in you, but now is the time for this chapter at King's Hollow to end, so politely and nicely, get out!"

We all rejoiced as we left the band room, each one of us shaking Mr. Undergrove's hand, giving him a high-five or a hug. "Thanks for always being the best," I said as I shook his hand.

"The pleasure has been all mine, Mitchell."

The halls buzzed with excitement all day long. No one was learning, but counting down to the final bell. It had been weeks since my fight during the band competition, and even though my black eyes had faded from my face, people still talked about me. You could feel the eyes burning into my head in the cafeteria, the whispers in the hall, the fingers pointing at me while we all waited for our rides to show up at the end of school.

"You know what you did?" Stephen said during lunch. "You really want to know what you did? You put us on the map!"

"What map?" I asked.

"The map, man!" Stephen replied. "Like, the map. People know who we are now. We're the guys that went to Snowfield and kicked booty booty."

"Booty booty?"

"Yes, booty booty," Stephen said with a grin. He put his hands in the air with excitement. "We're Stephen & Mitchell! We're the cool kids! Girls know who we are, man!"

"Um, not to disagree with you, but I don't recall you being in any of my fights," I said, "so us being the guys that went to Snowfield and kicked 'booty booty,'" I said using air quotes, "feels misleading."

"As your lawyer on retainer, I am legally obligated to ride on the coattails of the celebrity status of my client. Therefore, we are a unit. You get in a fight and win, and I get to help you bask in the glory of your victory."

"Fights," I corrected him.

"Fights indeed. Without that first black eye, we never would have...." Stephen hesitated. He knew it was a touchy subject. I already knew what he was going to say without actually saying it: Chassidy and Lauren.

I looked down at my feet and cracked my knuckles. After a minute, I asked the question that I didn't really want to ask but feel obligated to. "You ever hear anything from Chassidy or..." I stumbled on my words.

"Or Lauren?" Stephen asked for me. "Nah, not a peep. I called Chassidy once, left her a message on her answering machine. Never heard back." He took a deep breath. "I'm guessing the whole 'You're still in middle school' thing probably turned her off." He nudged the chair beside him at the lunch table and adjusted it to put his foot up. "That little skirmish you got in kinda got word out that we were only in middle school."

"Yeah, I'm really sorry about all that. I never really apologized to you about everything. I ruined everything for both of us when....when I..."Again my words left me.

"Kicked a high school football player's tush in front of all of his friends?" Stephen asked, a smirk across his face, his body leaned back into his chair, his hands in the front pockets of his shorts. "I don't think you need to apologize for that. And watching you take down the Wolfman like that was legendary. If anything, I'd say you earned your admission into *The Monster Squad*. If our town ever falls under attack at the hands of Dracula and his friends, I already know I want you on the team.

I laughed, then folded my arms on the cafeteria table and leaned forward. "Hey, Stephen?"

"Yeah?"

"If girls know who we are now and everything, then why are we still sitting by ourselves at lunch?"

Stephen glanced around the cafeteria. "It's the last day of school; let's not think too much about this." He then looked over at me. "The black eyes are almost all the way gone. You going to miss them?"

"I won't miss the weird looks I get from people, but then again, I hang out with you, so weird looks are nothing new."

Stephen sat up in his seat, a grin on his face. "Well, the boxer has jokes now." He readjusted his leg on the neighboring chair while his face slowly shifted away from his normal grin to a sense of seriousness. "Hey, so like, not to bum you out with bad memories or anything, but you ever hear anything from..." Stephen hesitated. "From...."

"Lauren?" I answered.

Stephen scratched his head. "Yeah, I didn't want to say her name any more than I needed to, you know, just in case her name is like a trigger word for you or something."

I shook my head. "No, it's ok. I don't think I'm THAT mentally damaged from her." I nervously moved my arms on the table, tapping the table top with my fingers. "I never called her. I just couldn't do it, ya know? Several times I had pulled her number out and found myself with the phone in my hand, my fingers ready to dial away, but I just couldn't do it. A few days after the fight, Mom said the phone rang one evening while I was outside mowing the grass. Said there was a girl on the other end and she sounded really upset, like crying and stuff, but when mom said I was outside and to hang on for a minute so she could get me, the girl just said it was alright and that she needed to go. Mom asked her for her name so I could call her back, but the girl just said to tell me that she was sorry; Mom said she hung up right there on the spot."

Stephen didn't need to say anything, because his face gave away his shock by how wide his eyes were and how far down his jaw had dropped. After a few seconds, Stephen asked, "Do you think it was Lauren?"

I shrugged my shoulders. "Only conclusion I can jump to. I can't be too mad for her not calling back when I never tried to call her either."

"Got that right," Stephen said. "What do you say in that conversation? 'Hey, thanks for sending your psycho Wolfman ex-boyfriend on me to kick my insides out.'"

"Yeah, some days I knew I didn't want to have that conversation, but then some days, I wanted that conversation." I hesitated for a moment. "Like I needed to hear her side of the story or something. Like a justification or closure or whatever"

"I'll be honest with you, bud," Stephen responded after a moment, "I don't think you need to hear her side of the story. Remember what Cooper said about cars? I think Lauren is just a car that's bound to leave you frustrated on the side of the road. Best to abandon ship now."

The flashbacks rolled through my brain again, for it was a daily occurrence: meeting Chassidy & Lauren, the bathroom incident, the mall, the fight. Everything all at once, hitting me. Plus the memories of Gabe actually hitting me. Whew.

"What is it that they call a brand new car that is actually a mess? A lemon?" Stephen squinted as he thought. "Yeah, I think it's a lemon. You definitely were put in a lemon situation with Lauren. Nice looking car, but just a terrible engine."

I nodded as I looked around the cafeteria. Hundreds of King's Hollow kids waited for the bell to release us to our last set of classes for the school year, and not a single one of them were probably aware that at some point in their future, whether close by or far away, their hearts were going to be completely broken or shattered by someone they least expect. It's a tragedy. Really.

The moment arrived that we had been waiting for: the final bell of the final day. As it rang, kids in every class rejoiced as we all flooded the halls. For all of us 8th graders, we were finally free of King's Hollow Middle School, headed onto bigger things at Northern Kent High School. Plus Mr. Undergrove was coming with us. Man, what a time to be alive.

Mr. Cooper stood out front of the school, waving goodbye to kids and shaking hands as they exited, but instead of his typical shirt and tie combo that he normally sported, Mr. Cooper was fashioned in a pair of shorts, sunglasses, a baseball cap, and this terribly bright orange Hawaiian shirt that I'm pretty sure could be seen blocks away throughout the various neighborhoods that surrounded King's Hollow. "Mr. Williams!" Mr. Cooper shouted to me and waved me over to him. He extended his hand and shook mine. "You made it!" A genuine smile covered his face. "Good luck in high school," he said, "and make me proud."

"Will do, Mr. Cooper," I said. "And thanks for always having faith in me." I looked his outfit up and down. "And nice shirt." Was I complimenting him? It was meant as a compliment, but it didn't feel like a compliment; I mean, the man was dressed kinda like my dad.

He patted me on the side of the arm. "You can thank Mr. Undergrove for that. He told me how much he believed in you, so I knew I could also believe in you. Mr. Undergrove is a good man."

"Yeah," I replied, "Yeah he is."

When I got home, I went upstairs to my room, opened my sock drawer, and pulled out the small scrap piece of paper that I had been holding onto since that day at the Snowfield mall. I opened it, picked up the phone, and began to dial Lauren's number. I was on the last number when my fingers began to tremble. I just stood there, holding the phone, scared out of my mind.

Stephen said she was a lemon, a car that would leave me abandoned on the side of the road, but what Stephen didn't know was why Lauren had felt so disgusted with me. I had, in her eyes, spied on her in the bathroom, even though I didn't actually spy on her, but yet, when looking at it from the other perspective, it looked like I was totally spying on her. She had her reasons when she told Gabe that I was bothering her.

To anyone looking at it from my view, Lauren was the lemon, but, if you stop and look at everything from Lauren's view, you can place the lemon status on Mitchell Williams, a middle school peepster from King's Hollow.

I placed the phone back on the receiver. I laid down on my bed, closed my eyes, and tried to imagine what life would have been like had I never accidentally found my way into the women's restroom at the band competition, but no matter what I tried to dream about in my head, it always came back to the look that was in Lauren's eyes when she realized I was the person in the bathroom stall while she poured her feelings out.

You know what? I deserved to be punched. Mr. Cooper's words about *Rocky* rang out in my head: sometimes the hero of the story doesn't always win.

Self-realization is a hard pill to swallow: it's bitter, jagged, and burns as it sits in your stomach.

Maybe Lauren addressed it best as she sat in the stall beside me in the girls' restroom back at the band competition: why does growing up have to be so weird?

APRIL - 10TH GRADE

Parents swarmed us with hugs and greetings as we tried to unload the bus in the Northern Kent High School parking lot. Brooks' parents had brought him a milkshake. Kirby's mom kept taking pictures with the flash on. David's mom had made homemade cookies that she was passing out. My parents were there, all smiles, just happy to see us back safe and healthy. My mom hugged me like she hadn't seen me in three years.

All our instruments, equipment and the ark were placed inside the band room. Mr. Undergrove thanked everyone for their efforts, shook our hands, and we went home. My parents asked me about three thousand questions about New York City, and it got to the point that I told them I was exhausted and just wanted to get some sleep. I had spent the money my dad had given me at the baseball game buying all three of us matching Yankees shirts, which made my mom practically lose a gasket at how awesome it would be if we all wore them on the same day; I pushed the shirts into their hands and then went upstairs to embrace the comfort of my bed.

I kinda felt bad about blowing them off, but, good golly, parents sometimes don't know when to stop asking questions. Right?

The weekend came and went; I think I slept for most of it. My mom kept checking on me to make sure I was ok, but I kept hearing my dad say that I was a teenager and teenagers are weird and they sleep a lot. He's not wrong.

By Monday, I was ready to get back to a normal routine at school. The halls of Northern Kent no longer seemed that crowded after a week in New York City. The kids seemed nicer, the traffic coming into school didn't seem as hectic, and even the roughest areas of the school that had been graffitied over the years didn't look as bad as I once thought.

When I entered the band room, I grabbed my trombone case and began assembling my instrument, as did the other kids, all smiling and equally relieved as I was to be back home. I watched as Veronica strolled into the band room, her notebook pulled tight by her arms against her body, her head down. She sat down at her chair at the keyboard, placed her music on her music stand, brushed the hair out of her eyes, and then looked up at me, our eyes locking before I realized I was staring and I looked away. Veronica then stood up and walked over.

'Here we go again,' I thought.

"Hey," she said, brushing her hair away from her eyes again and then crossing her arms across her chest.

"Hi," I said back, a smile on my face to try to keep things from getting awkward.

"Feels good to be back, right?" Veronica asked, her eyes showing her nervousness shining through.

"Oh gosh, yes," I agreed. "I didn't think I'd ever say that I 'missed' my own bed, but it felt great sleeping in my own bed again."

"I slept all weekend. I was so exhausted."

"Me too!" I responded, slightly louder than I wanted to sound. "I mean, me too," I said again, lowering my voice just a tad to try to sound not so excited.

Veronica smiled, looked down at the floor, and then back up at me. "New York City was nice. It was definitely an adventure."

I put my mouthpiece into my trombone, tooted it real quick to make sure everything was attached securely, and then said, "I'll honestly probably one day tell my grandkids about that trip and how I got to see the *Ghostbusters* firehouse in person."

"Speaking of *Ghostbusters*," Veronica said, uncrossing her arms and then recrossing her arms, "my mom said when she picks up her pictures from being developed, she's going to put the group picture that we took in front of the *Ghostbusters* firehouse in a frame and wrap it up as a gift to give to Mr. Undergrove from all of us."

"Oh, that's really nice. It doesn't seem like much since Mr. Undergrove has always gone above and beyond for us."

Veronica rolled her eyes. "I said something similar, like we need to do more, but Mom kept saying that he would love to have a picture to help commemorate the trip. I don't know. Adults just like different things."

I nodded along. "I wish I could bottle up the smell of the subway. That'd be a fun gift to give to someone you don't like."

"Or to a fan of the Teenage Mutant Ninja Turtles, since they live in the sewers and all, which got to smell way worse than the subway," Veronica responded with a smile.

"That is an amazing point," I said. "I take that back. Maybe I would want a bottle of the smell of the subway." Veronica laughed. For a moment, I forgot about how much I had upset her over the past couple of months.

As the other band members put their instruments together, Veronica glared around the room, as if she had a secret she wanted to tell but didn't want anyone to hear. She leaned forward, placing her head against mine, and whispered into my ear, "We're going to be ok, right? Like, still friends, right?"

I nodded my head. "I'm sor-" but Veronica cut me off.

"I know, I know, and I'm sorry too. It's ok. Really."

I nodded my head, Veronica wrapped her arms around my neck and hugged me, smiled, and then sat back down in her seat by the keyboard. Stephen leaned over to me. "What was that all about?" he asked.

I looked over at Stephen. "Teenagers aren't good people," I said, 'but we're learning."

Stephen smiled. "That we are, my good man, that we are."

Mr. Undergrove sat down in his band director's chair. We all got quiet and gave him our attention.

"What a blast last week was!" he said with enthusiasm, a smile breaking out across his face. Like our brains were connected telepathically, we all, in unison, began to clap loudly to show that we agreed.

And then we kept clapping. And clapped some more. I don't know who did it first, whether it was Stephen, or David, or Kevin, but someone stood up, and then we all stood up and kept clapping, like a standing ovation at a Broadway show or a concert at a fancy venue. Someone hooted. Some hollered. Mr. Undergrove's face turned red, and nodded, a tear forming in the corner of his eye, which he quickly wiped away, probably hoping nobody noticed.

When we finally stopped clapping and returned to our seats, Mr. Undergrove said, "Last week, you all played some of the finest jazz I've ever heard performed in my life. You were diamonds, reflecting the light of Northern Kent in one of the biggest cities and biggest jazz competitions in the world. I know I've said it so many times, but you all need to hear it again: I'm proud of you, and I believe in you."

"We believe in you too, Mr. Undergrove," Stephen shouted, which prompted another round of loud and appreciative clapping. When the clapping finally died down, Stephen followed up with, "What are we going to do now? I mean, we've rocked every gig we've performed at this school year, we went to one of the coolest cities in the world, and we went head-to-head with some of the best jazz bands in the nation. What else can we possibly do?"

"I know," Brooks said, "we can finally give our band a proper name."

"We're the Northern Kent Jazz Band," Mr. Undergrove said, a look of confusion on his face.

"Yeah," Brooks said back," but if we're going to keep making a run of this whole jazz band thing, we need a proper name, like something that identifies us."

"Like Nirvana?" I asked.

"Yeah, like a band name like Nirvana or Alice In Chains or Sonic Youth or something that helps with establishing who we are."

"What about the Terrible Treble?" Stephen said.

"I don't think the word 'terrible' should be in the band name," Mr. Undergrove advised.

"I actually already have a name in mind, something that I think would totally work, especially for us," Brooks mentioned, grabbing the attention of everyone in the band.

"What is it?" Mr. Undergrove asked.

Brooks took a deep breath. "What about Hey Jude?"

We all sat in silence for a moment to let the name settle in our heads.

Brooks continued. "It works on so many levels. It's an established song by The Beatles, a song that we also cover, and it stands out by itself as a name while also giving people something that they can already relate to."

"Technically, we cover Maynard Ferguson's version of 'Hey Jude', ya know, in case we're being specific," Stephen added.

We all looked around the room at each other. Mr. Undergrove spoke up. "Anything is better than Terrible Treble, but I like Hey Jude. Anyone got any other ideas?"

Kevin chimed in. "All in favor in renaming the Northern Kent Jazz Band to Hey Jude, raise your hand." United, we all raised our hands.

"I guess that makes it official then," Mr. Undergrove confirmed, "from now on, we're Hey Jude."

Hey Jude – maybe the most fitting name for our band ever. In a world full of Sonic Youths and Nirvana, we were Hey Jude.

"So, what kind of gigs or exciting adventures are awaiting the future of Hey Jude?" Stephen asked.

Mr. Undergrove smiled, stood up out of his chair, opened his music folder, and said, "Stephen, you used the word 'gig' correctly, so that's worth its weight in gold right there." We all giggled. Mr. Undergrove continued. "But to answer your question, we're going to do the same thing we do every day because it's our strongest connection to each other and the reason why we're all here: we're going to play jazz. And we're going to start with Maynard Ferguson's arrangement of 'Hey Jude'. Stephen, you take the solo."

I think we were all smiling as we arranged our music in preparation to play, because when you're doing what you love surrounded by the people that you love, you cannot help but smile.

Mr. Undergrove raised his baton, counted down from four, and then, just as it had so many times before, the sound of jazz music filled the air.

Acknowledgement

In the spring of 2020, I sat down to write what I thought would be a short story about a band teacher and the relationship he had with his students. The story grew and grew to the point where I thought I had a novella on my hands, but the story continued to morph to the point where I realized I was writing a full blown novel. Along the way, I had a lot of people give me tips and advice, including my wife, Ashley, my parents, Rick & Trish, and my friends Steven, Angela, Beth, and David. I also received advice (mostly scathing, but still advice) from my son Noah, the world's hardest critic to please. Without these people, completing *Jazz* would not have been possible.

While *Jazz* is a work of fiction, many of my characters received inspiration from some of the people in my personal universe. Mr. Undergrove has shades of some of my favorite teachers, including my band director from high school, Mr. Kuni. Stephen, Mitchell's best friend who seems like a character out of Kevin Smith movie, is a mixture of some of my personal friends from my childhood.

There are, of course, the Coach Briers of the world, for we seem to remember our worst teachers just as much as our favorites. While I hate it, the character of Coach Brier exists because teachers like Coach Brier exist, and that is sad.

While I didn't set out to write a superhero story, it has become clear to me now that maybe I did, for Mr. Undergrove feels like what a superhero should be: a reflection of the best of us.

As an educator and a parent, I can only hope that every kid out there has a teacher just like Mr. Undergrove that cares about them.

About the Author

Michael Bean is an educator from North Carolina that enjoys writing, despite that he is convinced that he's not very good at it. His wife is a rock star (not literally but totally literally), and they have three boys, three dogs, a cat, and a turtle that keep them busy. In his free time, Michael loves to read comic books, over-analyze movies, attend local theater productions, and support youth sports.

Jazz is Michael's first novel. You can interact with Michael on Twitter and Instagram by following @HalloBean82.

www.ingramcontent.com/pod-product-compliance
Ingram Content Group UK Ltd.
Pitfield, Milton Keynes, MK11 3LW, UK
UKHW041632190726
13854UKWH00006B/2447

9 798223 021476